To
Joe, Peter, Christopher and David
—my team—
which is splendid and fairly amazin'.

CASEY: THE LIFE AND LEGEND OF CHARLES DILLON STENGEL
by Joseph Durso

Library of Congress Catalog Card Number: 67-13566

Printed in the United States of America

T 12043

Prentice-Hall International, Inc., *London*
Prentice-Hall of Australia, Pty. Ltd., *Sydney*
Prentice-Hall of Canada, Ltd., *Toronto*
Prentice-Hall of India Private Ltd., *New Delhi*
Prentice-Hall of Japan, Inc., *Tokyo*

CASEY

THE LIFE AND LEGEND
OF
CHARLES DILLON STENGEL

BY JOSEPH DURSO

PRENTICE-HALL, INC.,
ENGLEWOOD CLIFFS, NEW JERSEY

CONTENTS

INTRODUCTION

It was with reluctance that I picked up the first galley proof of Joe Durso's biography of Casey Stengel. I didn't want to start reading.

I suppose the feeling was normal. At least normal in this era of the anti-hero. Because, to me, Charles Dillon Stengel *is* a hero. And today who can afford to see one of this disappearing breed destroyed, if only in print. Not I.

So I hesitated. Wondering if Mr. Durso would be able to capture the essence of MY Casey Stengel or would settle for the "public image." Would this be a biography of "scissors and paste" or a reflective study of a remarkable man? I said I hesitated. I also hoped.

And I needn't have worried.

Casey is a superb book. The author has seen far beyond the buffoonery and the bandy-legged walk, past the Stengelese and the quotable quotes. He has seen the man, and, at the same time, has captured the flavor, the fun, the wit, the intelligence, and the thoughtfulness of this irrepressible hero of a thousand and one irrepressible stories.

Writing accurately on Casey isn't easy. The legend keeps getting in the way. I myself was once guilty of "buying" the guy on the basis of the published reports. "Un-buying" would be more accurate. For that is exactly what I wanted to do.

During my days as the albatross around Uncle Sam's neck, back in one of our earlier wars, Charlie Grimm who had been managing (and partnering) for me in Milwaukee got a chance to go back to the Cubs. Now if managing is your racket, there's only one place to be. That's in the big leagues. So Charlie wisely caught the first electric to Chicago. Not, however, before convincing the semi-retired Stengel he should abandon his swimming pool in Glendale and go to work in Milwaukee.

When I heard of the maneuver some weeks later on some forgotten island I was annoyed. Livid would be more accurate. For although I had known Casey casually since early childhood, I still thought of him as a clown. A guy who put sparrows on his head, who let the fans select his pinch-hitters, a guy who didn't win. I had bought the then "public image."

So being a man of action, I wrote to my friend Jim Gallagher who was then General Manager for the Cubs and who had helped Grimm get Stengel as his replacement, berating the bunch of them for this travesty they had perpetrated during my absence.

This "travesty" turned out to be the best thing that happened to me in the wondrous world of baseball. Not just because Mr. Stengel developed and peddled enough athletes to insure winning clubs, a healthy gate, and a bigger bank balance (although these details aren't exactly a source of annoyance), but more because I gained a great friend in every respect.

When it was hearsay for any member of the mighty Yankee organization from Laughing George Weiss down to admit they even knew how to spell my name, it was Casey Stengel who invited me to breakfast each morning the Yanks played in Cleveland, St. Louis, and Chicago. In the main dining room it was Casey Stengel who showed up in the press room, not when his nine bested ours, but when he lost. "Gotta give Will a chance to celebrate" he'd say.

Casey Stengel wasn't a company man, but when you paid for his services you got them—all the way. He gave his employer twenty-four hours of his time, every day.

And don't let the Stengelese bit fool you. Casey can make himself understood anytime anywhere—when he wants to. He can be incomprehensible at a governmental hearing, but his athletes will get the message that night. And quickly. He knows more about the game, its nuances and intricacies, than anyone around today.

He's an innovator too. Look at the rookie camps, and the sneaky way he used platooning. That was the greatest job in sports history.

I remember when I was hanging around the Corona Naval Hospital a few years back, feeling sorry for myself, the Old Man, only recently recovered from his collision with a Boston cab, would wander down from Glendale to try and cheer up Ol Will. Seeing him doing knee-bobs and nip-ups on those gimpy gambs was greater therapy for the amputee ward than anything the government's covey of psychologists could ever produce.

I could go on. But why should I? Joseph Durso has done the job for me. And better too. He has produced a fascinating and honest account of the life and times of Casey Stengel. And in the process Joe has produced a history of baseball, for the game and Mr. Stengel are so interwoven that it's impossible to discuss one without the other.

Thank you Joseph Durso. And thank you too, Charles Dillon Stengel.

Bill Veeck

*"Something of insanity
has gone out of the performance."*
—BROOKS ATKINSON.

1

YOU COULD LOOK IT UP

His name was Charles Dillon Stengel, but because he had been born in Kansas City, Missouri, he was the man from K.C.—*Casey*. But he also was called "Dutch," because his family was German; "the Professor," because of his Socratic manner of presiding over baseball dugouts; "the Swami," because, under mild promotional prompting, he affected exotic headgear and stared wildly into crystal balls, and "Doctor," simply because he had an uncertain memory for names and called everybody else "Doctor."

Branch Rickey, the "deacon" of major league baseball, called him "the perfect link between the team and the public."

It was a link he had started to establish as a 19-year-old outfielder in a place called Kankakee, Illinois, in a league called the Northern Association in 1910. That was four years before World War I, a decade before Babe Ruth became a Yankee, half a century before the first big league game was played indoors. The league folded in July.

Stengel thereupon squirreled a couple of Kankakee uniforms into a suitcase and moved over to Shelbyville, Kentucky, in the Blue Grass League. The franchise collapsed.

He packed again and moved to Maysville, Kentucky, where a stream skirted the outfield grass, and one day he drifted back for a fly ball, sloshed a few feet farther back and caught the ball while standing in the stream. The link was taking shape.

For the next 55 years, Casey Stengel grew old, rich and famous while the United States moved from William Howard Taft to John F. Kennedy and beyond, with talking pictures, the automobile and the Lunar Excursion Module revolutionizing life, and baseball expanding as a multimillion-dollar business into the West Coast, the Deep South, Central America and even Japan. He had been transported to his early baseball games in horse-drawn surreys and he wound up a regular traveler from Los Angeles to New York in Boeing 727 jetliners.

He owned oil wells in Texas, was vice president of a bank in California and controlled real estate that made him a millionaire. His face was heavily wrinkled, his ears were floppy, his voice was guttural, his endurance beyond belief. Like Mickey Mouse and Charles de Gaulle, he was a household figure of towering identification.

But for all his status, he was best known as a baseball man, earned his "source" money in baseball and for 55 years exerted his greatest influence on baseball players, fans and franchises.

He had been a player, coach or manager on 17 professional baseball teams. He had been traded four times as a left-handed outfielder in the major leagues. He had been dropped or relieved three times as a manager in the big leagues. He had even been paid twice for *not* managing.

He had retired at the age of 71, had returned at 72, and had been re-hired at 73 and 74. Then, as he turned 75, he fell and broke his left hip somewhere between Toots Shor's restaurant in Manhattan and a house in Whitestone, Queens, and had to watch on television from a room in Roosevelt Hospital while 39,288 persons in Shea Stadium sang "Happy Birthday, Dear Casey, Happy Birthday to You."

One year later, to the day, he limped into the Baseball Hall of Fame alongside Ted Williams, having completed the course from Kankakee to Cooperstown as a national figure, an average player, a controversial coach, a wheeler and dealer of minor league talent, a second-division manager of dismal teams, a first-division manager of the Olympian Yankees, a man criticized as an expert at *over-*

managing wherever he managed—a mixture of Santa Claus and
Jimmy Durante as he duck-walked out to home plate with his
lineup card, wearing flannel pinstripes and No. 37 on the back of
his uniform.

Was he the greatest baseball manager who ever lived? Was he
the luckiest manager who ever lived? Was he simply a manager
whose fortunes oscillated with the talent available? Was he a meddler, a tyrant in the dugout, a slave to the "book," a wizard, a patriarch, a Merlin, a charming old man or an "angry old man" with
great press notices?

Whatever he was, when he signed his final contract as manager
of the New York Mets on September 29, 1964, he received the
following telegram from Rickey, then seven years younger than
Winston Churchill and eight years older than Stengel—who was
74 years and two months old:

"You are exactly the right age to manage a major league baseball
team in my book."

Later, sitting in his box seat between home plate and third base
in Busch Stadium, St. Louis, Rickey leaned forward on a gnarled
cherrywood cane, chewed on a cigar and watched the St. Louis
Cardinals bat their way into a tie for first place in the National
League.

Rickey had been born on a farm in Ohio 82 years earlier,
once had pedaled a bicycle 18 miles each way to teach school
and later had become a lawyer with three degrees, the creator of
baseball's first farm system and the dominant figure in the major
leagues in three cities. But what excited him now was that Casey
Stengel—in his 75th year—had just signed a $100,000 contract to
manage a baseball team. And he reacted as though he suddenly had
put his finger on something constant in the sweep of a busy life.

"Exactly the right age," he said. "You know, it's a great waste
for universities to force brilliant men to retire at 65, when they're
at the peak of their ability. And baseball needs men like that, too
—like Casey Stengel—who are so able, so alive, so articulate, so
aroused."

"People in New York have spent a lot of time and effort trying
to ferret out the reason for the Mets' astounding attendance," he
said, peering out beneath strong, bushy eyebrows, his hands folded

across the knob of the cherrywood cane. "You need look no farther than Casey Stengel. He is the perfect link between the team
and the public."

The perfect link between the team and the public, at that moment, was landing in Milwaukee aboard a jet airliner from New
York. In 72 hours, his team would arrive in Deacon Rickey's St.
Louis and cause panic in much of the Midwest by reaching up from
the league cellar to defeat the Cardinals twice at the climax of one
of the great finishes in baseball history. He had the knack, it seemed,
of living at the eye of the hurricane.

The Mets required one full page in their handbook that season
to record his three-quarters of a century, but somehow managed to
compress his vital statistics into these four lines of spectacular
understatement:

> STENGEL, Charles Dillon. 'Casey.' Manager. Born July 30, 1890,
> at Kansas City, Mo. Height: 5 ft., 10 in. Weight: 175 pounds.
> Batted and threw lefthanded. Married and lives in Glendale, Calif.
> Former outfielder.

Before he had become a "former outfielder," though, Stengel
had played baseball from 1910 to 1931 for four minor league
teams, five major league teams and two more minor league teams.
Then, as a manager, he lived through 25 seasons of almost
abject frustration in both the major and minor leagues, finishing
no higher than fifth in an eight-team league during one entire
decade, before suddenly graduating to the New York Yankees as
the 15th manager in their 46-year history of dominating the
sport. He won 10 pennants in 12 years and finally, at the age of
72, wound up with the Mets where he had started—at the bottom
of the ladder.

During the next four years, the Mets fielded a team that won
194 games, lost 452 and ran dead last in the National League
each time. But they fielded a team that was cast in the precise
image of the waddling old man who directed it, a team whose sins
were pardoned by an adoring public, whose life was surrounded by
legend—and could be understood only in terms of legend—and a
team whose bank credit grew as indisputably as the lore.

In 1965, Casey Stengel's last year in a baseball uniform,
1,768,389 persons paid up to $3.50 each to watch the Old

Man and his celebrated Youth of America in their new ball park on
Flushing Bay, and 1,075,431 paid to see them on the road.

Only the Los Angeles Dodgers, en route to the world championship, and the Houston Astros, en route to great wealth under
baseball's first roof, did better business at home, and with a World's
Fair enlivening the Meadow next to the stadium, Stengel completed
the "perfect link" to the public that had so enthralled Branch
Rickey.

But Stengel's rapport with the American public went far beyond the box office.

"He's not a clown," his wife Edna said after 40 years of marriage. "He's one of the smartest men in baseball, in business, in
anything he'd try."

He was a turn-of-the-century athlete, country boy and Broadway character rolled into one and, it was widely believed, was the
model for Carey in Ring Lardner's *Alibi Ike.* He drove a taxicab
as a husky, rather oldish teen-ager in Kansas City; played football
and basketball as well as baseball in high school; turned to semi-pro
baseball in 1910 to earn money for dental school; consternated
his laboratory instructors by attempting to practice dentistry left-
handed; was paid 25 cents for pumping the organ in St. Mark's
Episcopal Church in Kansas City, $1 a day for pitching with the
Kansas City Red Sox, $135 a month for playing the outfield with
Kankakee and, 55 years later, $100,000 a year for managing the
New York Mets.

When he was poor, he was duly impressed by small wealth. "I
found they'd pay me $135 a month for playing ball," he told the
members of the Senate Antitrust and Monopoly Subcommittee on
July 9, 1958, during hearings on baseball's business growth. "I
thought it was amazing." But, he said later when private conver-
sations got around to his personal fortune, "people are always
talking about how much money I got; they never remember how
much money I lost."

He earned all this to the loud accompaniment of theatrical antics both on and off the baseball field, until he was accused of carrying on in order to distract people from the less effectual
performances of his teams. But even in his heyday as skipper of the
lordly Yankees, he performed from a full repertoire of practical
jokes, pantomime and anecdotes.

"He can talk all day and all night," John Lardner said, "on any kind of track, wet or dry."

His talent for outlandish behavior outraged owners like Barney Dreyfuss of the Pittsburgh Pirates, officials like Judge Emil Fuchs of the Boston Braves, commissioners like Kenesaw Mountain Landis and umpires like Bill Klem.

"Every time two owners got together with a fountain pen," observed Quentin Reynolds, "Casey Stengel was being sold or bought."

"I never played with the Cubs, Cards or Reds," Stengel acknowledged. "I guess that was because the owners of those clubs didn't own no fountain pens."

When he was installed as a one-man triumvirate—president, manager and outfielder—for the Braves' farm club at Worcester, Massachusetts, in the Eastern League in 1925, he fretted through his first assignment as an executive for one season. He even played in 100 of the team's 125 games and the team finished third. But at the end of the season he executed a monumental front-office triple play to escape. As manager, he released Stengel the player. As president, he fired Stengel the manager. And as Stengel, he resigned as president.

He once slid into a potted plant in the Sheraton-Cadillac Hotel in Detroit to demonstrate Ty Cobb's famous fallaway slide. But when he was criticized in 1918 for not sliding home during a close game when he was, according to his own judgment, a grossly underpaid member of the Pittsburgh Pirates, he replied: "With the salary I get here, I'm so hollow and starving that I'm liable to explode like a light bulb if I hit the ground too hard."

Putting him into the outfield was likely to become an adventure for both sides. When he returned to Ebbets Field in Brooklyn for the first time as a member of the Pirates, he was welcomed back with a rousing round of catcalls from the same fans who had applauded his tricks for his first five years in the major leagues. In reply, he marched to home plate, bowed with courtliness to the grandstand, doffed his cap, and out flew a sparrow.

When he took over right field for Montgomery of the Southern Association in the spring of 1912, he achieved a complicated variation of the fly-ball-in-a-stream routine that had helped launch his histrionic career two years earlier. He found a drainage hole in the outfield and simply disappeared from sight. A short time later he rose like Triton from the sea, drainage cover under his arm, just in time to grab a fly ball. His manager, Kid Elberfeld, was not amused.

When umpires pulled rank to thwart his tricks, he sometimes counterattacked with passive resistance. He would swoon in a mock faint and just lie down on the ground while they raged. He did this effectively one day against Beans Reardon, one of the National League's senior umpires, but Reardon trumped Stengel's ace by lying down alongside him.

"When I peeked outa one eye and saw Reardon on the ground, too," he recalled later, "I knew I was licked."

When another umpire rejected his suggestion that it was growing too dark to continue playing, Stengel goaded him by signaling his pitcher with a flashlight. When yet another umpire appeared to give him the worst of a series of decisions, he stripped off his uniform shirt on the field, held it out and said impudently: "You try to play on our side for a change."

When John J. McGraw, his idol as a manager, attempted to stifle him, Stengel rebelled somewhat more gently. McGraw hired a private detective to shadow Stengel and Irish Meusel, the two most celebrated hell-raisers on the New York Giants. So the two players simply split up, forcing McGraw's man to track one quarry and neglect the other. Stengel, with pretended petulance, then went to McGraw and complained: "If you want me followed, you'll have to get me a detective of my own."

Later, when he became a manager himself, Stengel looked back on his wayward years and said: "Now that I am a manager, I see the error of my youthful ways. If any player pulled that stuff on me now, I would probably fine his ears off."

Indeed, he was frequently accused of intolerance in the face of others' antics, though the degree of intolerance appeared to fluctuate with the degree of the culprit's success with ball, bat and glove.

When he was a new manager at Toledo in the American Association in the late nineteen-twenties, his players, like most other working adults in the country, became Wall Street buffs who played the soaring stock market and showed more frenzy over the stock averages than over their batting averages. The team dropped off from first place in 1927 to sixth in 1928 and plunged to eighth in 1929 just before the market plunged even deeper.

He called the team together one day at the height of the boom and said, with a tone of formality: "You fellows better start buying Pennsylvania Railroad and Baltimore & Ohio stock, because when we start shipping you out to the bushes next week those roads are going to get rich."

A quarter-century later, his New York Yankees eased into a game of Twenty Questions aboard a train en route from a catastrophic series against the meek Philadelphia Athletics. When he could stand the frivolity no longer, he poked his head around from the manager's front seat in the special car and growled: "I'll ask *you* a question. How many of you fellas think you're earning your salary?"

Still, he proved unregenerate himself no matter what rank he occupied. Arthur Daley wrote in *The New York Times:* "His humor is constant and ever-flowing, but most of it is strictly visual. You have to see him in action to appreciate him, an item which perpetually confounds those chroniclers who strive to capture his hilarious antics in print. He acts funny but he doesn't write funny because his violent pantomime and mimicry need a much broader stage than the confining limitations of type."

He displayed this bent on a sufficiently broad stage sometimes in situations that might have been perilous for a less-talented mimic. On a tour of the Pacific he once devoted an entire 20-minute "speech" at a rally to a violent pantomime of arm-waving, finger-pointing and head-shaking, clenching his fist and going through all the signs of an orator without actually saying anything, while the crowd roared.

He was not insensitive to the possibility of diplomatic or physical dangers, however, exhibiting a kind of Charlie Chaplin stoicism to the tightrope course he often plunged along.

In the spring of 1915, his third with Wilbert Robinson's Dodgers, a sports writer was driving across the trestle between Charles Ebbets's "beautiful Daytona" and the beach when his headlights caught the figure of a man leaning over the railing toward the water. He stopped, ran over and looked into the anguished face of Casey Stengel. "I'm sick," the young outfielder moaned, "and Uncle Robbie doesn't like me and I can't hit, and I'm deliberatin' whether to jump in."

When he became manager of the same Dodgers 20 seasons later, he slumped into a barber's chair after the team had fumbled away a doubleheader with flourishes, ordered a shave and cautioned the barber: "Don't cut my throat. I may want to do that later myself."

When he became manager of Oakland in the Pacific Coast League in 1946, he noted the geographical advantages of the area with appreciation. "Just like Brooklyn," he said, "wherever I go they throw in a bridge as part of the service. Every manager wants to jump off a bridge sooner or later, and it is very nice for an old man like me to know he don't have to walk 50 miles to find one."

He did not have to walk 50 miles to find an audience, either, for his nonstop, marathon, circuitous style of speaking that became known as "Stengelese."

It was a kind of rambling semi-doubletalk laced with ambiguous, assumed or unknown antecedents, a liberal use of "which" instead of "who" or "that," a roundabout narrative framed in great generalities and dangling modifiers, a lack of proper names for "that fella" or simply "the shortstop," plus flashes of incisiveness tacked onto the ends of sentences, like: "And, of course, they got Perranoski."

When a listener's interest appeared to wane, Stengel recaptured his attention by suddenly exclaiming, "Now, wait; let me ask you," etc. And he would then pose a question in the form of a lengthy monologue. Finally, when the central point was delivered, he would extend a finger, wink with exaggeration and ask: "Got it?" Strict followers of Stengelese always found a point at the end of the trail, though often an hour later; between the layers of dangling participles and fused phrases, a point lurked.

Sometimes the point was made rather quickly in a form of short, clipped, Stengelese, most frequently to summarize a baseball player's ability or idiosyncrasies or to define a situation starkly.

Of Jim Bunning, who had pitched successfully for both the Detroit Tigers of the American League and the Philadelphia Phillies of the National League, he said: "He must be good. He gets 'em out in both leagues."

Of Van Lingle Mungo, his impetuous pitcher with the Dodgers in the nineteen-thirties: "Mungo and I get along fine. I just tell him I won't stand for no nonsense—and then I duck."

Of Roger Maris, the aloof, arch power-hitter of the Yankees: "That Maris. You'd tell him something and he'd stare at you for a week before answering."

Of baseball itself and the nature of the game: "You got to get 27 outs to win."

Of the logic of the double play: "It gives you two twenty-sevenths of a ball game."

Of a pitcher who throws sinking balls that tend to be hit onto the ground into such double plays: "He throws grounders."

Of ball players and their occasional lack of hustle: "I ain't seen no one die on a ball field chasing flies. And the pitchers. I bet I lost six games fieldin' by a pitcher. He's got an eighteen-dollar glove, ain't he?"

Of Willie Mays, who played for the San Francisco Giants in windy Candlestick Park: "If a typhoon is blowing, he catches the ball."

Of a ball player with a problem: "That feller runs splendid but he needs help at the plate, which coming from the country chasing rabbits all winter give him strong legs, although he broke one falling out of a tree, which shows you can't tell, and when a curve ball comes he waves at it and if pitchers don't throw curves you have no pitching staff, so how is a manager going to know whether to tell boys to fall out of trees and break legs so he can run fast even if he can't hit a curve ball?"

Stengelese flowered, though, in even longer, fuller public utterances that reached Olympian heights in Congress, where a rambler of Stengel's range might be accused of carrying coal to Newcastle. When he testified in 1958 before the Senate's Antitrust and Monopoly Subcommittee, he took the members back in history and syntax as he reviewed the ramifications of Oliver Wendell Holmes's decision of 1922 that baseball was not a business subject to trust laws but was "a local exhibition."

"I had many years that I was not so successful as a ball player, as it is a game of skill," Stengel said, appearing as the manager of Yankees and the patriarch of the national game. "And then I no doubt was discharged by baseball, in which I had to go back to the minor leagues as a manager and after being in the minor leagues as a manager I became a major league manager in several cities and was discharged, we call it 'discharged' because there is no question I had to leave."

But should there be a new law governing professional baseball's relations with its players?

"Well," the Professor replied into the microphone, "I would have to say at the present time that I think baseball has advanced in this respect for the player help. That is an amazing statement for me to make, because you can retire with an annuity at 50 and what organization in America allows you to retire at 50 and receive money?

"I want to further state that I am not a ball player, that is, put into that pension fund committee. At my age, and I have been in baseball, well, I will say that I am possibly the oldest man in baseball. I would say that when they start an annuity for ball players to better their conditions, it should have been done and I think it has been done."

Estes Kefauver, the tall Tennesseean who became a Presidential contender after staring down Frank Costello and other powerful starers in other Senate hearings, received the loudest laugh of the day when he cleared his throat and said: "Mr. Stengel, I'm not sure I made my question clear."

The feeling persisted, after performances like these, that Stengelese was at least 50 per cent "put on" and 50 per cent "personality." As a vice president and director of the Valley National Bank of Glendale, which he and his wife's family controlled, Casey was considered as clownish as a barracuda despite straight-faced monologues like this one during an exposition on his bank's branch at Toluca Lake:

"We're a national bank and this is what you call a subsiduary. That's correct. Our main office is over in Glendale and this is a subsiduary—a branch. You can't ask me to go downstairs and run an I.B.M. machine without a college I.B.M. course. And I'm not supposed to talk about the banking business at all, because gold is leaving the country.

"Now this is the board room. See over there on the chart—capital assets and all that. Now you ask me: if this is the board room, where is the board, and I say this ain't the day the board meets. Okay?

"Now, in there where it says 'escrows' is where they can take people in and talk about escrows so it won't be out in public."

Part of the anatomy of Stengelese consisted of certain understated adjectives, like "fairly" as in "fairly amazing," and certain rich or mid-Victorian words or usages that he dropped neatly among the "ain'ts" and "fellas," such as "commence" and "numerous" and "splendid."

When 1,400 banners were paraded around the perimeter of Shea Stadium in New York during the Mets' annual Banner Day contest, "numerous splendid" hand-made signs carried messages in short, pure Stengelese, including one that caught the essence of the Stengel philosophy toward his astonishingly forlorn ball club in the Professor's own metier: "Commence Bein' Amazin'."

Even the Stengel telephone had a touch of the legend. His home number in California for years carried the exchange "Citrus"; his office exchange, appropriately, "Popular." One day in January 1965, just before he began what turned into his final season as a manager, the phone rang in the bank and the vice president, who had been alerted for a call from this writer on the East Coast, answered.

"I feel fairly good, yes, sir," he boomed, his flair for understatement in mid-season form. "We've been going to all them big football games at Southern Cal. And now we're going ahead with our new bank building here in Glendale, and then there's a branch in North Hollywood that we're goin' to dig ground for, and if I had Berra and Spahn and some of those pitchers here I'd see that they'd dig in and I'd show 'em who's the boss—around the bank, anyway."

"Spahn and Berra the opening-day battery?" he asked, barely pausing to field a question. "Well, I tell you. You know the amazing fans we have in Shea Stadium, which have stormed us with mail from all over, and now we have a girls' group and a women's group. There's nobody in the world I've seen will buy more tickets, and more fans are going to show up on opening day whether the Dodgers show up or not. So maybe we'll fill the park anyway and let those boys play 'em another day."

The point being delivered was that Stengel the Banker never let Stengel the Manager indulge in non sequiturs in money matters. The Los Angeles Dodgers, with Sandy Koufax, Don Drysdale, Maury Wills and many memories of the team's 67 years in Brooklyn, were scheduled to open the season three months later in New York. It was to be a one-day stand and a certain sellout, followed for two days by the Houston Astros, who were certain not to sell out the stadium. So behind the doubletalk lay the seeds of a plan to fill the Mets' coffers on those quieter days with Stengel's "money" combination of Yogi Berra and Warren Spahn, two of the game's ranking stars who had been signed by the Mets near the end of their careers.

"I think we have a number of spots open on the ball club," Stengel went on, having, as usual, all of his time-outs left. "We have numerous jobs which our men can fill on the pitching staff, in the outfield and in the infield, too. You could look it up, but very few players last more than five years, or maybe ten, and you'll find that the annuities are made out that way."

Did he know that his second-baseman, Ron Hunt, had returned his contract unsigned?

"Is that so?" he asked with interest. "Well, Mr. Hunt has given 100 per cent, and he'll probably have to be a second-baseman again this year. I have a proposition with Hunt that he'd have to beat out several outstanding players, and he did win the job against competition without ever being in Triple-A baseball."

Translation: Hunt resented suggestions that he shift to third base to make way for unproved players at second base, and he probably was right.

Edna Stengel added a postscript to the conversation, displaying some Stengel understatement herself, by saying: "We're kind of an active family, you know."

Stengel's entourage of baseball players and writers had watched one-half of the active family that season in cities from San Francisco to Philadelphia, as they traveled the country with their 74-year-old manager, watching him in action before the public around the clock.

In Milwaukee, we watched him rush onto the field when the Mets and the Braves got into a ninth-inning rumble one night. Some players said later that they were so surprised to stumble over "the Old Man" in the dust that they broke up laughing. Hours after, the Old Man was enthralling friends and writers by re-enacting great team fights of two generations earlier.

In Pittsburgh one day, a family named Stengel sent a birth certificate into the dugout with the name David Casey Stengel written on it—their son, who had been born nine years earlier after Casey's Yankees had won their fifth straight championship.

He bounced over to the dugout railing and held court with his namesake for 20 minutes.

In St. Louis, before a glittering mink-and-tails crowd on Robert Goulet's opening night in the ballroom of the Chase Hotel, Goulet eased into his first number, cruising around a raised dance floor murmuring a love song to the ringside tables. He turned left and ("Why not take all of me?") came face to face with the unmistakable features of Casey Stengel, who was sitting at the ringside, too. The singer did a double take, fell to one knee, stopped his show and, to deafening applause, introduced the manager of the Mets, who stood and croaked: "You know, I've got a way with the ladies myself." After that, Goulet sang and Stengel was besieged by dozens of stunningly gowned women, who thronged his table pleading for autographs, and it became the Robert Goulet and Casey Stengel show.

In Cincinnati, a radio interviewer asked about Washington's place in the national life and Casey said proudly that "people want to see three things there, don't they? the White House, the Washington Monument because Gabby Street once caught a ball dropped off it and the ball park—because in what other sport does the President throw out the first ball every year?"

In Houston, a man brought his skeptical son to the visiting team's dugout and said hesitantly: "I wonder if you remember me. I pitched against you when you broke in with Kankakee." The Mets had just traveled from the Coast, were sleepless and, as usual, somewhat hopeless, and they were showing signs of total collapse as a baseball team. But the old manager looked at the visitor and his son and said: "Sure, sure. The old fireball himself. Why, I was sure glad when you quit that league. Did you make me look bad. I never could hit you."

In San Francisco, a minister leaned over the visiting team's dugout, introduced himself and said he had pitched batting practice to Stengel in 1910 in Kankakee. The census listed Kankakee, Illinois, at 27,666, and that was half a century after Stengel and all of his visitors supposedly had crowded the little town, but he showed no flicker of disbelief this time, either. He turned in astonishment to a man standing near him in the dugout and, spanning the 54 turbulent years since Kankakee, said warmly: "You know, he helped me hit."

That was a depression, two world wars, three generations and a dozen leagues earlier. And now, Branch Rickey was saying on that mild September evening in 1964 just before Casey Stengel headed into his last season as the most splendidly flamboyant, influential and controversial figure in the game, "he is exactly the right age to manage a major league baseball team."

2

KANKAKEE

Casey Stengel, the manager of the New York Yankees, winners
of three straight American League pennants, was 62 years old
in 1952 and Mickey Mantle was muscular, inexperienced and
21. Mantle had been signed to a professional contract by Tom
Greenwade, a Yankee scout, on June 13, 1949, had been braced
with a $1,000 bonus, had played one season at Independence,
Kansas, one at Joplin, Missouri, then had taken the giant step to the
major leagues.

Now he was being billed as the successor to Babe Ruth, Lou
Gehrig and Joe DiMaggio—the premier New York Yankee players
of the century. But he was at the stage when life seemed a constant
torture of third strikes on offense and line drives on defense that
caromed unpredictably off the low outfield fence in Yankee
Stadium.

So now Mr. Stengel stood in right field alongside him, faced the
wall, trapped an imaginary baseball as it rebounded, and wheeled
as if to throw it in to one of the infielders. Mantle, it seemed to the
Old Man, appeared reasonably bored, skeptical and unimpressed.

"He thinks," Stengel said later, diagnosing their relationship in
a few words, "that I was born at the age of 62 and started managing immediately."

If so, Mantle had a faint point. Stengel probably did look, to a
rookie outfielder two generations younger, as though he had been

born at the age of 62 and had started managing immediately. He had had a kind of old, strong, eagle look about him even as a child, in an era that Mantle might read about but that might only confirm his suspicions that the Yankees' manager of 1952 was an anachronism, misplaced in time and miscast as an expert on the angle, carry and velocity of caroming baseballs.

Victoria had been Queen for 53 years on July 30, 1890, when Charles Dillon Stengel was born to Louis E. and Jennie Jordan Stengel in Kansas City. Benjamin Harrison was President of a country that was slipping from the post-Civil War period into the so-called Gay Nineties, and Grover Cleveland, who had already served one term, was about to confound the statisticians of Presidential succession by returning for a second term four years later.

Louis Stengel's father had emigrated to the United States from Germany in 1851 at the age of 13, had settled in Rock Island, Illinois, married Katherine Kniphals and died in 1865 when Louis was 4. Rock Island was typical farm country, across the Mississippi River from Davenport, Iowa, which is where Louis Stengel found, courted and married Jennie Jordan. She was the daughter of John B. Jordan and the niece of a judge of the Iowa Supreme Court, John F. Dillon, who also served as counsel for railroad companies that had spread their tracks south and west from Chicago.

Louis and Jennie Stengel had moved from the Davenport-Rock Island area to Kansas City and had two children at that time—Louise, born in 1886, and Grant, born in 1887. Louis Stengel was a short, strong man who made a comfortable living as an agent for the Joseph Stiebel Insurance Company, which also owned a commercial street-sprinkling system. For a fee, a wagon with a wooden water tank pulled by horses would sprinkle the main street of town and the wealthier, more fastidious neighborhoods. The company persuaded Stengel to take over this part of its diversification. He did, and became a familiar figure riding behind the horses on the streets of Kansas City until the city commandeered the sprinkling itself in 1915 and he more or less retired.

"Charley," meanwhile, was living the unhurried life of any midwestern boy at the turn of the century. The family switched houses fairly frequently, his mother became locally renowned as a formidable cook, and in grammar school he had to undergo the usual

transformation faced by thousands of other children with one of
the outstanding social afflictions of the day: he was left-handed.

Being left-handed proved no affliction, though, when it came to
the things that became his chief interest in life—games—as he moved
through Woodland grade school and Kansas City Central High
School, displaying a neat right hand for penmanship and an increasingly neat left hand for throwing baseballs, footballs and
basketballs. He was the leading athlete in his class at Central High,
halfback and captain on the football team, a member of the state
championship basketball team, and the third-baseman, pitcher and
captain of the baseball team, which also won the state championship.

Baseball steadily outgrew the other sports as a way of afternoon
life, though. For one thing, it didn't cost much to come up with a
ball or even a glove. For another, Kansas City was blessed with
enough vacant lots to accommodate the teen-agers who were trying to copy the great Ty Cobb, who had reached the big leagues in
Detroit in 1905 and, starting two years later, won nine American
League batting championships in a row; or Hans Wagner, who
led the National League in batting eight times between 1900 and
1911.

The ball yards were likely to have tremendous bumps and ruts,
or even ravines, across the outfield, unlike Yankee Stadium a generation later, which, Stengel noted, had an outfield turf "like a pool
table." But no matter. Nor did it matter that the customary way
to get to a ball game, aside from a bicycle, was by horse-drawn
surrey, the kind that carted the Armour packinghouse team
around, including the teen-aged Stengel brothers, Charley and
Grant.

Grant, who was three years older, had managed to get his
brother a spot on the team. They played together until a day
when the team was coming back from a game and Grant was
scuffling with some of the other boys on the surrey, slipped, caught
his foot in the brake and lost part of his heel. "He was a good outfielder, an accurate thrower and very bright on the bases," his
brother recalled, but Grant's career in baseball was ended and
Charley was on his own.

During his last two years in high school, "Dutch" Stengel—or
Casey, as he was being called—traveled during summer vacations

with the Kansas City Red Sox. They even got as far as Cheyenne, Wyoming, playing for $1 a day and fringe benefits like candy and snacks.

Then, in his junior year at City Central in 1909, he pitched the final game for the state championship against Joplin, a town that was to send Mantle to the major leagues 40 years later. He pitched 15 innings, won the game, 7–6, left high school the following year without actually graduating, walked into the front parlor of his home one spring day in 1910 holding a paper in his hand and said to Louis Stengel, "Hey, Pop, sign this, will you?"

"So I put down my paper and pipe and signed," his father said. "You never could change the boy's mind, even then. He had been working out with the Kansas City [professional] club, the manager liked his looks, though not as a pitcher, and thought he'd make quite an outfielder. But he needed his parents' consent to join the club."

Strictly speaking, joining the Kansas City Blues was a means to an end, though two years later the means grew into the end. The end was to collect enough money to stake Casey through dental school, and, having secured his financial flank, so to speak, and having earned enough high school credits even without a diploma, he enrolled in the Western Dental College in Kansas City aiming for a career in dentistry.

This became a part-time effort that lasted two winters and that finally foundered for three reasons, any one of which would have been adequate: He really wanted to become a full-time baseball player, no strings attached; left-handed dentists had a considerably more obscure future in Kansas City in 1910 than left-handed baseball players, and, as he acknowledged later, the college did not have the daring to turn him loose with a "weapon" in his hand.

In fact, he recalled, his first clinic patient was also his last. While still a student, he was entrusted (under supervision) with the task of extracting a tooth from "a guy who must've been nine feet tall and which was the strongest man around." Casey bent to his task without hesitation, but the harder he tugged the more impossible his task became. The patient, he noticed, seemed to be growing taller and taller as he yanked on the tooth. He just could not get any leverage, had almost encircled the victim's head with his arm and extracted the patient almost completely from the chair, the tooth unmolested, when his instructor came running up, halted the farce and cried: "You're left-handed, you're left-handed!"

"I did everything right," Casey reported, "except switchin' hands."

As things turned out, his debut as a professional ball player that summer ran a gantlet of mishaps, too. They were typical of the primitive state of baseball economics then and untypical of the situation 40 years later when 16 clubs would pursue a college boy with bids as high as $200,000 and nurse him painstakingly toward the major leagues. Or, 50 years later, for that matter, when the first draft of "free agents" was put into effect and more than 800 amateur players were drafted, or claimed, by 20 major league clubs for future consideration and consignment.

For one thing, though he joined the Blues and even trained for his professional debut at Excelsior Springs, Missouri, he was relegated to a considerably more obscure station when the season began: Kankakee of the Northern Association. He also abandoned his career as a left-handed pitcher, became an outfielder for good and reported for work in the dim minor leagues in rural Illinois.

"I found they'd pay me $135 a month for playing ball," he told the Kefauver committee in his celebrated Senate appearance 48 years later. "I thought that was amazing."

He was even more amazed, though, when the league collapsed from financial anemia midway through the season. He had appeared in 59 games, gone to bat 203 times, made 51 hits (including one home run), batted .251, stolen the respectable total of 16 bases and was owed a month's pay when the league went bankrupt—"blew up," according to a footnote in an otherwise staid baseball guide that chronicled his career 15 years later.

"The team didn't last the season," he said, "and I was out of work before I had a job."

So, he packed his suitcase and moved down the road to Shelbyville, Kentucky, in a league with a picturesque name, the Blue Grass League, but with no cash to speak of. This time, the Shelbyville franchise collapsed.

However, it staged a comeback of sorts a few days later by reviving itself in a nearby town, Maysville, which, except for the stream flowing past the outfield, was on more solid footing.

Stengel also finally got a line in a record book that outlived the

league. He played in 69 games for Maysville in 1910, went to
bat 233 times, made 52 hits, including 10 two-baggers, 5 three-
baggers and 2 home runs; scored 27 runs, and finished his first
season in the minor leagues with two franchises shot out from
under him and a batting average of .223.

That winter he was back in dental school, a comic-opera figure
in a Prince Albert frock coat, he said later; but a bright student
trying to work out his future in something more secure than the
Blue Grass Baseball League. But too many things were stirring to
let a 20-year-old of his assertive nature become secure and settled
in a dentist's parlor in Kansas City.

Glen Curtiss had just won $10,000 from the New York
World for making the first nonstop flight from Albany to New
York City, 137 miles in 152 minutes. A dynamite explosion had
rocked the Los Angeles *Times* building during a dispute between building contractors and structural ironworkers, killing 21
persons and touching off a legal hassle in which Clarence Darrow
argued for the defense and Lincoln Steffens finally was enlisted as
a conciliator. And Sir Robert Baden-Powell was transplanting his
Boy Scouts from England to America, though more boys in
Kansas City that year probably had their eyes on Ty Cobb, the
"Peach" from Narrows, Georgia, who had signed a baseball contract for $500 and now, in his sixth season in the big leagues, was
batting .385 with eight home runs.

When spring came in 1911, Stengel quietly said good-by to
his instructors at Western Dental, appeared briefly on the roster
—but not on the field—for his old Kansas City team, and then settled
into the lineup of Aurora, Illinois, in the Wisconsin-Illinois League.
This league survived, and he made the most of it: 121 games,
420 times at bat, 115 singles, 23 doubles, 6 triples, 4 home runs,
and a batting average of .352.

Aurora was only a short run down the line from Chicago, and
a rookie with a batting average of .352 was worth a look by the
major league scouts, even in those days. So a scout for Brooklyn
named Larry Sutton made the trip to watch Stengel play. When he
left, Aurora had a check for $300, Brooklyn had first rights to
Casey Stengel and Stengel had a contract to play eventually for
Brooklyn, a team variously nicknamed the Superbas, the Bride-

grooms and the Trolley Dodgers—but a major league team. Before
another year was out, he would be standing in Washington Park,
Brooklyn.

That winter he severed his last ties with the dental profession
and, when spring arrived in 1912, he arrived at the Brooklyn
farm club in Montgomery, Alabama, having leapfrogged all the
way from the "low" minor leagues to the "high" ones and being
now just a telegram away from the major leagues. He had played
only one complete season, not counting the misadventures in Illinois and Kentucky in 1910, but he latched onto a regular job
playing the outfield in the Southern League, which he did for
136 games. He was batting .290 for Montgomery that September when the telegram came. He had been called up by Brooklyn.

When Stengel arrived in the big leagues in September 1912,
baseball had evolved from rounders and cricket in England to
town ball in America, then into a gentleman's game called "base
ball" and finally into a fairly roughneck sport.

Seven years earlier, when he was a 15-year-old starting through
Kansas City Central High, the presidents of the two major leagues
—Harry C. Pulliam of the National League and Byron Bancroft
Johnson of the four-year-old American League—had organized a
commission to search out the origins of the game.

Pulliam and Johnson outdid themselves in selecting the commission. They named Morgan G. Bulkeley, onetime Governor of
Connecticut and first president of the National League; Arthur P.
Gorman, former Senator from Maryland; A.G. Mills, third president of the National League; Nicholas E. Young, fourth president
of the National League; Alfred J. Reach, second-baseman for the
Philadelphia club in the first professional league, the National Association, in 1871, and later the head of a giant sporting goods
company that produced, among other things, the baseballs used in
the American League; George Wright, shortstop for the first professional club, the Cincinnati Red Stockings, and James E. Sullivan,
president of the Amateur Athletic Union.

For three years they researched the subject, trying to distinguish
between primitive forms like "one old cat"—or, phonetically, at
least, "one o' cat"—or two o' cat, in which the batter had one or
two swings at a ball of twine with a stick or paddle; and town
ball, a more organized form of mayhem in which the whole town

was invited to take part and each side grew frequently to a mob of 30 or more players.

One thing seemed constant: all the variations involved hitting a ball and trying to run to a base before a defending player could retrieve it.

The commission, having pursued witnesses and descendants of witnesses as far west as the Rockies, finally decided that these earlier forms had been developed into "base ball" by Abner Doubleday in the farmland around Cooperstown, New York, in 1839—just before he left home to enter West Point and 21 years before he gained considerably less fame as the captain of artillery at Fort Sumter, South Carolina, who fired the first shot for the Union in the exchange that escalated into the Civil War.

Several kinds of "base ball," though, were being played at about the same time Doubleday was laying out a diamond-shaped area with four bases at Cooperstown. In New York City, the Knickerbocker Baseball and Social Club was organized in 1845 and two or three times a week split into two teams for a game of ball, with the first team to score 21 runs winning the game.

Rules, though, were as numerous as the players sometimes had been in the old town ball matches, and they remained that way until one of the well-to-do sports of the Knickerbocker Club, Alexander Joy Cartwright Jr., headed a "committee" to draw up a set of rules. Cartwright had been playing ball for three years with other more or less wealthy young men on open land near Madison Avenue and Twenty-seventh Street, and he was already a superior ball player. He promptly performed a monumental job of standardizing rules that lasted: a diamond with bases 90 feet apart, nine men to a team, unchangeable batting orders, three outs to a side in each inning, and no throwing the ball at a base runner to put him out, like a clay pigeon.

Once this amount of order had been established, the game spread with a speed that might have astonished even the 20 major league clubs who, 120 years later, were paid $25,510,000 by television stations for the right to broadcast games coast to coast. On June 19, 1846, the Knickerbockers played the first match of record, a four-inning contest umpired by Cartwright and won, 23–1, by a rival club, the New York Nine, and how the mighty had fallen. The game was played at Elysian Field in Hoboken, New

Jersey, across the Hudson River from Manhattan, and the niceties
were maintained with some difficulty by Cartwright, who established perhaps an even more revealing precedent by fining one of
the players 6 cents for "cussing."

In 1849, the Knickerbockers appeared in the first baseball uniforms—long blue woolen trousers, white flannel shirts and straw
hats. Cartwright himself was too preoccupied with another project
to take part, having bought a covered wagon and headed west in
the gold rush, and later growing into an imposing figure with
white hair and a long beard by the time he died in Hawaii in
1892.

As usually happens when the boys leave home and take their
banjos, songs and games with them, the game that Doubleday had
helped start got its greatest momentum from the war that Doubleday had helped start. Union and Confederate soldiers alike played
camp baseball games, sometimes against each other when prisoners
of war were allowed a few hours' free time.

With this momentum, the Nationals of Washington, D.C., took
baseball on its first road trips after the war, covering 2,400 miles
in three weeks, which became par for the course even in chartered
jetliners a century later. The Nationals were tough, and their
scores tended to get out of hand. They won games by 113 to
26 and 88 to 12, and were subdued only when a teen-ager
named Albert Goodwill Spalding outpitched them in Rockford,
Illinois, 29 to 23.

The first professional team, the Red Stockings of Cincinnati, was
formed in 1869 and immediately enjoyed a season to end all
seasons. The Red Stockings traveled 12,000 miles, won 65 straight
games and, more significantly, played before 200,000 persons,
unfortunately including hordes of gamblers who began to follow
baseball teams eagerly and make book openly in the grandstands.

Worse, for a few dollars, the new professional players could be
tempted to jump to other clubs, which they began to do in droves.
When the situation got out of hand, ten of the clubs met in New
York in 1871 and organized the National Association of Professional Base Ball Players, a governing body that tried to keep
house against long odds. The association also authorized the first
"world's championship," a title bestowed on the team that finished

the season with the highest playing percentage of games won and that thereupon was entitled to fly a "championship streamer," or pennant.

The Athletics of Philadelphia won the first such streamer, in 1871, then the Red Stockings of Boston the next four with unusual flourishes, including an excursion to Canada during the season. The Red Stockings met and defeated teams from Guelph, Toronto, Ottawa, London, Dundas and Montreal before recrossing the border to resume their "pennant race."

When the gambling and raiding of players continued to increase in spite of the association's surveillance and, more important, the gate receipts started to decrease, eight of the professional clubs banded in 1876 into the National League. Hulbert, who was president of the Chicago White Stockings, drew up a constitution along with Spalding, the teen-aged pitcher of the eighteen-sixties, who was to succeed him six years later as head of the club. The cities were Chicago, Boston, New York, Philadelphia, Hartford, St. Louis, Cincinnati and Louisville, in that order of admission. Bulkeley, who headed the Hartford team, also headed the league for one year, after which Hulbert took over and ran the league and the Chicago franchise simultaneously until he died in 1882.

The National League's outlook was fairly austere. No Sunday baseball was permitted, no beer was allowed in the grandstand and no ticket-scalping was countenanced. For all three reasons, dissent was sure to set in, and it did after just six years in the form of a rival league, the American Association, which berated the National League owners as fat cats who thrived on exorbitant admissions of 50 cents and saddled the public with intolerable restraints. The National League replied by deploring the corruptive influence of a "beer and whiskey" organization, a league that included teams in Baltimore and Louisville that were owned by breweries and distilleries and in St. Louis by Chris Van Der Ahe, a prosperous saloon-keeper, and that charged only 25 cents for a ball game.

The "beer and whiskey" issue, as it turned out, was an omen that survived many other aspects of the game, including legal spit-balls and 46-ounce bats. Eighty-four years later, the New York chapter of the Baseball Writers Association of America, in their 1966 winter follies, satirized this aspect of ownership and of the

sponsorship of television broadcasts by depicting four members of
the New York Yankees as singing this lament, to the tune of "The
Whiffenpoof Song":

> From the bar in Newark Airport
> To that joint in Lauderdale,
> We're accused of impropriety and sin,
> Even though the ones who pay us
> Make their dough from beer and ale
> We are punished if we sip a little gin.

The feuding of 1882 was not exactly dissipated, either, when
the White Stockings of Chicago challenged the American Association's best team, the Reds of Cincinnati, to a "world series." The
association had forbidden its teams to compete with the "rowdy"
National League, but the Reds ignored the injunction, went
through the motions of disbanding after the season, then revived
themselves as an "independent" club—and promptly knocked off the
Chicago team, 4 to 0, causing dancing in the streets of Cincinnati
and consternation in the older league.

Chicago recovered its poise the next day, though, and tied the
series by winning, 2 to 0. However, the clandestine match was
halted when H.D. Denny McKnight, president of the association,
threatened to expel the Cincinnati players if they continued. So,
the first "world series" ended in a one-to-one tie.

This sort of skirmishing led, as skirmishing often does, to a treaty
of sorts—the National Agreement of 1882. The "agreement,"
the first code for professional baseball, tried to end the talent raids
between clubs by declaring contracts off-limits to raiders and by
assuring each club firm control over its players. However, as
treaties often do, the agreement led to disagreement. Slavery, it was
called by many players; and a new issue was created that was to
hound baseball owners as long as contracts reserved such rights
to the clubs.

As might be expected, a third force soon appeared on the scene
to offer the disgruntled players an alternative: a new organization
calling itself the Players League, which promptly challenged the
original "major" league, the National League, and its principal
rival, the American Association.

Now the situation became chaotic. Most of the ranking players in both the National League and the American Association began crossing over to the new league in a mutiny against the National Agreement of 1882, and by 1890, the year Stengel was born, baseball was embroiled in a civil war of its own.

The Players League, however, survived only one season in spite of its ready-made issue. But before it collapsed, it weakened the American Association to the point of collapse, too. So frantic was the infighting that one entire team, the Brooklyn team, switched en masse in 1890 from the American Association to the National League. Worse, for the association, Brooklyn had won the championship the year before and, worse still, it made good its escape by promptly winning the championship of the National League, too.

The confusion lasted far into the autumn. Brooklyn, the renegade, met Louisville in a "world series" between the feuding leagues that started late, October 17, was delayed four days by rain and was finally deadlocked at three games apiece with one tie when everybody decided nothing had been settled and called it a season on October 28.

The association, though, had clearly begun to totter. So the National League maneuvered clear of the tangle by annexing a total of four of the association's clubs, expanding from 8 to 12 teams, and for the next 10 years at least it was not seriously challenged again—until the American League was formed in 1901 and the modern pattern of the game, hinged on two equal major leagues, took shape.

The American League was not exactly welcomed when it crowded its way into the act. It evolved from the strong Western League, whose president, Ban Johnson, announced in 1899 that his group would be known as the American League. Johnson then invaded the National League's pioneer city, Chicago, moved quickly into Milwaukee, Cleveland, Detroit, Washington, Boston, Baltimore and Philadelphia; staged a series of punishing raids on National League talent; subtracted Milwaukee and Baltimore, added New York and St. Louis, and by 1903 confronted—and won equal status with—the National League.

The newcomers cemented their grip in the first World Series between the leagues, too, a series played over a two-week period in

1903 with the Boston Pilgrims, or Puritans, as they were known, defeating the Pittsburgh Pirates of the National League in eight games.

The crowds in that historic series contributed almost as much action as the players. The Pirates' Exposition Park in Allegheny seated only 8,000 persons. Yet, twice that many were crammed into the stands and behind ropes that were stretched down the foul lines, hemming the infield and making the outfield a ground-rule hazard that came to be known as "triples paradise," and, in fact, 17 three-baggers were hit into the crowd in four days.

When the series shifted to Boston, the Pilgrims' park, which reportedly could seat 16,242 persons, bulged with 18,801 and fights broke out in the grandstand when squatters refused to move for late arrivals whose ticket stubs, however legitimate, simply led to blows.

Anyway, when the sound and fury faded, there were two major leagues. And when Stengel took the train from Montgomery to Brooklyn nine seasons later, the pattern was firmly set.

The Dodgers in those days were playing out their last season in Washington Park, a wooden bandbox typical of the antiquated ball yards that were just beginning to be replaced. Connie Mack had built the first "modern" stadium, Shibe Park in Philadelphia, a park that was three years old in 1912 and that seated 25,000 persons at a time when big league clubs often played to capacity crowds of 10,000.

Washington Park held 12,000 persons with lots of overhanging seats on nearby buildings and Stengel, getting his first glimpse of New York, recalled how the tempo rose inning by inning, with the players of both teams caught in the middle:

"It cost 10 cents for a can of beer to sit up on the fire escape, and they didn't get real insulting until the beer had begun to take effect—in about the fourth inning. It was like playing for Harvard against Yale."

The ball players who were thus egged on were largely a breed that was perfectly suited for rough-and-tumble. The dominant player in the game was Cobb, the hellcat for the Detroit Tigers, who wound up with the highest career batting average in the game, .367, and who was so tough that the manager of the St. Louis Browns advised his players before Detroit came to town to "keep him in a good humor." The dominant manager was John J. McGraw, whose New York Giants won 10 pennants after he had ended his career as third-baseman for the famed Baltimore Orioles of the nineties, a defensive star so grim that Connie Mack later recalled the "horror" of advancing as far as third base.

The players were hungry, too. Hans Wagner held out one year for $10,000, but salaries rarely exceeded $6,000 in Stengel's first years. The great Christy Mathewson earned no more than $6,000 until his later years. Hal Chase, who played first base and also managed the Yankees in 1912, was paid $6,000 for both jobs.

As a result, the players tangled not only with each other but with the fans and the executives of the game, too. When the Polo Grounds burned in April 1911, the Giants shared the Yankees' Highlander Park for four months while their own park was being rebuilt and fitted with an upper deck. The Yankees thereupon switched to the new Polo Grounds along with the Giants, and the clubs reversed their landlord-tenant roles. But when they did, the Giants found it too much of a strain to adjust from a park that seated 12,000 persons to one that seated 32,000.

The strain showed when newspapers announced that crowds as high as 50,000 were attending the World Series that fall in the new Polo Grounds. The Giant players, whose share of the series revenue was based on the gate receipts, were incredulous at what they sensed was a "short count." After all, if 50,000 persons actually had crammed into the park, the "official capacity" of 32,000 was pretty obsolete.

So they dispatched a delegation led by Chief Meyers, a California mission Indian, to carry a protest to the National Commission, which presided over baseball then. To their amazement, the commissioners ranted right back at them and issued stern reprimands to the players for casting aspersions on the integrity of the game.

On the playing field, order was maintained precariously. Frederick G. Lieb, the baseball writer and historian, saw his first big league game as a boy in 1904 and watched one umpire call balls and strikes and "work" the bases as well, stationing himself behind the pitcher's mound and roaming as the action warranted.

By 1912, two umpires were being assigned to games, one working behind home plate and one on the baselines. They wore blue uniforms, as the teams of four umpires later did (six at World Series games), but they held no pre-game meeting at home plate and they helped hustle the players through games that rarely lasted more than two hours.

The players themselves were a trifle more civilized in appearance, if not in temper, than they had been during the more violent nineties. John Titus, right-fielder for the Philadelphia Phillies, sported a stubbly blond mustache early in the century. Jake Beckley of the St. Louis club even displayed a bit of a handlebar, contrasted with the full-flower handlebars that Wilbert Robinson and John McGraw and their cronies had grown 10 years before. The decline of the mustachioed ball player had set in, though Wally Schang, the catcher for the Philadelphia Athletics, grew a mustache as late as 1914 before shaving it off under mild duress.

Stengel, who was described by an eyewitness as "petulant, perhaps truculent, maybe even bellicose," as a player, underwent a somewhat understandable change of heart on the subject of flamboyant players in his later years as a manager. When Frenchie Bordagary appeared in Brooklyn in 1934 with a substantial mustache, Stengel fumed.

"Every time you get on base," he said, "I have asked the catchers in this league to throw the ball at your mustache. If they happen to kill you, I will pay the funeral expense."

Bordagary removed the offending mustache, but it was by no means likely that he would have done so if the incident had occurred in 1912. Life was considerably more casual then. On the road, for example, the teams traveled around the 16 cities in the major leagues in Pullman car expeditions—one car for the writers accompanying the team and perhaps a second-string pitcher or two, and two cars for the team's regulars. Promptly after a game on "getaway day," the train would pull out of town, taking 20 hours or more from New York to Chicago, with occasional obnoxious variations like the "Owl Train" that left New York for Boston at midnight.

The players whiled away the hours by endless hands of poker or hearts or, much less frequently, bridge. No dice-rolling was permitted aboard, however. Many players sported peaked caps, though McGraw insisted that his Giants wear hats. One disadvantage of the trains, Stengel noted, was that they gave managers like

Uncle Robbie "time to get sore after we'd lose a series, and he'd call me over and give me hell."

In most overt matters of public morals, the baseball clubs hewed a straight line. The only cities that permitted Sunday baseball were Chicago, Cincinnati and St. Louis. In the nineteen-twenties, Cleveland and Detroit acceded, along with New York, which received authorization from the Legislature through a bill sponsored by State Senator James J. Walker. The last holdouts, Philadelphia and Pittsburgh, did not capitulate until ten years later, though not for the loftiest of motives. In Pittsburgh, Barney Dreyfuss had often pointed out that Sunday baseball was dangerous because it was likely to kill the Saturday gate.

On other days of the week, ball games did not start until 3:15 in the afternoon or later, a holdover from the eighteen-eighties, when a starting time of 4 o'clock gave members of the Stock Exchange and other businessmen time to make it to the park after work.

Public recognition was just beginning to be accorded the game in high places, in ways that would almost be taken for granted later. William Howard Taft was from a baseball-oriented family; his half-brother, Charles P. Taft, owned the Chicago Cubs and Mrs. Charles P. Taft owned the National League ball park in Philadelphia. The President was known to go out to the ball game when he was spending vacations back home in Cincinnati. When he consented to throw out the "first ball" on opening day in 1910, he erected an institution that has amused, sometimes annoyed, Presidents since then.

One other institution that was revered with almost total enthusiasm in 1912 was hazing, ignoring or insulting the "busher," the boy from the bush leagues, the rookie, the rube.

On the day Stengel joined the Dodgers, he was greeted only by Zack Wheat, an Indian from Missouri who, like Stengel, had been "discovered" by Larry Sutton and routed to Brooklyn through the Southern Association three years before. The other players in the clubhouse ignored him. So, Stengel put his best foot forward to break the barrier; he begged into the crap game that was at full tilt in the locker room before the Dodgers took the field. He was rattling the dice for his first roll when he felt a heavy hand on his shoulder. He turned and looked into the steady eyes of Bad Bill

Dahlen, who had played for 20 years as a shortstop, who had earned the nickname because he had been ejected from so many games by umpires and who was now the manager of the Brooklyn ball club.

"Are you a crap-shooter or a ball player?" Dahlen asked.

"I guess I'm a ball player," Stengel said.

"Then get out there and shag some flies," Dahlen thundered.

A short time later, Stengel was astonished when Dahlen called to him and said: "You start in right field for me today."

So, a few hours after he had arrived by train from Montgomery, suitcase in hand, he was standing in right field for the Dodgers. Then he was batting against Claude Hendrix, the best pitcher on the Pittsburgh Pirates, the best in the National League that season with 24 victories and 9 defeats, and a spitball artist of the front rank.

Stengel singled the first time up, then the second, third and fourth times up, and he had the comforting total of four-for-four in his first major league game when he went to bat a fifth time and found that the Pirates had just switched to a left-handed pitcher named Hank Robinson. So, to the amazement of Dahlen, Wheat and the rest of the Dodgers—to say nothing of Robinson and the rest of the Pirates—the rookie from Kankakee turned around at the plate and batted right-handed.

"It was probably the only time I ever batted right-handed in the league," he said. "And I'd built such a reputation by that time that he walked me."

Stengel got into 16 other games for the Dodgers that September before the season ended, but his gaudy debut had made him a marked man. "I broke in with four hits and the writers promptly decided they had seen the new Ty Cobb," he recalled. "It took me only a few days to correct that impression."

He went to bat 53 other times in that first month, made 14 other hits, including a double and a home run, batted in 12 runs and finished with a batting average of .316. On defense, though, he made four errors, averaging one for every nine fly balls that he caught. But his reputation as a "fresh busher" who had made a flamboyant, almost insulting, start was secure.

In fact, his reputation preceded him to Chicago, where the Dodgers played a series against the Cubs and where Stengel would have his first nose-to-nose confrontation with one of the lions of the game, Johnny Evers. Evers, who had weighed 95 pounds in his first season in professional baseball, had matured to 135 by 1912 and still resembled a small child in a Chicago Cubs uniform, except for the fact that he carried himself with such authority and tenacity that he became known as "The Crab." He also became known as the youngest member of baseball's most legendary trio: Joe Tinker, Johnny Evers and Frank Chance.

Joe Tinker was a third-baseman from Muscotah, Kansas, who also could play shortstop. Johnny Evers was a shortstop from Troy, New York, who also could play second base, and did for most of his 1,776 games in the major leagues. Frank Chance was a catcher from Fresno, California, who had played at the University of Washington before joining the Cubs in 1898, converting to a first-baseman in 1901 and becoming manager in 1905.

They made their first double play on September 13, 1902; helped to make Chicago dominant in baseball for a decade; were so temperamental that Evers and Tinker ignored each other off the field for two years; were so sought-after that Evers was offered—and refused—$30,000 in cash and $15,000 a year for five years to desert to the "outlaw" Federal League, choosing to remain with the Cubs, who then traded him to Boston; and were so cohesive on the playing field that they were voted into the Baseball Hall of Fame as a unit. They also moved Franklin P. Adams to these lines:

> These are the saddest of possible words,
>   Tinker to Evers to Chance.
> Trio of Bear Cubs and fleeter than birds,
>   Tinker to Evers to Chance.
> Pricking our gonfalon bubble,
> Making a Giant hit into a double,
> Words that are weighty with nothing but trouble,
>   Tinker to Evers to Chance.

Now the great Evers was at second base for the Chicago club when Stengel and the Dodgers arrived in September 1912, and Casey later described the unequal relationship between a rookie and a regular under even the least provoking of circumstances.

"It was rougher then," he said, looking back on his hazing days. "Now, when a pitcher happens to get a ball close to a hitter, the hitter comes back to the bench and says, 'I think he was throwing at me.' Boys, when I broke in, you just knew they were throwing at you. The first month I was in the league, I spent three weeks on my back at the plate."

On the day he met the Cubs for the first time, he conceded, "they had me pretty scared at first, since I was just a busher and they were a lot of famous ball players. Jimmy Archer was catching and the first time I went up to hit he said to me: 'So you're Stengel, eh?' "

" 'Yes,' I said, 'I'm Stengel.' "

Then, Casey recalled, the conversation grew pointed.

"I see you broke in pretty good," Archer said.

"Yeah, pretty good," Stengel replied. "Four for four and stole a couple of bases."

"Well," said Archer, squatting behind the plate with an air of expectation, "when you get on there, let me see you run."

"Not today, Mr. Archer," Casey said politely. "I know you."

"But the last time up," he recalled years later, "I got on with two out and I had to run, and this Archer threw me out from here to there. But I wasn't giving up easy, so I rode in feet first to try to knock Johnny Evers out of the way. He tagged me and then, while I was still lying on my back, he bellowed at me: 'You fresh busher. The next time you come into me like that I'll stick the ball down your throat.'

"Up to then I was scared, but now I was mad. So I jumped up and bellowed right back at him. 'That's the way I slid in the bushes and that's the way I'll slide up here,' I said. 'My name is Stengel, Evers. Take a good look at me, because I'll be up here a long while.' "

3

KING OF THE GRUMBLERS

The two greatest influences on Casey Stengel's life in baseball after he arrived in the major leagues in September 1912, were Wilbert Robinson and John J. McGraw. They had played side by side for the old roughhouse Baltimore Orioles in the eighteen-nineties, Robinson a barrel-sized catcher with an enormous handle-bar mustache curling out from behind his face mask, and McGraw a demon third-baseman with the imperious stance, stride and spirit of a Little Napoleon, which was his nickname during his 42-year career.

When Robinson joined the Orioles in 1890, the year Stengel was born, the team belonged to the American Association, which was then caught in a giant pincers between the established National League and an interloper, the Players League. The following year, McGraw joined the Orioles—not yet 18 years old and, at 5-foot-7, an inch below Robinson's maximum height.

One year later, the Orioles stepped over the corpse of the American Association, which had just collapsed along with the Players League; switched to the surviving National League, and began to create baseball legends.

Besides McGraw and Robinson, the short dynamos who once made 10 hits between them in a game in 1892, the Orioles included Hughie Jennings, a red-haired, freckled-faced shortstop who batted .357 in 663 games before becoming manager of the

Detroit Tigers and chief keeper of Ty Cobb during his most hellbent years; Wee Willie Keeler, 5 feet 4½ inches tall, a left-handed infielder who became an outfielder, hit .393 in 642 games and, swinging the lightest bat in baseball, used to "hit 'em where they ain't"; Dan Brouthers, 10 inches taller than Keeler and a .348 lifetime hitter who had hit three home runs in a single game in 1886, when home runs were rare; and Joe Corbett, the brother of the heavyweight champion, Gentleman Jim Corbett, who would have felt comfortably at home among the team's roughnecks.

The Baltimore Orioles wasted no time organizing the National League to their liking. They won the championship in 1894, 1895 and 1896, and five of their eight regulars eventually were elected to the Baseball Hall of Fame, including McGraw and Robinson.

When the American League was formed in 1901, the National League reacted by regrouping, pulling in its horns to meet the competition and raiding of a new baseball war. It reduced its franchises from 12 to eight, with Baltimore among the victims, though most of the Oriole stars were switched over to the Brooklyn Club. That is, except for McGraw and Robinson. They moved instead to St. Louis, but reappeared a year later back in Baltimore, which by then had just been awarded a franchise in the new American League.

McGraw now became the manager of the Orioles and Robinson his chief deputy as well as the team's catcher. The understanding was that the Orioles' wanderings would be ended when the American League engineered one more shift: the Baltimore club would move to New York, with McGraw as manager and the Giants of the National League as their combined target.

But McGraw shortly sensed that the scheme was about to be altered without his knowledge or approval. So he abruptly engineered a spectacular shift of his own: He left the Orioles in July and switched himself to New York as manager of the Giants.

Until he died in February 1934, he was the impresario of New York Giant baseball, winning 10 pennants and establishing a record that would stand until Stengel himself won 10 as manager of the Yankees. However, McGraw's defection to New York broke up his act with Robinson, who stayed behind in Baltimore, then broke a finger in 1904—an occupational catastrophe for a catcher —left baseball and finally opened a cafe, with McGraw as his absentee partner.

In 1911, McGraw revived their partnership on the baseball field by inviting Robinson to work with him as a coach of the Giants, who had won the pennant in 1904 and 1905 and were headed for another. Robinson accepted, and he was once more side by side with his old crony as the Giants won in 1911 and again in 1912 and 1913, Robinson coaching at first base and Mc-Graw at third.

Then, on one play in the 1913 World Series against the Philadelphia Athletics, their friendship was shattered. A Giant runner was thrown out while trying to steal second base, McGraw loudly blamed Robinson for concocting the play, argued bitterly with him all day and most of the night and finally uttered the magic words, "You're fired."

Robinson thereupon switched to Brooklyn, their teams became blood rivals, the two old Orioles rarely spoke to each other for the next 30 years and they died six months apart in 1934.

When Casey Stengel arrived in Brooklyn late in 1912, the Dodger-Giant rivalry was already in flower, though McGraw and Robinson were still together on the Giants. But the 1913 season was approaching, putting them all on a kind of collision course. Brooklyn was scheduled to open the season against New York, the Dodgers were moving into a new park—Ebbets Field—and Stengel, a veteran of 17 big league games, was packing for the great day.

He went south to his first major league training camp that winter, to Augusta, Georgia, where the Dodgers were preparing for the 154-game season in a series of exhibition games. Spring training games were played chiefly against minor league clubs in the region, since travel was difficult and teams within the same league were discouraged from playing one another, at least until the policy was changed in the mid-twenties.

The great spring-training boom was just beginning in Florida that year, with the Chicago Cubs pitching their camp in Tampa, in a beach area on the Gulf of Mexico that would have as many as eight teams in training at one time half a century later. The New York Yankees showed the greatest flair, training that spring in Bermuda, moving in 1914 to Houston, in 1915 to Savannah and in 1916 to Macon.

Stengel had two things going for him that spring in Augusta: he had a reputation as a clever runner and he played right field in an outfield that also included Hy Myers in center and Zach Wheat in left. Myers and Wheat had professional experience and suitably off-beat personalities, providing a buffer in both respects for the shenanigans that the rookie left-hander was about to hatch during 12 seasons in the National League.

Casey also had a "caddie," a right-handed hitter named Jimmy Johnston, who took over right field for him frequently when a left-hander was pitching against the Dodgers—the theory being that when a left-handed pitcher throws to a left-handed batter, or a right-hander to a right-handed batter, the pitcher has a commanding advantage since he delivers from the batter's blind side and his curving pitches break away.

It was a theory that Stengel used to considerable advantage— and considerable criticism—as a manager with the Yankees later, the criticism being that he adhered to the strategy slavishly. But it was not one that he invented, and it did not keep him on the sidelines when the Dodgers went north in April 1913, to open the season in their new ball park in an exhibition series against the Yankees the weekend before the regular season started.

It was a gala, and somewhat bizarre, weekend. Frank Chance, the old double-play partner of Joe Tinker and Johnny Evers, was making his debut as manager of the Yankees. Ebbets Field had 25,000 seats, double the capacity of Washington Park, but it also had an unfinished playing surface with grass on the infield only and a solid "skin" of frozen dirt in the outfield.

So, when the inaugural game got under way and Stengel drove a ball between the Yankee outfielders, it skidded past them on the frozen ground, shot like a rocket to the deepest corner of the park and ricocheted around while the 22-year-old rookie ran around the bases for the first home run hit in Ebbets Field.

When the regular season opened two days later, Stengel was in right field, Nap Rucker was the pitcher and 25,000 persons again were in the new grandstand. The Giants had McGraw strutting in the dugout as manager, Christy Mathewson and Rube Marquard pitching, and four fast outfielders—Josh Devore, Fred Snodgrass, Red Jack Murray and Beals Becker—who had been instrumental in setting a record number of 347 stolen bases for the team the season before. The Giants also had won two straight pennants and were about to win a third. But the Dodgers had an inning or two that day—as they were to have on other days in their rivalry with the more affluent Giants—and won the first regular game in Ebbets Field, 3 to 2.

Stengel played in 123 other games that season, his first full one in the league. He went to bat 438 times, made 88 singles, 16 doubles, 8 triples and 7 home runs, batted in 44 runs, caught 270 fly balls, threw out 16 base runners, made 12 errors and batted .272. And the team finished sixth.

"I was fairly good at times," he said later, reviewing his first days in the big leagues with a kind of objectivity. "But a lot of people seem to remember some of the stunts I pulled better than they do the ball games I helped win."

One of the people who remembered some of his stunts better than the games he helped to win was Robinson, who was then 50 years old and only a semi-reformed stuntman himself. He made his appearance in Ebbets Field at the start of the 1914 season as manager of the Dodgers and also now as the sworn enemy of Mc-Graw, who was presiding over the Polo Grounds across the East River and a few miles north.

Uncle Robbie was still a broad-shouldered little man with a barrel shape, but without the handlebar mustache of the old Baltimore Oriole era in the nineties. He was given to atrocious malapropisms, like Stengel a quarter-century later, such as "Lumbago" for "Lombardi." He still prided himself on his background as a catcher, too, and this was shortly to make him the principal victim of an incident that became increasingly typical of his Dodgers' pranks, which in turn became increasingly attributed to his right-fielder.

Stengel, during Robinson's first year in Brooklyn, had completed his transition from ignored "busher" to acknowledged regular, and was in fact well along toward becoming a clubhouse ringleader. He played in two more games than in the season before, 126, and though he went to bat 26 fewer times he made 11 more hits, batted in 12 more runs and added 44 points to his batting average, bringing it to .316, the same figure he had reached during his 17-game break-in month and the highest figure he would reach for a full season during the next 10 years.

The Dodgers, who had ranked seventh two years earlier and sixth the previous year, crept to fifth place.

Then it was the spring of 1915 and the Dodgers were headed

for the first division of the league for the first time in 13 years since Ned Hanlon, already notorious as the late manager of the old Baltimore rowdies, had made it to second place. But the owner of the Dodgers, Charles Ebbets, was already expressing forebodings about the state of the world and later would "retrench" to align his ball club with the international situation, which was marked that year by the sinking of the British liner Lusitania by torpedoes, with 128 Americans and a thousand other persons as victims.

The "big stick" had already given way to "dollar diplomacy," which in turn had yielded to "watchful waiting." But while others watched and waited, Robinson's Dodgers nested in Daytona Beach and one spring day there appeared Ruth Law, the pioneer woman flier, puttering over the ball field in a biplane with flat sail-like wings supported by rods and wires, and there were the Superbas looking up and remembering that Gabby Street had recently caught a baseball dropped from the Washington Monument, and wondering if you could catch one dropped from an airplane.

Wheat and Stengel and the other clubhouse regulars were among those considering the problem and, Stengel said later, "we had this here Jack Coombs, a very brilliant man which could figure out the velocity of a baseball, and he would even know when people said which weighed more, a ton of feathers or a ton of steel, and he could tell you."

The experiment being so irresistible, and Coombs's calculations being regarded as inconclusive, it was decided to test the velocity theory directly. The team's trainer would climb in behind Ruth Law, fly over the field and release the ball while the "gloves" on the team would try to catch it. In the excitement—or, Robinson long suspected, in the evil machinations of Casey Stengel—a grapefruit was substituted for the baseball, and soon the biplane was chugging over and everybody was looking up at it.

"Uncle Robbie had a belly out like this," Stengel recalled, "and he was warming up this pitcher on the sidelines—we didn't have six coaches in those days. And this *aviatorix*—it was the first one they had—she flew over and dropped it. And Uncle Robbie saw it coming and waved everybody away like an outfielder and said, 'I've got it, I've got it.' And the thing kept coming closer and getting bigger.

"Robbie got under this grapefruit, thinking it was a baseball, which hit him right on this pitcher's glove he put on, and you know, the insides of it flew all over, seeds on his face and uniform, and flipped him back right over on his back. He lay there, looking like a ghost. Everybody came running up and everybody commenced laughing, all except Robbie, who got burned up. And six months later, we didn't have that trainer."

Robinson's tribulations were only beginning. Stengel was now the ordained ringleader of a clubhouse clique known as "the Grumblers," with a deputy named "Jeff" Pfeffer, a pitcher who had earned his nickname because of a rowdy resemblance to Jim Jeffries, the heavyweight champion. Stengel was bold and even pugnacious himself, and he led the Grumblers through a series of barroom adventures in 1915 and 1916 that kept the team's front office in a chronic state of anxiety.

One Sunday night they had somehow been inveigled into a brawl in Coney Island, there being no Sunday baseball then and, supposedly, no Sunday brawling. Ebbets had joined the Dodgers in 1890, had later taken control in 1898, had still later sold tickets outside his own ball park and finally had sold 50 per cent of his stock in 1913 to Stephen and Edward McKeever in order to build Ebbets Field. He tended to keep a close, baleful eye on details, and so the day after the fight he summoned Stengel and asked in exasperation:

"What kind of hoodlums do we have on this club, anyway?"

Stengel, with an air of injured respectability, replied: "No, Mr. Ebbets, we only had four beers," and he help up four fingers to illustrate. ("But," remarked Uncle Robbie, after Stengel had got off the hook with this bit of piousness, "they were as big as pails.")

For years after, the Grumblers were taunted around the league by other players who held up four fingers in a silent, mocking salute to their sobriety.

"I was always in a lot of damn trouble," Stengel acknowledged, looking back on his misadventures. "We didn't have any Landis in those days, and players used to give even the umpires hell."

He illustrated, giving full credit to the Dodgers' pitcher, Leon Cadore.

"Cadore was my room-mate," he said, "and he was an exceedingly handsome man which was very good at card tricks; he could hand you the jack of diamonds. And he said to me one night, 'I bet I can control an umpire.' So one night on a Pullman coach, he was showing us these card tricks and he had Bill Klem there, riding with us, and he told Klem he'd give him the nine of spades. And I was standing behind Klem and slipped it under his collar, and Cadore was shuffling the cards and dealing them and he suddenly says, 'Look under your collar, Mr. Klem.' And in front of all these ball players—which Mr. Klem didn't like.

"Anyway, it didn't stop there. We had concrete walls then and you could scuff the ball pretty good. But Cadore used to stop between pitches in the game and I was the right-fielder, and he'd look out toward right as if he was shifting me around, but he was just saying to me: 'Don't miss this one. Watch.' And then he'd wave his arms at the catcher as though he didn't get the sign, waving with one hand while scuffin' up the ball with the other, he was so slick. Between pitches, with one hand.

"Then he'd pitch, and for five innings he'd call every pitch himself as he was throwin' it. 'Strike one' and 'Strike two,' and finally Klem came out and stood between home plate and first and yelled at him: 'You don't call them on me, Cadore, damn it. I'll call the pitches here—you're not dealing me those card tricks now—so cut it out.' "

Stengel was undeterred from his pranks by the fact that the 1915 season developed into a personal decline for him on the ball field. He played in 132 games,, missing only 22 in spite of the "platoon system," but his batting average plummeted 79 points to .237. By contrast, Ty Cobb batted .369 that year, so any resemblance between the two that might have been encouraged by Casey's 4-for-4 performance the day he arrived had long since been adjusted.

The Dodgers, though, responding to Uncle Robbie's insistent ambition to overtake McGraw and the Giants, advanced from fifth place to third. They now had crept almost imperceptibly from seventh place in 1911 to sixth two years later, when Stengel joined them; then fifth the next season, when Robinson joined them, and finally third in 1915.

They may have been gaining reputations as the foremost rascals in baseball, but they were winning games in a steady, almost mathematical, progression, too. They won only 58 and lost 95 at their low point in 1912, then won 65 the following year, then 75 and now 85.

Then it was 1916, and Wilbert Robinson was about to have his revenge on McGraw. How he accomplished this was a little vague, since the defending champion Philadelphia Phillies had another fine team led by Alex the Great, Grover Cleveland Alexander, the hard-drinking, hard-throwing Nebraskan who had won 28 games in his first season—more than any rookie in the twentieth century—and who won 30 or more games for three straight years, starting in 1915.

Boston and New York stayed near the top of the league, too, and the Giants even won 26 games in a row as the four clubs struggled through September. But the Dodgers won 94 games, lost 60 and ended the season in first place by 2½ games over the Phillies, with Boston third and the Giants fourth. McGraw angrily left the stadium during the final Giant-Dodger doubleheader, grousing: "I want no part of this," while his old crony Robinson accused him of trying to dilute the taste of Brooklyn's first World Series since 1900.

The Dodgers were actually not a particularly formidable team. Not as formidable, say, as they were after hours, when the Grumblers rode high. Robinson managed a team composed mainly of discards from other teams: Coombs from the Philadelphia Athletics of the American League; Mike Mowrey, the third-baseman, from Pittsburgh; Ivan Olson, the shortstop, from Cleveland; Larry Cheney, a pitcher, from Chicago, and Rube Marquard, Chief Meyers and Fred Merkle from the unloved Giants. The president of the National League, John K. Tener, surveyed the situation and remarked: "I never saw a club go into a series so willing to settle for the loser's end."

Still, the Dodgers had three of the most colorful outfielders in the game in Wheat, Hy Myers and Stengel, and Stengel had just redeemed himself somewhat during the season by adding 42 points to his batting average—making up half of the decline that had set in the season before. He finished at .279, with 8 home runs—only four below the leaders of both leagues—and 8 triples, 27 doubles and 53 runs batted in.

When the World Series opened in Boston on October 7, the feeling lingered that the Dodgers were slightly miscast. The feeling was intensified as the Red Sox, who had won the American League pennant for the second straight year, hit Marquard freely and took a 6-to-1 lead.

World Series games started at 3 o'clock then and often ended in semi-darkness on chilly October afternoons. And, as the shadows began to fall and many in the crowd of 36,117 persons began to leave, the Dodgers, in their unpredictable way, came to life.

Jake Daubert, the team's captain, first-baseman and batting champion of the league two straight years, started the trouble by getting a base on balls. "Charles Stengel," who was listed in semi-formality in the official record as the right-fielder, hit a single. A walk to George Cutshaw loaded the bases, and then a Boston error, another walk and an infield single gave the Dodgers four runs. But they were stopped there when Everett Scott made a fine play at shortstop to cheat Daubert of a hit, while Charles Stengel knelt in the chalk circle in front of the dugout waiting to bat next.

The next time he batted was in the following game, two days later, and the Red Sox pitcher was the 22-year-old strong boy from Baltimore, Babe Ruth. Stengel was to meet Ruth in a World Series seven years later, after Ruth had ended his career as a left-handed pitcher who won 92 games, lost 44 and compiled a winning percentage of .676 that was almost as unassailable in its way as his lifetime batting average of .342 and the 714 home runs he hit as a left-handed batter.

Now, in the 1916 World Series, he was about to start a string of pitching 13 scoreless innings, adding 16 more two years later for a record of 29. He never lost a World Series game as a pitcher and, having won 23 games in the regular season that year, he wasn't about to lose the second game of the series against Robinson's Dodgers. In a drawn-out struggle that lasted 14 innings and that ended in the dark, Ruth outpitched Sherry Smith, 2 to 1. Smith had one consolation: at bat, the great Ruth got no hits in five times up, which was no small accomplishment. But now the Dodgers trailed, two games to none, and the series was slipping from their reach.

In fact, except for the third game, which the Dodgers won, 4 to 3, the series slipped from their reach without interruption. Boston won the fourth game, 6 to 2, and the fifth game, 4 to 1, and the only exceptional developments were Casey Stengel's batting average of .364 (four singles in eleven times at bat), making him No. 1 on the frustrated Brooklyn club, and two financial crises.

The first crisis arose when the series shifted from Boston to Brooklyn, and Ebbets quietly raised the price of a grandstand seat from $3 to $5, and only 21,000 persons appeared. Exactly twice as many had paid to see the last game in Boston, and 20,000 persons had been left milling around outside the park.

Crisis No. 2 arose when the Brooklyn players met after the series and decided how their shares of the players' pool were to be divided. They promptly made a decision that was as unpopular as Ebbets's price scale. They allotted nothing to the coaches, locker-room staff and other attendants, but instead pocketed $2,834 each, a record share for a losing team in a World Series. The Red Sox players were each $3,910 richer, but everybody aimed their darts at the ungenerous Dodgers—from the president of the league, who had been critical, on down to the writers, who had been skeptical, and the fans, who had paid $5 apiece in Ebbets's grandstand caper and who now got their money's worth of comeback by berating his players for their "greed."

Their revenge became complete the following season, when the Dodgers made a spectacular plunge from first place to seventh, while two shadows began to fall across the club. One was the shadow of McGraw, whose Giants rebounded in 1917 as convincingly as the Dodgers declined. The other was the shadow of the war, which had begun to reach to the United States during the World Series the previous fall, when German U-boats roamed the near-Atlantic in packs and began picking off ships near Nantucket while the Dodgers struggled with the Red Sox in Boston.

So impressed was Ebbets by the approaching menaces of the war that he began to retrench even before his team went into the tailspin of 1917. The axe fell on Stengel, for one thing. Despite his mild heroics as the team's regular right-fielder, batting leader in the World Series and foremost after-hours personality, his salary was cut by $2,600—almost the amount of his World Series bonus. In fact, he did not agree to the terms of his contract until March 28, just in time to join the Brooklyn-Red Sox Special as it left Hot Springs, Arkansas, at 1 o'clock in the afternoon, headed for

Memphis and the next stop on the "World Series train," where it arrived eight hours later. And nine days later, the United States entered the war and Stengel entered his final season in Brooklyn.

If he thought that his relations with Ebbets had grown a bit strained, however, he was in for an even greater shock at the end of the season. It was a full season: 150 games and 549 times at bat, the fullest of his six seasons in Brooklyn. But it had depressions. Though he made 141 hits, his batting average slipped 22 points to .257, the Dodgers won 24 fewer games than the year before and only one club fared worse—Pittsburgh. And it was to Pittsburgh and to Barney Dreyfuss that Stengel was sold in January 1918.

The trade sent Stengel and George Cutshaw, the Brooklyn second-baseman, to Pittsburgh for Chuck Ward, an infielder, and two pitchers, Burleigh Grimes and Al Mamaux. It involved Casey in one of those riches-to-rags switches that he seemed addicted to throughout his 55 years in baseball. The riches had materialized in the Dodgers' grand march to the World Series; the rags now appeared even before he climbed into a Pittsburgh uniform for the first time. He immediately became embroiled with Dreyfuss in a long hassle over salary, did not sign his contract until just before the season opened and went out to right field with strong advance billing as the bête noire of Pittsburgh baseball.

First, though, a little score was to be settled with the faithful in Brooklyn, who had reacted in rage at the tight fists of the Grumblers and their clubhouse cronies. Stengel was still known variously as "Casey" or "Dutch" by most of the players, including his new teammates, though Bill McKechnie and a few others still preferred "Charley." But, by any name, he was undismayed when the Pirates paid their first call on Brooklyn in 1918 and in the last half of the first inning he trotted out to right field while the crowd whistled and hooted and called after him with the mixed affection and derision that followed him around the National League for 14 seasons.

The next inning, when he went to bat for the first time in Brooklyn in a Pittsburgh uniform, the catcalls reached a peak. In complete courtliness, he advanced to home plate, bowed deeply toward the grandstand, removed his cap—and out flew a sparrow. He had given them the bird.

Where did the bird come from? Tracking down any of his

comic-opera plots could become as complex as trying to follow and solve Harry Houdini's sleight-of-hand, especially when Casey's own testimony was heard. Later he laughed and said that when he had taken his post in right field during the first inning, he had found the bird lying on the grass as though stunned, so he slipped it under his cap. Another time he acknowledged a little help from the bullpen, where, he said, "one of my buddies, Cadore, had found the bird and slipped it to me over the bullpen railing."

Wherever he acquired his menagerie on that occasion, and his elaborate changes of costume on others, Dreyfuss was no more amused than Kid Elberfeld had been over his disappearing act down the drainage-hole five years before. But Dreyfuss's trials were mercifully short. Stengel played in only 39 games with the Pirates before finding temporary refuge somewhere else, the Brooklyn Navy Yard, to be exact. But to reach that haven back in his old stomping grounds, he required an incident and a cause.

The incident arose the day after he had outraged the umpires by removing his Pittsburgh uniform shirt, offering it to one and suggesting impudently, "You try playing on our side for a while."

For this irreverence, he was fined $50 by the president of the National League, with the towering approval of his harassed owner, Dreyfuss. But the next day, Stengel found the "cause" that would deliver him from both the fine and Dreyfuss.

"I went down and enlisted in the Navy," he said. "I beat the league out of fifty bucks, but it wound up costing me seven hundred fifty in pay. They put me to work in the Navy Yard in Brooklyn, not far from the ball park; I was supposed to paint ships, they found out I could paint. But then one day this lieutenant commander walked in and said, 'You're the manager of the ball team.'"

So, for the rest of 1918, Barney's Bad Boy survived in a no-man's-land between the Western Front and Pittsburgh. He was safe from Dreyfuss, at least, and that was something. Then, turning his Machiavellian talents toward the job at hand, he contrived to win ball games with psychological twists that the Navy might have found useful in tactical situations.

"I used to board them ships," he said, "as soon as they got in, and make a date for a game the next day. I found if they'd been on land too long, we couldn't beat them."

He suffered one setback in brinkmanship—at the hands of a child —and it was recorded in magnificently exaggerated straight-faced language on September 1 by *The New York Times:*

> The astute police have been requested by Casey Stengel, one-time outfielder with the Brooklyn and Pittsburgh National League baseball teams, but now a toiler in a shipyard, to find the boy and the $50 which disappeared simultaneously yesterday from that part of Prospect Park where Mr. Stengel was practising baseball.
>
> Stengel is captain of a shipyard nine, which is to play another shipyard nine today. He led his men into Prospect Park yesterday for a little necessary practice.
>
> In the old days the man at the clubhouse used to look after Stengel's bankroll and bibelots. In the park yesterday, no other repository being available, he left his coat and wallet with a boy from the sidelines, who stepped forward and offered himself as custodian.
>
> There the matter rests. There was $50 in the money sack. Boy and money were missing when the practice hour ended, and although Stengel has made all the traditional motions of informing the police, his expectation of ever glimpsing his cash again is exceedingly small.

He never did. But 48 years later, when he was reminded of an "incident" during his Navy days of 1918, he laughed and said without hesitation, but with a trace of admiration: "The kid and the fifty bucks. He was just a little kid on a bicycle, and when practice ended I can still see him riding away on that bike with my fifty."

The armistice of November 1918 meant no particular armistice between Stengel, who was now 28 and saucier than ever, and Dreyfuss, who was finally driven to the only way out for a sensitive soul who owns a bugbear. He sold him. Stengel actually had returned to Pittsburgh from his semi-comic Navy hitch in outstanding fettle. He raised his batting average 47 points to .293, hit 4 home runs, 10 triples, 10 doubles and 70 singles in 89 games and much to his relief—and Dreyfuss's—he was traded to Philadelphia in September of 1919 in a straight swap for another, though vastly more inhibited, outfielder named George Whitted.

"I was glad to get away from Pittsburgh," he confessed, "if for no other reason than that I wouldn't have to listen to a loud-mouthed guy in the right-field stand who used to holler at me every day: 'Hey, Casey. How's Big Bess?' "

And who was Big Bess? he was asked.

"I never found out," he said innocently.

However, life in Philadelphia was no joy, either. After six years of moving onward and upward with the Dodgers, he now was retreating steadily downhill—from the World Series in 1916, to seventh place with Brooklyn, fourth with Pittsburgh and now last with Philadelphia. Worse, the Phillies were a tattered bunch of miscast ball players who performed in a bandbox ball park while their manager, Bill Donovan, watched and suffered. Donovan's trouble was that he cared, and he was reported to be the only man on the team who did care, except for Cy Williams, his center fielder. For eight years, the Phillies ran either last or next to last in an eight-team league before rising to sixth place; but then they lapsed back to last place for three more years, as though caught in the act of something unethical.

"At that," Stengel recalled, "playing right field for the Phillies was the softest job in baseball. I had the wall behind me, the second-baseman in front of me, the foul line on my left and Cy Williams on my right. The only time I had a chance to catch the ball was when it was hit right at me."

People who watched ball games in Philadelphia in 1920 and 1921 confirmed the stationary nature of playing right field for the Phillies, and more. Irish Meusel, the left-fielder, was afflicted with a sore arm and couldn't throw; Stengel, the right-fielder, was beginning to feel his legs growing unsteady at the age of 30, and couldn't run. That left Williams, the center-fielder, who could do both, and so wherever Stengel and Meusel played, as they did together on the Giants a short time later, the cry was raised: "Hey, Cy, you take it."

The closing days of 1920, though, veered from mild nonsense of this sort to a more serious matter. The World Series of 1919 had been played between the heavily favored Chicago White Sox and the Cincinnati Reds, descendants of the first professional baseball club, who had finally made it to their first National League pennant. To considerable surprise, but with no great suspicion as yet, gamblers were seen openly, almost desperately, trying to get money down on the underdog Reds in the lobbies of Cincinnati hotels on the day the series opened.

The Reds immediately won the first two games. Chicago won

the next, but Cincinnati won two more and took a 4-to-1 lead in games, five victories being required that year (and the next two) under a change in the 4-out-of-7 rule that had been initiated, ironically, to improve the financial return to the players in the series.

The White Sox rallied to win two more games, but were demolished in the final game, 10 to 5. With even greater irony, the White Sox players survived the rumors that began to circulate and became embroiled in a lively pennant race against the Yankees and Cleveland Indians with one week left in the following season before evidence was finally submitted to a grand jury in Chicago that the series had been fixed. Eight of the Chicago players were indicted.

The fact that one of them, Joe Jackson, had hit .375 while presumably living up to his part in the fix was only one of the far-fetched developments that surrounded the case. Arnold Rothstein, foremost of the big bettors, testified in court that he had been offered a chance to underwrite the scheme but had declined the invitation. The grand jury's findings, including three confessions from ball players, were stolen from the District Attorney's office in Chicago. The White Sox, now being referred to as the Black Sox, still finished second to the Indians and ahead of the Yankees, although eight of their players were indicted in the waning hours of the season.

It wasn't until August 2, 1921, however, that a jury in Cook County reached a verdict—not guilty of criminal conspiracy. But a Federal judge, Kenesaw Mountain Landis, had been installed as the first Commissioner of Baseball on November 12, 1920, replacing the National Commission—one of whose members, Garry Herrmann, had simultaneously been president of the Cincinnati Reds and, as such, had found it difficult to accept the suspicion that his underdog ball club had won a tainted World Series.

Landis, who had been appointed to the Federal bench by Theodore Roosevelt and who was named for the Civil War battle at Kenesaw Mountain where his father had lost a leg, disregarded the jury's finding. He immediately issued a statement that said with remarkable idiom:

"Regardless of the verdict of juries, no player that throws a ball game, no player that entertains proposals or promises to throw a game, no player that sits in a conference with a bunch of crooked players and gamblers where the ways and means of throwing games are discussed, and does not promptly tell his club about it, will ever again play professional baseball."

None of the eight ever did. Judge Landis, though, required an accomplice to move baseball out from under the cloud, and by considerable luck he found one in Babe Ruth, who had pitched for the Boston Red Sox in the 1916 World Series against the Dodgers and who now was being sold to the New York Yankees for $525,000 in cash—$400,000 of which was considered a loan to help bail the Boston club owner, Harry Frazee, out of the financial narrows.

Ruth was worth the half-million to the Yankees' owner, Jacob Ruppert, and inestimably more to Landis because he had already displayed a great flair that had recaptured the public's interest in baseball: he hit home runs.

Stengel, who had been chafing with the Phillies during this strained period, had suffered a certain slowing down as an outfielder but none that was apparent as a clubhouse comic.

His talent for theatrics reached a zenith of sorts one spring afternoon in 1920 when the Phillies stopped in Fort Wayne, Indiana, for an exhibition game against the local team. At game time, Stengel was observed neither at the team's hotel nor at the ball park, and the Phillies, who had ranked eighth and last the season before, took the field without him but with a constant torrent of heckling from one corner of the grandstand. The heckling became louder and louder, and in the second inning was traced to a farmer type, dressed in country clothes, complete to bandana handkerchief and straw hat.

"You're a bunch of city dudes," he yelled to the Phillies, "and you're a bad apology for ball players."

One of the Philadelphia players sauntered over to the grandstand, looked toward the big-voiced heckler and said: "I guess you could play better."

"You bet I could," the hick shot back.

"Well," he was told, "come out and try."

So he came out and tried, and to the amazement of everybody —except the Phillies, who were in on the prank, and Casey Stengel, who had produced, directed and starred in it—the "rube" whacked the ball over the fence for a home run.

The "unknown marvel" of Fort Wayne actually played one of

his better seasons with the Phillies, though it was one of his least happy ones. In 1920, he recovered from his detour in the Navy, played in 129 games, the most since 1917; batted in 50 runs and hit .292, with 90 singles, 25 doubles, 6 triples and 9 home runs, the most he hit in 14 seasons in the major leagues.

In 1921, however, the Phillies were securely in last place and Casey, who was 31 now, was suffering from a strained back. He was showing signs of becoming prone to knee and back injuries, in fact, and played in only 42 games the entire season. One day in June, it was raining hard in Philadelphia, the game had been postponed and the Phillies were back in the clubhouse changing into their street clothes. Jim Hagen, secretary of the club, went up to Stengel and handed him a note.

"Things had been pretty hot in the clubhouse that summer," Casey recalled, "and as I had been dressing next to Donovan, I had my locker moved into a little room off the dressing room where I couldn't hear old Bill rave. One day one of the players told him I was dressing in the little room after a game and he hadn't noticed it, I guess, so he said: 'He is, eh? Well, he'll be dressing farther away than that pretty soon.' I said to myself, 'Oh, oh, he's going to send me to Kalamazoo.' "

So when Hagen handed him the note, Casey guessed that he had had it. To his surprise, the note advised him that he and Johnny Rawlings had been traded to the lordly Giants for $75,000. Having grown suspicious of pranks in his long, distinguished career as a prankster, Stengel quietly placed a long-distance call to New York to confirm the "trade." It was no gag.

With a well-developed sense of the moment, and with great relief at putting Philadelphia behind him, he went to his locker and put on a clean Phillies uniform. Then he trotted out the runway onto the muddy field, looked up into the wet sky, put his head down and charged toward first base.

He reached the bag in a spectacular slide through the mud that sent water cascading into the air, then headed for second base, sliding in with another torrent of mud. At third base, he did the same, and at home plate he outdid himself, churning water and dirt high in the air and completing a flamboyant farewell to Philadelphia before 20,000 empty seats.

In the clubhouse, Donovan said simply: "You can settle your

Philadelphia in 1920: a serene city, except on certain summer afternoons when the King of the Grumblers would hold court in the Phillies' ball yard. On the right, Fred Luderus; in the center, Cliff (Gabby) Cravath, who became a judge in Laguna Beach, California, and on the left, the real Gabby, who grew up to be Charles Dillon Stengel.

The Roaring Twenties had some of their most roaring moments at the Polo Grounds in Manhattan. And one of the reasons was the Giants' rightfielder, Casey Stengel: hero of Ethel Barrymore and Al Jolson, fiancé of Edna Lawson, bane of John J. McGraw.

United Press International

Casey at the Bat: "I had many years that I was not so successful as a ball player," he told the United States Senate 35 years later, "as it is a game of skill." However, 1922 with the Giants, when he hit .368, was not one of them.

This is the way old Casey ran his inside-the-park home run home in new Yankee Stadium on October 10, 1923, for the Giants against the Yankees in the World Series: collapsing at Wally Schang's feet.

Casey, who hit two dramatic home runs in the 1923 World Series, was upstaged by Babe Ruth, who hit three, and by Graham McNamee, who made historic first broadcast of a series and described all five.

After 21 seasons as a baseball player and after seven as a manager of minor league teams, he became a rookie all over again in 1934 as manager of a big league team, that splendid collection of oddballs, the Brooklyn Dodgers. After that, there was no place to go but up.

United Press International

Portrait of the man from Kansas City. Stengel's the name, it's 1936, the Depression is still on, World War II is gathering, the manager of the Brooklyn Dodgers is all buttoned up—and check those huge lapels.

George M. Weiss, the pride of Yale, had his eye on Casey back in the Eastern League in 1925. "He would find out whenever I was discharged," Casey said, "and would re-employ me." In 1948, though Stengel was employed this time, Weiss "re-employed" him for the New York Yankees.

Act I, Scene 1 of the Stengel era with the New York Yankees, October 12, 1948. Dan Topping beams, George Weiss beams, Casey signs his contract and confesses: "I scarcely know where I am at."

The Hot Stove League in plenary session for the start of spring training, March 1, 1949, at St. Petersburg, Florida. Those present for the Professor's debut with the Yankees include Phil Rizzuto, Ralph Houk, Joe DiMaggio, Charley Keller and Hank Bauer.

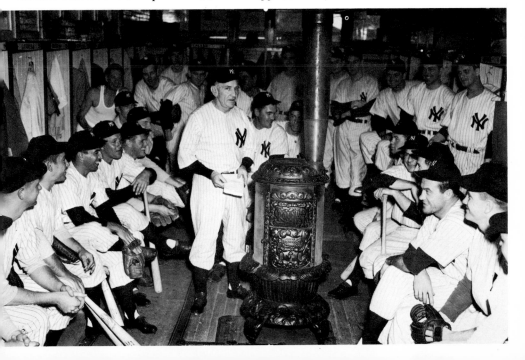

1949: Master of the Yankees. The 12 most splendid years begin in Yankee Stadium, scene of "the" home run a quarter of a century earlier. The Doctor directs traffic against his old club, the Dodgers, in the first of 10 World Series.

The Yankees won the 1949 pennant on the last day of the season, then won the opening game of the World Series in the last inning on Tommy Henrich's home run against Don Newcombe of the Brooklyn Dodgers as 66,224 persons roared and No. 37 danced on the dirt.

They could have danced all night. The Professor and his lady celebrate the Yankees' World Series victory of 1949 with a Stengel Polka. The suit came back in style years later.

New York Daily News

Glendale, California, and Edna Lawson are both proud of Casey Stengel as he brings home the bacon after the 1949 World Series. It was a long way from Kankakee, Illinois.

United Press International

Casey and Joe Page wait for the rain to let up in Washington on September 9, 1950. They just heard that Detroit shut out Chicago, 7-0, sinking the Yankees deeper into second place. And now they would like to get at the Senators with those bats and get back into the race.

September 29, 1950: The race is run, the victory won. The Yankees learn in their hotel rooms in Boston that they just clinched the pennant because Detroit was eliminated by Cleveland. The happy people include old hero Joe DiMaggio (far left), future managers Ralph Houk and Yogi Berra and the boy wonder Whitey Ford.

Stengel welcomes a 20-year-old rookie outfielder to spring training in 1951. The youngster arrived from Oklahoma with one suit and a $1,000 bonus, and had to use Cliff Mapes's bat. Name: Mickey Mantle.

Mr. Berra, "which is my assistant manager," watches the Doctor check the laws of gravity while waiting for the bullpen to produce a relief pitcher. It's May 23, 1951, and the Detroit Tigers have just scored three runs in the second inning. Casey was famous for juggling lineups, too.

July 12, 1952, Yankee Stadium: Billy Martin tagged Clint Courtney at second base a trifle hard. Courtney came up swinging, and the riot was on. No. 37, who was 62 years old, went to Martin's rescue in a swirl of Frank Crosetti (2), Tom Morgan (28), Irv Noren (25), Johnny Mize (36), Jim Brideweser (27). Fight was draw, but Yankees won game, 5-4, in 11th inning.

In the catacombs of Ebbets Field, it's difficult to tell who won as Stengel leads the Yankees to their clubhouse and Jackie Robinson leads the Dodgers. The day was October 4, 1953; the game was No. 5 in the World Series, and the Yankees just won it by the tidy score of 11-7.

Once he used a flashlight to signal his pitcher to stress his contention that it was too dark to continue playing. Once he carried an umbrella to home plate to suggest that it was raining too hard. But a poncho in Yankee Stadium?

Baseball—just a gleam in the eye of Dr. Stengel. The eye is clear, the ball is white, the signature is "William Harridge." On a clear day, you can see all three.

affairs around here tonight and leave tomorrow to join the Giants in Boston."

Casey's reaction, he said later, was: "Leave tomorrow? Boys, I was leaving right now. I caught the 6:14 from North Philadelphia for New York and the midnight out of New York for Boston. Rawlings waited over until the next day, but I wasn't taking any chances on the deal being called off."

From Boston, the Giants returned to New York, where Stengel appeared for the first time in a Giant uniform. He had played six seasons in Brooklyn under Uncle Robbie; but this was New York, and he was playing for Robbie's nemesis, John Joseph McGraw. He looked over the Polo Grounds when he arrived and said to himself: "Wake up, muscles! We're in New York now."

His muscles didn't actually have too much waking up to do that first half-season in New York. McGraw already had more muscles than he needed: Long George Kelley at first base; Rawlings, the expatriate from Philadelphia, at second; the talented youngster, Frankie Frisch, at third; Dave Bancroft at shortstop; Irish Meusel in left field; Georgie Burns in center, and Ross Youngs in right. Frank Snyder and Earl Smith were the catchers, while Art Nehf, Phil Douglas, Jesse Barnes and Fred Toney did most of the pitching.

Stengel mostly watched, but he watched a great show. The Phillies had been doomed tail-enders; the Giants were perennial contenders. They were 7½ games behind Pittsburgh on August 24, but in one spectacular series won five straight games from the Pirates and narrowed the gap to 2½ games. They closed it completely in September and won the pennant by four games.

An even more intriguing situation developed in the World Series, the first for the Giants since 1917 and the first for Stengel since Brooklyn's one year in the sun in 1916. The American League in 1921 was being treated to a spectacle that appealed to Judge Landis in his first year as commissioner following the Black Sox scandal and that thrilled the public to an extraordinary degree.

With Babe Ruth completing his transformation from a superior pitcher to a home-run hitter of record proportions, Yankee attendance leaped from 619,164 in 1919 to 1,289,422 the following year, and was keeping pace in 1921 as Ruth slugged the far-fetched total of 59 home runs.

Even in the hands of Frank "Home-Run" Baker, the home run had been a rare sight; in 1911, Baker won the American League leadership as a power hitter with nine home runs. He went to 10 the next year and all the way to 12 the year after that. When Ruth, in 1919, hit 29 for Boston, he surpassed all of the home-run hitters in the game, and in his first season with the Yankees, with Baker as a teammate, he hit 54 while Fred Williams of Philadelphia led the National League with 15.

The Yankees had finished third the year before, but now they outdistanced the defending champions, the Cleveland Indians, and won the first pennant in Yankee history—a history that would see them reaching the pinnacle of success in baseball by winning 29 pennants in the next 45 years.

The World Series, being the first between New York's two principal teams, was spiced by the fact that the Giants were the Yankees' landlord in the Polo Grounds, since Yankee Stadium was still two years away. It was also the last of the 5-out-of-9 series, and the Yankees got off to a fine start by winning the first two games by identical scores of 3 to 0, and winning the first game in exactly one hour and 38 minutes. The Giants, in fact, did not score a run until the third inning of the third game. But they scored four then and went on to win the game, 13 to 5.

No team had ever spotted an opponent two games in the 17 previous World Series and survived, let alone a club led by Babe Ruth. But somehow the Giants survived. They won the fourth game, 4 to 2, despite Ruth's first home run in a World Series, but lost the fifth, 3 to 1. Now the Yankees lost Ruth because of an abscess on his left elbow, and McGraw was never one to miss an opportunity like that. The Giants swept three straight games, 8 to 5, then 2 to 1, and finally 1 to 0.

Stengel took no part in the series, the first one that the Giants had won in 16 years, but he took part in the division of the spoils: $5,265 worth. And his muscles had already followed his call to wake up. He had hit .284 that first season in New York, then went fairly wild in 1922 by raising his average 84 points to the highest in his career: .368, with seven home runs and 48 runs batted in, though he appeared in only 84 games out of 154 with the well-stocked Giants.

"I never hit that high before," he said, "and I thought to myself, that's amazing. But I woke up on the last day of the season and found that Hornsby was leading the league 33 points higher."

Rogers Hornsby, whom Casey called the toughest right-handed batter he had seen, indeed was leading the league with an average of .401, so Casey was eclipsed in his finest hour. And worse, in the American League, George Sisler hit .420. The following year, Stengel outreached himself again, batting .339 in 75 games, but Hornsby again led the league with .384 while Harry Heilmann of Detroit hit .403 to lead both leagues.

Being part of McGraw's traveling circus, though, helped to make up for little frustrations like these. The Giants won the pennant again in 1922, with Cincinnati second and Pittsburgh and St. Louis tied for third. In the American League, the Yankees won over St. Louis, Detroit and Cleveland in that order.

Judge Landis decided that the series had wearied the public when forced to a decision in five games out of nine, so he restored the 4-out-of-7 rule. But it still proved dismally long for the Yankees. Ruth was finishing a relatively poor year in which he hit only .315 and had been ineligible to play until May 20 because he had gone barnstorming after the 1921 series against Landis's orders.

In the series, Ruth hit .118, while Stengel went to bat five times, got two singles and wound up batting .400. The Giants, meanwhile, swept all four games, though the Yankees salvaged a tie in the second game, with the umpires causing a storm of insults when the game was halted "because of darkness" with the score 3 to 3 in the 10th inning and the clock pointing to 4:40 P.M. in fairly broad daylight.

One of the high spots for Stengel came off the field, when Ruth and Bob Meusel barged into the Giants' locker room in fighting mood after the third game looking for Rawlings, the second-baseman who had waited overnight in Philadelphia while Stengel high-tailed it to New York. The Giants were removing their coats to accept the challenge when McGraw entered the room and ordered Ruth and Muesel out.

Another high spot came in the next game, the fourth. Casey was sitting in the dugout this time, watching as his substitute, Bill Cunningham, played center field. Ruth hit a tremendous drive behind the monument near the bleacher wall, but Cunningham raced behind the slab and made a sensational catch.

This time, winning the series was worth $4,470 to each Giant. But the most significant result of the Yankees' defeat in four games was an argument it caused between the owners of the team, Colonel Jacob Ruppert and the magnificently named Colonel Tillinghast l' Hommedieu Huston, who was all for dispensing with Miller Huggins as manager of the Yankees.

Huston, who had been a contractor and engineer during the Spanish-American War, was already far along with plans for Yankee Stadium, which was opened the following year. But by then Ruppert had resolved the argument by simply buying him out.

Fate was about to play a perverse trick on Stengel, too. Having played only a minor role in the Giants' two consecutive successes over the Yankees, and having reached the advanced baseball age of 33, he suddenly was projected into the limelight in 1923 as the Yankees and Giants won their third straight pennants and faced each other for the third straight year—this time with the new Yankee Stadium ready for its prime tenant, George Herman Ruth.

Ruth had rebounded dramatically from his "off" year by hitting 41 home runs and batting in 130 runs, while the Yankees finished 14 games ahead of Detroit. But now, like star-crossed lovers, he and Stengel were headed for each other in the World Series—and Casey was headed for a "fairly amazing" surprise after the series.

As the series opened—the first one ever broadcast by radio, with Graham McNamee at the microphone and a record crowd of 55,307 in the new concrete stadium at 161st Street and River Avenue in the Bronx—Stengel went to right field not knowing two things: He was about to live the most memorable moment of his career as a ball player, but 30 days later his career as a Giant would abruptly end.

However, he had more on his mind that October than either Babe Ruth or the Yankees' new stadium. He, the "team bachelor," had met a girl, and her name was Edna.

4

EDNA

Edna Lawson was one of those fearsome combinations: beautiful but smart. She was a tall, willowy brunette accountant when she met Casey Stengel at a baseball game in 1923, and he was playing right field for John McGraw's Giants. They were married on August 18 the following year, and then Edna followed baseball teams around the circuits of a dozen leagues for 41 years while the fortunes of Casey and his teams fluctuated wildly.

Her thinking, though, never strayed far from their home at 1663 Grandview Avenue in Glendale, California, and she practically commuted from it to baseball games all over the country. So, whether the year was 1925 and Worcester was in third place in the Eastern League under a rookie manager or whether it was 1955 and the New York Yankees were in first place under a patriarch—the house, the palm trees, the swimming pool, the Oriental furnishings, the playhouse in the garden were all there awaiting the return of Charles Dillon Stengel.

It all started on a kind of blind date at the Polo Grounds. She had gone to the game with Mrs. Emil Meusel, the wife of the ball player best known as Irish Meusel, who in fact was of Alsatian descent and who had played with Stengel in Philadelphia as well as in New York. Casey was one of the few bachelors in the lineup—the "team bachelor," in some ways—and when McGraw removed him from the lineup in the seventh inning in order to send in Jimmy O'Connell for defensive purposes, he changed Stengel's life.

O'Connell was sent in because of "that fence," Edna said years later, referring to the difficult carom shots that bounced off the short right-field fence in the Polo Grounds and that made right field an obstacle course at times for a pair of legs as uncertain as Casey's had become. Anyway, when O'Connell went in, Stengel went out. He went straight to the clubhouse, showered, dressed and then appeared in the box-seat section reserved for the players' wives and guests, where Edna Lawson was sitting with Mrs. Meusel. All four went out to dinner after the game, and that was the beginning of that.

"Just think," he would say 40 years later, "if I hadn't been taken out of that game, Edna might've wound up with somebody else."

Edna, in fact, almost did wind up with somebody else, since she had an "understanding" at the time with a young doctor. But she wound up with Casey, and from the first day became the gyroscope of his life. He was already 34 years old and had led the life of a galloping nomad. But Edna wasted no time providing him with a base of operations that he never relinquished.

The base was in Glendale, where she had been raised while her father, a building contractor, had constructed some of the early movie sets, Glendale being one of the early capitals of silent films. As a schoolgirl in the seventh grade, she and her classmates would stop to watch scenes being shot while on their way home from school. Later, as an 18-year-old, she began to get into the act, so to speak, as did other people in the town who were being trotted in as extras.

"I was a good dancer," she recalled, "so they put me in western dance-hall scenes. Once I knocked over the whole set. Nobody made much money in those days. The most I ever got was 85 dollars a week. But I acted with Lillian Gish and Hoot Gibson and other stars. I guess I photographed well, but it wasn't for me."

In 1924, her father built something else, not far from the movie sets he used to build: a house. And Casey and Edna moved into it as a wedding present and settled down.

It was a big two-story house on a street lined with palm trees, a street that sloped upward to the foothills of the Sierras. And

wherever Casey roamed around his acres for the next half-century
—to the flower gardens, the tennis court, the pool out back, the
orange and lemon trees—he could look over his shoulder and see
a majestic gray mountain peak looming up a couple of miles away.

Better yet, wherever he roamed outside the acres—New York,
Florida, Japan—he could know that Edna was worrying less about
batting averages than about the windstorms that occasionally blew
dust all over their living-room drapes.

The only thing missing was children, a fact that encouraged
Casey to dote on teen-aged baseball players after he had become
a manager or on the hordes of Edna's relatives who lived nearby.
Her brother Jack and cousin Margaret lived in houses not far away,
and "Uncle Casey" became the paterfamilias of a booming, traveling, enterprising clan of Lawsons.

Thriving, too. When Casey later invested in some oil-well properties along with Al Lopez, Randy Moore and several other baseball cronies, they literally struck oil and the cash started to flow.
When Edna's family set up a bank in Glendale, more cash flowed.
When they invested in real estate, they found Glendale expanding
and their dividends multiplied, too.

The strength of the Stengels' life together, though, rested not
so much on their taste for the good life, nor their increasing ability
to finance it, nor the riot of adventure that they seemed to incite
from the start; it was more the fact that each thought the other
was a card, and each was right.

Casey, for example, liked to sit by his wife's elbow at home, in
hotel lobbies, in railroad stations or in airport terminals and make
impertinent asides as she described the windstorms, rainstorms and
even forest fires that created household emergencies back in Glendale.

For one thing, Edna was a tireless interior decorator who always
was remodeling the house into "Chinese rooms" and other exotic
styles with imported Japanese beds and the like. For another thing,
he could tweak her with the impunity of a man who fully appreci-
ates a woman's business skill and often lets the world know it.
After all, she had been a professional accountant and actress when
they met, and she revived her skills later by managing apartment-
house properties and serving as chairman of the board of the company that operated their bank's headquarters building.

"Tell 'em about the time you played with Hoot Gibson," he would say, interrupting her at a serious moment.

Or, while she was relating a plan to save both an insurance company and herself some money by caching the family silverware in the swimming pool to protect it from dust and fire, he would ask off the back of his hand in a stage whisper: "What good silver? Do we own any?"

He conceded, though, that an ill wind might blow some good in Glendale. He used to have a room in the house, he said, that was so flawless that Mrs. Stengel in exasperation finally gave it to "some relation." So now, he went on, he was stuck with a Chinese room and a Japanese bed, inspired by a baseball junket to the Far East.

"That Japanese bed of mine," he said, "the one that took two years to build—it had to be so perfect—I wish the storm would blow that thing away."

Edna was undismayed by his flippancy. "One advantage," she replied with a sly grin, "is that Casey doesn't have to look for his room any more. He just looks for the Chinese room."

Even during the baseball season when he would leave this California oasis for eight months, she would try to keep one foot in Glendale while following the baseball trail herself. One reason was that nobody could keep up Casey's whirlwind pace, anyway— up at dawn; meals taken on the run; long afternoons and, later, long evenings in stadiums; drinking with the Giants or Braves or Toledo Mudhens or "my writers" until 2 or 3 A.M.

Another reason was that her roots were deep in Glendale, and she simply liked it there. When the bank was established, she sold most of the stock for it and enlisted the most depositors. She also rang doorbells and made speeches to help her brother in his campaign for mayor of Glendale and, she said a trifle triumphantly, "of course he won."

When she finally would hit the baseball trails with Casey, though, she traveled in full plumage and rivaled him for energy and zest. She had a rich, smart, expensive wardrobe and the long, lean figure to go with it. She indulged herself in dramatically ornate hats. Her jewelry was usually glittering, and she was as vivacious and outspoken in a high voice as Casey was in a low voice.

But, whether at home or on the road, Edna was a tower of

strength and a buffer shielding him from the world. She undertook to answer his stacks of fan mail, setting up a little office wherever they traveled and drafting replies to letters for him to sign, separating the autograph requests from mail that required information; getting him to sign baseballs that were sent to them, then repacking the baseballs and often paying the return postage; adding to their Christmas list, which grew into the thousands, and in general performing the work of a staff of secretaries and stenographers.

When the World Series became a regular part of their life—long after the 1923 World Series the first year they had met—Edna sifted through hundreds of requests for tickets, often from persons who simply put the bite on them or who were willing to pay if Casey could produce the seats.

One day there came a knock on the door of their suite in the Essex House in New York during a World Series, and she opened it to find a man and a 3-year-old boy standing outside. It would mean a lot, he said, for the boy to have a ticket to that game that day, so he had simply called for it. Edna forked over two tickets.

"I thought he was a friend of Casey's," she said later. "I assumed Casey had promised him tickets and he *was* just calling for them."

The confusion was understandable, since Casey tended to be as imprecise about the mechanics of some things as she was precise. One of his closest friends in baseball was Al Lopez, who was a catcher for 24 years and a highly successful manager at Cleveland and Chicago for 15. They were boon companions, and yet, Lopez recalled, "I don't ever remember getting a letter from Casey during all that time."

"We might not see each other for a year or so," he said, "and we would not write to each other. But we could always resume the conversation when we got around to it, without any loss of communication."

Besides this stream-of-consciousness quality of Stengel's friendship, Lopez detected one overriding characteristic of life with Casey: "He was warm. I mean, on the ball field, he had one great goal: to teach. But as a friend, he was simply warm."

The crevasse in his personality was noticeable to others, too. With ball players, he could be short, he could be brusque, he could even be mean. With "civilians" like his sister Louise, who lived alone in Kansas City in later years, he could be devoted to the point of doting. He would simply stop off at Kansas City en route from East Coast to West Coast and see that she was provided for. With a blind man brought to him in a ball park, he could be gentle to the point of letting his visitor run fingers over that great stone face in order to picture it and frame it in memory.

That is, he could be careless about the fringe details of friendship like writing letters; but he cared. He did not go to church as Edna did each Sunday, checking the schedule of masses and attending faithfully; but he was compassionate. She would worry about a meal; he would merely eat it.

In a word, Edna kept the books. She even preferred this type of administrative duty to some of the more prosaic household chores, like cooking.

"I never really liked to cook," she said, looking back on the early years of their marriage. "I was never what you would call a good cook. Oh, I could cook, all right; but not really well. And yet we always seemed to have great crowds of people around, so I'd have to cook. We'd plan a quiet Sunday at home, with maybe my brother or some other close member of the family, but before long other people would start to drop by the house. The Irish Meusels lived up the street and they would show up, and I might not even have enough to go around, really. Casey didn't mind; he loved crowds. But I worried."

Edna worried about other people's bookkeeping, too. Years after she and Casey had settled in Glendale, she expressed interest one day during spring training in the fact that this writer had a room with a kitchenette with a refrigerator in the Colonial Inn at St. Petersburg Beach.

"When do you defrost the refrigerator?" she asked, sensing a flaw in mid-sentence.

"When do I do what?" I asked.

"Defrost the icebox," she shot back. "Do you keep anything perishable in it? Oh, ice cream, oranges and things like that, eh. Well, I'll take care of that."

Bright and early the next morning, a knock at the door introduced the assistant housekeeper of the hotel, who announced: "Mrs. Stengel sent me. She told me to defrost your refrigerator, and to send your ice cream over to *her* refrigerator until yours is done."

The Stengels supplemented each other like Romeo and Juliet, all right. They liked to globe-trot and they liked little trips to Lake Tahoe and Las Vegas, which were within jaunting distance of Glendale. They liked good food and good drink and horse races, and they liked to eat pancakes—which they did at department store lunch counters. Best of all, they liked each other.

Edna also had an abiding no-nonsense attitude toward his reputation for nonsense, which was already well-established when they met in the Polo Grounds in 1923 and which flourished after that.

"He's not a clown," she would say with emphasis. "He's one of the smartest men in baseball, in business, in anything he'd try. He's given his life to baseball, and baseball owes Casey more than Casey owes baseball."

Later, when he was berated in The Saturday Evening Post as "an angry old man," Edna weighed in with this defense:

"I think I know the man better than almost anyone. I must say that Casey, to me and to my entire family—well, we have worshipped the ground the man walks on.

"When we go out to a restaurant, he walks behind me. He doesn't want any favors. He doesn't call ahead and say, 'This is Casey Stengel. I want a table.'

"The man has never said anything detrimental about any ball player he has managed. Never once did he begrudge anyone in baseball anything or come home and blame any outfielder, infielder or pitcher for losing a ball game.

"He used to say to me, 'Edna, can't you find a place in your business for this player?' He would have liked nothing better than to have ball players come home and stay with us so that he could work with them longer. He might bark and talk out loud, but 30 minutes later he would change.

"Why, Mickey Mantle has called Casey a second father to him. Each and every ball player has meant the best in life to Casey."

In pursuit of her hero, Edna led a kind of limited nomad's life away from Glendale herself. But she kept order wherever they went.

In New York, they customarily lived at the Essex House on

Central Park South; in St. Petersburg, at the Soreno Hotel or the Colonial Inn on the beach in later years. She would join him in Florida in the spring, or would accompany him there, and they would share a double suite and keep house while he ran the ball club after he had advanced to managing. If the team opened the season in New York, she would accompany him there for the big day, but was likely to fly home to Glendale when Casey and the boys took to the road a week later.

Then, when they returned to New York, she would fly there for the two-week home stand, often timing her flight from Los Angeles to arrive in New York just as Casey was arriving from, say, Chicago. And they would have a trancontinental rendezvous at the airport, Edna sitting by chattering gaily with the coaches and players while Casey rooted around for his baggage.

Sometimes the exigencies of travel would put a bit of a strain on their relaxed relations. Once, when she was late for a chartered airplane that was transporting his Yankees to New York after a World Series game in Cincinnati, he gave the command to depart without her.

Another time, in March of 1964, his New York Mets spent a weekend in Mexico City on their first "intercontinental expedition" to play exhibition games. They flew from St. Petersburg to Miami, then to Mexico City, and after the weekend—which was a solid success at the box office—they headed back. Everybody was at the airport ready for the takeoff when a hitch developed: Mrs. Stengel, the manager's wife, had lost, misplaced or simply forgotten her exit visa. The airport official was inflexible on the subject and stood by rigidly while she searched her handbags and then her baggage. And while she did, the manager, vexed that the delay to his ball club was being caused by his own wife, quietly fumed.

A taxicab was dispatched back to the hotel and a search there was undertaken; still no visa. And as the manager fumed less quietly and the time passed, a tenseness settled over the party. When the visa was finally found, they took off for Miami, good and late and good and grim.

All the way to Miami, silence enveloped the "manager's seat" on the chartered airliner, where he sat side by side with her, letting her crimes sink in. All the way from Miami to Tampa Airport on the west coast of Florida, he let the silence grow thicker. Finally, they left the plane at Tampa and boarded a chartered bus for St. Petersburg, where the Mets were living, and as they got seated in the front row, the enormity of his response to her faux pas seemed to grow apparent to him. He relented.

"I'll check and see that your bags are okay," he said, breaking several hours of silence in a belated attempt to be solicitous and to make up for the exaggerated strain between them since the airport incident in Mexico. So, he hopped down the steps of the bus and disappeared toward the baggage-loading hatch to the rear. Ten minutes later he returned, trundled on board, sat alongside her and said, in an obvious but overplayed effort to make it up to her:

"Yeah, they're all right. They've got all three of them packed in."

Edna, given her "shot" at him after hours of suffering in silence, made the most of it. Tersely, evenly, unemotionally, yet triumphantly, she replied:

"I had four."

One thing that irritated Casey constantly was the fact that his comfort and wealth were taken for granted, carelessly and anonymously as though he had not labored mightily to achieve both.

"People always say I'm rich and the director of a bank," he said after he had reached a state of considerable affluence, "but they never say which bank."

Well, it was the Valley National Bank, with John E. Lawson chairman of the board and trustee of the Lawson Estate, and Charles D. "Casey" Stengel vice president. The main office was on North Brand Boulevard in the heart of Glendale, and Stengel could be reached there in the off-season through a telephone number with the appropriate exchange of POpular 6.

He wasn't exactly a captain of finance; seven years after it had opened in 1957, the bank listed deposits of 19 million dollars, and the following year edged closer to 22 million. But he was at least a lieutenant, and by September of 1964 the Valley National Bank had a "Toluca Lake Office" in North Hollywood and Casey donned a yellow helmet to break ground for a new main-bank building in a spacious lot adjoining the headquarters.

"We might even strike oil," he said as he dug a golden spade into the ground.

He was finishing his third season as manager of the Mets at that time and the team had just ended a weekend series in Los Angeles. Monday was an off-day, and while the rest of the team flew up to San Francisco to open a series with the Giants on Tuesday, Stengel peeled off to spend a day at home with Edna, their mementoes and their little business empire.

The ground-breaking was accomplished with full flourishes. Cameramen had been alerted, baseball writers traveling with the club had been invited and a small army of businessmen, contractors and relatives from Glendale stood by watching as Casey tried to turn a shovel-full of dirt alongside a cement parking lot.

Then the whole cavalcade drove off to a ceremonial luncheon at a restaurant, where Jack Lawson acted as master of ceremonies and Casey acted as Casey. Lead pencils shaped like little baseball bats were passed out along with matchbooks inscribed "Valley National Bank." Then Stengel packed a couple of dozen writers and friends into more cars for a guided tour of the area before leading the caravan to 1663 Grandview to spend the rest of his "off-day" with Edna in the big house at the foot of the mountain.

There, he climbed into what might best be described as an Oriental cabana outfit, and with a lordly sweep of his hand told his guests in a loud voice to "have a good time for yourselves." He settled into a chair on the manicured lawn alongside the swimming pool, not far from old grandstand seats from the Polo Grounds inscribed "Edna" and "Casey"; directed a band of caterers who soon arrived to set up a steak dinner for 40, and, a fugitive from the circus world of baseball for 24 hours, surrounded himself with the best of both worlds in his own backyard.

Inside the house, Edna cheerfully showed off the family heirlooms—gilded Louisville Slugger bats from each of the 10 Yankee teams that had won pennants, glasses monogrammed with the Yankee top hat symbol in red, white and blue, and hundreds of photographs.

"Look," she cried, as though discovering something, "here's one of Casey and King George."

Sure enough, there was Stengel the outfielder lined up shoulder to shoulder with his touring teammates and other ball players in the winter of 1924 while George V, magnificently bewhiskered and bearded, passed along the line shaking hands. Out of camera range that day stood Edna herself, a bride of three months taking a delayed honeymoon with a traveling baseball troupe.

At the ball park, Edna usually sat in the front-row box just to the right of the dugout, not 30 feet from Stengel as he waddled around in the pin-striped uniform with No. 37 printed across the back of the shirt. She did not keep "official" score for him, as Johnny Keane's wife did all during the years Keane managed in the minor and major leagues. But she paid strict attention, whether her companion was a close friend like Dorothy Heffner, the wife of the Met coach who later became manager of the Cincinnati Reds, or Joan W. Payson, principal owner of the Mets.

One night when Casey was running the Yankees, Edna's maid at the Essex House suggested that it might rain and that Mrs. Stengel might better wear rain gear to the game. Edna did, and walked into Yankee Stadium 30 minutes later under glowering clouds. Then she noticed "a lot of people and policemen around, down near the box behind the dugout on the first-base side." She guessed something was up. She was right. The Duke and Duchess of Windsor were soon escorted into her box, and for the rest of the cloudy evening the son of George V sat alongside the wife of the former outfielder, Casey Stengel—30 years later.

"They were great," Edna recalled. "They asked about the game, and the Duchess kept talking with me about it all the time."

"You know, she was from Baltimore," Edna concluded, establishing a good case for the Duchess on the odd chance that she might turn out to be a red-hot Oriole fan.

Casey's fortunes in baseball gyrated, but Mrs. Casey remained fairly stoical, even when the Yankee years were followed by the Met years. It was a little like going from knighthood to serfdom, but Edna was unruffled.

"The major difference," she said, "was that Casey and I used to have a reunion of our family during the World Series. We'd even have a formal dinner in the hotel for all our relatives and friends. But we adjusted to the Mets very well."

The final adjustment was made in the spring of 1965, his last as a major league manager.

First, Edna strained her back and had to stay home when he

flew to St. Petersburg for spring training for the third week in February. Then, a week later, three young prowlers forced their way into the Stengels' home. She woke up and called the police, who arrived a few minutes later and arrested the intruders, but Edna had slipped getting out of bed to make the call and had injured her back again.

Finally, she flew to Florida two weeks later to join Casey, endured the 3,000-mile flight well, but was immediately racked with back pains when she landed, and spent most of the time in St. Petersburg in bed. Casey made a notable adjustment, too. He had been his old night-time self until then, conversing and drinking far into the night with his baseball friends. But when Edna arrived in distress, he stopped carousing with the boys, babied her for weeks and waited on her with the gallantry of a bridegroom.

Edna returned the devotion four months later when their baseball lives unexpectedly reached the turning point.

She was back home one week before his 75th birthday when he fell on July 25 and fractured his left hip. She still wasn't feeling too chipper herself and had intended to stay home until his birthday. But when George M. Weiss, president of the Mets, telephoned the news to her, she set out for New York.

She arrived the next night at 11:30 on a United Air Lines jet from Los Angeles. Dorothy Heffner, Harold Weissman, the Mets' public relations director, and I met her. She was worn out and half-sick herself, but she took time to thank the crew members who had looked after her during the five-hour flight. Then she walked down the long corridor at Kennedy Airport to Mrs. Heffner's car outside, posing for pictures on the way and even sitting in a phone booth as though chatting with Casey in the hospital.

It wasn't until they were getting into the car for the drive into Manhattan that she was told Casey would have an operation early the next morning, and it wasn't until then that she broke into tears.

"Oh, dear," she said, weeping freely, "do you think I'll get to see Casey before they take him in for the operation?"

She did get to see him, though he was under heavy sedation and was sleeping. But for months after, she spoke of one happy memory that night that outlived the apprehension and anxiety. He had told the nurse to ask Edna for three things: his electric razor, his toothbrush and the lump of clay he'd been using for his hand exercises to strengthen his right wrist, which he had broken at West Point two and a half months earlier.

One month later, when Casey made his farewell appearance at Shea Stadium, she was there in the familiar spot alongside him, dressed to the nines and proudly carrying his baseball shirt—No. 37—into retirement. Six weeks later, back home, she drove him to Dodger Stadium for the World Series, at which Casey was scheduled to throw out the first ball. She had two worries: whether there would be an elevator to take him up and down five flights to his seat, mending hip and all, and how to get an aspirin tablet into him to ease his pain. She finally disguised it in a Coca-Cola while he signed autographs, posed for pictures leaning on a cane and answered dozens of questions from radio reporters who lugged tape-recorders into their dugout-level box.

That's the way life with Casey always had been, since the day they met at the Polo Grounds with Irish Meusel and his wife. Edna Lawson was chief of staff, financial wizard, homemaker and housekeeper, traveling companion, executive secretary, auditor of the family books and girl friend. In short, the woman behind the man behind the baseball team.

For their 40th wedding anniversary—August 18, 1964—they posed in a hansom cab in Central Park, she chucking him affectionately under the chin while he tried to look abashed. They had it reproduced in a golden tint and sent it out that December as a Christmas card to their mile-long list of friends, with the single word: "Joy."

That was the quality of their feeling for each other, beneath his crustiness and her smart energy. They liked each other, and the "rube" from Kankakee did not let her forget it for long after the day McGraw took him out of the game and into her life.

"They tell me," he said with an air of discovery one day after 40 years of marriage, "that your cream pie is very good."

Another time—a typically whirlwind day in St. Petersburg in the spring—he cut through the fanfare and noise that surrounded them all the time and put things in the perspective that had taken shape the day of the blind date in 1923. He popped his head out of the dugout at Al Lang Field and searched through the Mets' box, where Johnny Murphy, the club's vice president, sat with Lou Niss, the traveling secretary, and Bill Dickey, the old Yankee catcher who was batting consultant to the Mets. Casey seemed to be ticking off a crowded agenda in his mind, and then suddenly he found himself face to face with his wife, sitting in the front row.

He did a double take but, without breaking stride, added her to the mental "agenda," pointed toward her and said: "And you want to see me when the season's over, right?"

Edna Lawson, perhaps thinking of those drapes covered with dust back in Glendale, nodded and smiled and said, "Right."

5

THIS IS THE WAY OLD CASEY RAN

The Roaring Twenties had some of their most roaring moments in the Polo Grounds, at 155th Street and Eighth Avenue, in upper Manhattan. There, stock brokers, politicians, actors, Gibson Girls and mobsters would abandon the cares of the spiraling stock market and the escalating warfare of the Prohibition feuds for a few hours' fantasy in the home of John J. McGraw's Giants.

There, George M. Cohan would sit, untroubled and unmolested by his public, and watch the titans of New York baseball, the Giants, play the seven other teams in the National League. There, Ethel Barrymore, the prima donna of the grandstand, would observe carefully and intelligently, tracking the ball games on a scorecard as meticulously as the critics of the day would scrutinize her performances on stages downtown. There, Al Jolson would appear from a runway behind first base, dressed magnificently in the high fashion of the affluent of the theater, walk deliberately around the perimeter of the grandstand behind home plate, acknowledge the cheers and shouts of "Hi, Al," by clasping his hands over his head in a victory salute as though he were Jack Dempsey and had just knocked out Luis Firpo, and slowly make his way to a reserved seat behind third base.

Then, with perhaps 50,000 persons seated in this island alongside the Harlem River, famous umpires like Bill Klem would station themselves behind home plate and "the batteries for today's game" would be announced. The advent of radio broadcasts and public address systems relieved umpires of the duty of turning to the throng and bellowing this information, plus changes in the lineups during the game, such as "For New York, Lindstrom now playing third base." But as late as 1928, Klem maintained his role as narrator at least in spring training games, in Sarasota and other cities on the west coast of Florida, where major league teams had been exercising for 15 springs. And nearly 40 years later a professional waiter named Pat Piper still sat on a camp chair near the screen behind home plate at Wrigley Field in Chicago, keeping track of the supply of new baseballs, often narrowly escaping foul balls that bounced off the screen and conferring with the umpires on pitching changes, which he would then announce to the crowd by a hand microphone in monosyllables that were often hard to decipher and that were sometimes several pitches late.

The Polo Grounds fans of the twenties would get their money's worth by direct participation, too. They kibitzed their heroes loudly, reserving special vocal effects for the more celebrated comics like Casey Stengel, who would be goaded into histrionics by good-natured booing no matter which team he happened to be playing for that season. Stengel always rose to the occasion, turning to the grandstand and bowing low with exaggerated courtesy.

Sometimes, he would make the afternoon exceptionally worthwhile by demonstrating his unusual talents for pugnacious behavior and, later, wounded sensitivity. In 1922, his first full season with the Giants, he experienced one of his better moments in both respects, in addition to exhibiting another peculiar talent: an ability to plague the team that had most recently traded him.

In this case, the visitors were his old, unlamented teammates, the Philadelphia Phillies. And for their appearance in the Polo Grounds, Stengel had preened himself with extreme care. "The full treatment," he had instructed the barber, and then he settled back for a haircut, shave, shampoo and double dose of hair tonic.

Right on schedule that afternoon, his well-groomed head became involved with the Phillies, who remembered his insultingly rapturous farewell to Philadelphia baseball the season before. Phil Weinert, the Philadelphia pitcher, let one of his fastballs fly straight toward the Stengel haircut, and Casey promptly hit the dirt. But he bounced back up with delighted fury, swinging away at Weinert. It was an exceptionally bruising fight, and the umpires finally were forced to send an SOS to the police to break it up.

At that point, Stengel's talent for wounded sensitivity took over, as he recalled later with some pleasure because he had spread the discomfort from Weinert to McGraw, the great reformed brawler of the Baltimore Orioles who now kept order on the Giants with piety as though brawling were tasteless.

"That will cost you 75 dollars," McGraw bellowed. "That fight was the dumbest thing I ever saw you do."

"But what could you expect," he added, wildly misjudging Stengel's pre-game grooming rituals, "what could you expect from a cheap lout who comes to the park smelling like cheap gin."

When the baseball season ended, McGraw, Stengel and the rest of the denizens of the Polo Grounds sometimes put their violent little world on display for people across the country who suffered the double disadvantage of not living near the Giants' ball park and of not yet living in a time when television would bring the ball park to the country. They even put the show on the road in faraway places, earning themselves six weeks or so of globetrotting and introducing the "national game" to an international audience that a generation later would start to send Japanese, Cuban and Latin American ball players back to America in return.

McGraw, in fact, had organized the first overseas barnstorming tour in the winter of 1913-14. It was an ambitious project that featured the Giants and Chicago White Sox, and that carried them around the world. Eight months later, World War I started and baseball junkets were out of the question for several years. But, in 1922, a former ball player named Herb Hunter, who had visited Japan and had business contacts there, put the globetrotters back in business.

He organized an Oriental trip in the fall of 1922, starring half a dozen members of the Yankees and Giants, who had just met in the World Series—including Stengel, who had been a "busher" at the time of the first tour nine years earlier but who was now a veteran of 10 seasons in the National League and who was fresh from his famous tiff with Weinert.

They toured Korea, China and Japan, bringing Stengel into touch with Oriental styles that would find their way into his home

20 months later after he had met and married Edna Lawson. In fact, two winters later, in 1924, Edna accompanied him on another barnstorming trip, this time to England, Ireland and France, where he played baseball and met crowned heads of Europe like George V while Edna, who had been married to him during the baseball season that year, celebrated a delayed honeymoon.

Later, the trips abroad became more glamorous and more significant. In 1931, Frederick G. Lieb, the writer, directed a tour that lasted six weeks and that featured six players who later were elected to the Hall of Fame: Lou Gehrig of the New York Yankees, Rabbit Maranville of the Boston Braves, Frankie Frisch of the St. Louis Cardinals and Lefty Grove, Mickey Cochrane and Al Simmons of the Philadelphia Athletics. Lieb had been offered $25,000 for Babe Ruth's appearance with the company, but Ruth was committed elsewhere, though he did make it to Japan with Connie Mack in 1934.

Lieb's tour was a resounding success in promoting baseball and in promoting profits. The players generally got expense money and a free trip abroad, but Gehrig also collected $5,000 this time as a world-famous "name." In Japan alone, the team played 17 games before 450,000 persons. Professional baseball had not yet been organized in Japan, but baseball was already "the fall sport" the way football was in the United States, and the big leaguers had no trouble lining up Japanese college teams and an "All-Nippon" amateur team as opponents.

"They played a lot more baseball then in Japan than they did in the United States," Lieb recalled later. "We went to Yokohama one Sunday to see a Buddhist shrine, and the entire shoreline was choked with ball games, so crowded that the outfielders from one game would overlap with the fielders from another. And the roads were nearly clogged with ball players on bicycles going to games that were held in rapid sequence—one would follow another as soon as the diamond was clear. One day at 6 o'clock in the morning, we even saw bank clerks and other business men playing a game before they went to work—that's how baseball had taken hold in Japan."

Baseball became such a popular export, though, only after it had survived the Black Sox scandal of 1919 in America and had taken hold in the new stadiums like Ebbets Field, the rebuilt Polo Grounds and the Yankee Stadium in New York, with towering new personalities like Babe Ruth, Rogers Hornsby and Walter Johnson. And Stengel, who was 33 years old and who ran on unsteady legs in 1923, was about to live his most memorable moment as a player in a World Series that included the most towering personality of all, Ruth, and the stadium he had just "built."

The Giants had won two straight World Series over the Yankees, but now the worm was about to turn. The Yankees had swept through to the American League pennant by the runaway margin of 14 games over their nearest pursuer, the Detroit Tigers. Yankee Stadium had gotten off to a resounding start in its first year, and it was about to share the "first million-dollar World Series" with the Polo Grounds.

McGraw fired the opening salvo by outraging the Yankees' owner, Colonel Jacob Ruppert, the beer tycoon and National Guardsman, by refusing to allow the Yankees' prize rookie, Lou Gehrig, to play. McGraw's permission was needed because Gehrig had played the season at Hartford, Connecticut, and had been called up by the Yankees after September 1, the traditional cutoff date for eligibility in a World Series.

Properly piqued, the Yankees took the field October 10 with everything going for them—the new stadium, the goading of two straight defeats to the Giants, McGraw's "ungenerosity" on Gehrig and the booming bat of Babe Ruth. They also had Waite Hoyt on the pitcher's mound, but by the ninth inning Hoyt had been relieved by Joe Bush, the score was tied 4-4, and Casey Stengel—of all people—was coming to bat.

Stengel, batting left-handed, as usual, hit a line drive toward the opposite field over the head of the Yankee shortstop, Everett Scott, and between the left-fielder, Bob Meusel, and the center-fielder, Whitey Witt, who were pulled around toward right in normal defensive alignment against a left-handed hitter.

"I didn't think the ball was hit too hard," said Fred Lieb, who was covering the game in the press box, not far from where Graham McNamee's first broadcast of a World Series game was building to a fine crescendo. "It looked to me like a single."

But, with Witt shaded far over toward right field, the ball skipped through center field unmolested on two bounces and caromed off the fence 450 feet from home plate. Witt finally overhauled it and threw it to Meusel, who was chasing it, too. But a hundred yards away, old Casey Stengel was churning around the bases, amazed that his "single" had met clear sailing and excited that he might break the stalemate in the game and just plain worn out from all that running. Later, he recalled saying—or thinking—to himself, as the crowd of 55,307 followed him around the bases with roars: "Go, legs, go; drive this boy around the bases."

Rounding third, he half-lost a shoe, but he staggered on anyway as Meusel fired a long relay to Scott and Scott fired on to home plate. Finally, as Wally Schang, the Yankee catcher, reached for the ball, Stengel, one shoe flopping and both feet dragging, pitched himself toward the plate, collapsing in a heap at Schang's feet.

Damon Runyon described the incident in these words:

> This is the way old Casey Stengel ran yesterday afternoon running his home run home.
> This is the way old Casey Stengel ran running his home run home to a Giant victory by a score of 5 to 4 in the first game of the World Series of 1923.
> This is the way old Casey Stengel ran running his home run home when two were out in the ninth inning and the score was tied, and the ball still bounding inside the Yankee yard.
> This is the way—
> His mouth wide open.
> His warped old legs bending beneath him at every stride.
> His arms flying back and forth like those of a man swimming with a crawl stroke.
> His flanks heaving, his breath whistling, his head far back. Yankee infielders, passed by Old Casey Stengel as he was running his home run home, say Casey was muttering to himself, adjuring himself to greater speed as a jockey mutters to his horse in a race, saying, 'Go on, Casey, go on.'
> The warped old legs, twisted and bent by many a year of baseball campaigning, just barely held out under Casey until he reached the plate, running his home run home.
> Then they collapsed.

Anyway, he was safe with an inside-the-park home run, and the Giants now had a 5-to-4 lead over the Yankees that McGraw wisely protected by escorting Stengel to the bench and sitting him down while Bill Cunningham took over his defensive post in center field. The Giants held on, and Stengel was suddenly the toast of New York, though Edna Lawson's father, reading newspaper accounts of his wobbly dash around the bases, asked her:

"What kind of old man are you marrying? He looks as though he should be in an old man's home."

Two days later, however, Casey was back in center field and the series was back in Yankee Stadium after a one-day switch to the Polo Grounds. The Yankees had recovered their poise in the second game, as Herb Pennock pitched them to a victory over the Giants and Ruth trumped Stengel's opening-day ace by hitting two home runs—which was the story of Stengel's life.

But now, for the third game, a record baseball crowd of 62,450 filled Yankee Stadium and watched Sad Sam Jones shut out the Giants for six innings while Art Nehf was shutting out the Yankees for six. So, when Stengel advanced to the plate in the seventh, he found the score tied again as it had been 48 hours earlier and he found the entire Yankee bench hooting, catcalling and in general riding him for his theatrical performance in untying it.

This time, Stengel made certain that he would not have to undergo the torture of running the bases. He lifted one of Jones's pitches into the right-field bleachers for his second home run of the series, and having nothing better to occupy his thoughts as he plodded around the bases this time, he artfully thumbed his nose in the direction of the Yankees' new dugout.

"I made like a bee or fly was bothering me," he said, "so I kept rubbing the end of my nose, with my fingers pointing toward the Yankee dugout."

Ruppert, whose pitcher had allowed only four hits against six off the Giants' pitcher, was stung, not only by the final score of 1 to 0 and the way it had been decided, but by Stengel's impudent ounce of revenge in broad daylight. He indignantly told Landis, who was watching from a box seat, that Stengel had insulted players and fans alike.

"I heard about that in a hurry," Stengel recalled. "Commissioner Landis called me over and said he didn't like that kind of exhibition before 60,000 people, and he told me, 'If you do that again, I promise you one thing: You won't receive a dollar of your World Series share.' "

To emphasize the point, Landis fined Stengel $50 on the spot. But Stengel did not know at the time that the Judge also had refused sterner punishment and had put off the furious Ruppert by saying: "Well, Casey Stengel just can't help being Casey Stengel."

As things turned out, Babe Ruth just couldn't help being Babe Ruth, either. His bat was still booming after Stengel's two great moments had come and gone. Casey batted .407 in the series with two home runs, while Ruth hit .360 with three home runs, and the only two games the Giants won were won by Stengel's home runs. Ruth, though, belted one as late as the sixth game, by which time the Yankees had a secure lead in the series and were winning their first championship in an unmatched line of world championships in baseball.

The smart talk described the series as "four games for the Yankees, one for the Giants and two for Stengel." But Casey, upstaged in his finest hour by the king of the upstagers, said the score was "three for Ruth and two for Stengel." He even found that a contract he had signed during the series for a stand-up vaudeville skit was promptly topped by a much better one Ruth signed after the series. And the crowning indignity came when Casey was invited to dinner at the home of Bill Slocum, the writer, and later that evening was taken in to meet Slocum's young son, Frank, who 35 years later became an assistant to Ford Frick, the third Commissioner of Baseball. The little boy was sleeping but his father woke him up, assuring Stengel that he would be thrilled to meet a real live ball player, especially one who had been so eminent in the World Series. But, Casey said years later, the tot knew his heroes. He rubbed his eyes sleepily, shook his head, blinked, looked at the craggy face of Charles Dillon Stengel and burst into angry tears, wailing, "I want to see Babe Ruth."

In spite of these little setbacks to his new fame, Stengel had reached a peak of sorts and had also pocketed $4,112 as the Giants' share of the series pie, while Ruth and the Yankees collected $6,143 each. But less than a month later he picked up *The New York Times* on November 13 and read:

> True to his promise to rebuild the Giants from the bottom up, Manager John J. McGraw last night engineered one of the biggest trades of his career. In exchange for Billy Southworth, outfielder, and Joe Oeschger, pitcher, of the Braves, the Giants' manager sent to Boston Shortstop Dave Bancroft and outfielders Casey Stengel and Bill Cunningham. Bancroft will become manager of Boston to succeed Fred Mitchell.

Years later, Stengel would reflect on the irony of the trade—coming just after his most flamboyant performance in a World Series, it made him more or less an extra added attraction in an exchange that really focused on Bancroft as a manager. "Nobody," said one observer of the trade, "regarded Stengel as a likely person to become a manager in those days."

The Times's account of the trade conveyed in full phrase the ornate language used by baseball owners even then to rationalize dealings that might have perplexed or angered their public. The report went on:

> Involving as it does the captains, Bancroft and Southworth, of two National League teams, the deal is the most sensational of recent baseball history. Bancroft is probably the leading shortstop in the game and Southworth is one of the best outfielders. Stengel, by winning two games single-handedly with home runs, was the great hero of the late World Series for the Giants. Cunningham is a coming outfielder, and Oeschger is the pitcher who won fame on May 1, 1920, by pitching the longest game in the history of baseball—a 26-inning contest to a 1 to 1 tie against Leon Cadore of the Brooklyn Robins.
>
> The deal was completed in the offices of the Giants at about 6:30 last night. Manager McGraw and President Charles A. Stoneham represented the Giants, and President Christy Mathewson and Judge Emil Fuchs, vice president, were present for the Boston club. Bancroft, who was first consulted to make sure that he was willing to become a major league manager, was also there when McGraw made his announcement to the newspapers.
>
> The Giants are giving up one of the best shortstops in baseball, if not the very best, but they are getting in return an outfielder who will effectively solve McGraw's outfield problem. With Meusel in left, Southworth probably in center and Youngs in right, the Giants will have an outer cordon vastly stronger than anything McGraw has had in many years.
>
> To fill the vacant shortstop position, McGraw said he would use Travis Jackson, the 20-year-old sensation from Little Rock, who made good overnight last summer.

Still, the Giants were trading away some of the permanent fixtures of their palmiest days in the Polo Grounds, and McGraw now undertook to defend, or at least to explain, the depth of his shake-up. His explanation, though, was couched in remarkable terms of piety, self-sacrifice and platitudes, and might be considered a prototype of the circular, almost devious, language that baseball officials lapsed into to explain why last season's demigods were next season's expendables.

"The New York Club," he said, softening his Little Napoleon tones, "realizes that in giving up Mr. Bancroft it is losing the best shortstop in baseball without a doubt. We have several reasons for making the sacrifice, the three particular ones being as follows:

"For the good of baseball and with the desire to do something big for my old friend Matty, and finally to give to Bancroft the opportunity which is due him to become a big league manager."

Having thus sacrificed his own pleasures for the good of baseball, his old friend Matty and finally, "Mr." Bancroft, McGraw turned to the other elements in the trade, including his World Series hero of a month earlier, plain old Casey Stengel.

"We also," he said, "have exchanged outfielders Cunningham and Stengel for Pitcher Oeschger of the Boston club."

That seemed to McGraw to cover the Stengel situation, and before anyone could delve more deeply into it, he waved the flag of past Giant glories even more hallowed than the 1923 World Series. He turned the forum over to Mathewson, the All-America boy of McGraw's early years with the Giants almost 20 years before.

"What do you want me to say?" Mathewson asked with a smile, and then, pointing to Bancroft, the only one of the expendables who had been invited, he said: "Here's my statement."

"And a good statement, too," chimed in McGraw patronizingly.

"Matty is the only man in baseball who could get Bancroft away from me," he went on smoothly, ignoring stern statements he had made after the Giants had lost the series to the effect that he would trade anybody on the club except Frankie Frisch, Ross Youngs and Travis Jackson, because on these young turks he was staking his chances for a fourth straight pennant.

The Times, at least, gave Stengel a measure of praise even if McGraw felt constrained to dust him off rather lightly.

"With Bancroft go two other prime favorites of Giant fans," it reported. "Except for Frank Frisch, Casey Stengel was the most popular and colorful of all the McGraw gladiators. After a career with Brooklyn, Pittsburgh and Philadelphia, the veteran, then a second-string outfielder, was thrown in as ballast in the deal that brought Johnny Rawlings to New York in June, 1921. After spending the rest of the season on the bench, the oldtimer was suddenly placed in the outfield in 1922 and came through with flying colors."

Flying colors, indeed. "It's lucky I didn't hit three home runs in three games in the series," Stengel remarked after being advised of the most sensational trade of recent baseball history, "or Mc-Graw would've traded me to the Three-I League."

Then, in a letter to his longtime friend Long George Kelly, he wrote: "It's just as well. We were in two World Series while I was with the Giants and they gave us watches, rings, fobs, cuff links and necktie pins. If we win another, the only thing left to give us is earrings and old Casey would look great walking around with earrings bobbing out of those big sails of his, wouldn't he?"

Still, earrings or not, the switch from the Polo Grounds to Braves Field in Boston was a trip to the salt mines, and it meant as drastic a change in Stengel's day-to-day fortunes as his earlier trips from Brooklyn to Pittsburgh, Pittsburgh to Philadelphia and, in reverse, for a change, Philadelphia to New York. From a winner, he now went to a loser.

The Braves, who had made baseball history in 1914 by winning the pennant and World Series after standing last on July Fourth, had subsided since the "miracle team" days. While the Giants were winning three straight pennants between 1921 and 1923, Boston ranked fourth, eighth and seventh, and after Mc-Graw traded Stengel and Bancroft to Boston, the Giants made it four straight pennants while Stengel and Bancroft promptly made it from first place in New York to the cellar in Boston.

So, when Stengel went south in February 1924 for the first time with the Braves, he left the heyday of New York baseball for good, as a player, at least, to the new generation of young men like Frisch, the Fordham graduate, "which has gone to college and is so smart." He also left the little luxuries of life with a winning team, as he discovered when he checked into the Braves' training camp at St. Petersburg, Florida, and was quartered in the Beverly Hotel.

What he discovered was Rube Marquard, Cotton Tierney and three other boys on the club, making six Braves in all in one hotel room, dormitory style. He later recalled how this communal style of life had contrasted with the calculated comfort of life with the Giants, even in little ways, like fighting for the bathroom the half-dozen shared.

"I had to give those guys the elbow," he said, as matter-of-factly as Custer discussing the demands of frontier survival. "Banny didn't want anybody late for morning practice, and I didn't want to be the one."

By the time the Braves had returned north and started the season, though, he had made the adjustment to the rigors of second division life and was in mid-season form, "with flying colors," as *The Times* chronicled on May 7:

> Casey Stengel, veteran outfielder of the Boston Braves, was fined $100 and suspended indefinitely yesterday by John A. Heydler, president of the National League, for disgraceful [sic] conduct in Monday's game with Brooklyn in Ebbets Field. Stengel was ejected from the game by Umpire Jack Powell after a heated argument over the arbiter's decisions on strikes. Stengel defied the umpire for several minutes and took his regular post in right field until a threat that his action would forfeit the game persuaded him to depart.

Life in Boston offered one compensation besides the opportunity to raise a ruckus on visits to Brooklyn, where Stengel had raised his first ruckuses in the big leagues: Since the Braves were hurting for players, a 34-year-old outfielder with creaking legs was more likely to get into baseball games than he had been, say, in the Polo Grounds. So Stengel found himself in great demand in Boston, appearing in 131 games—more than he had played in any season since 1917 in his last year in Brooklyn. He hit .280, a decline of 59 points in one year and 88 in two years, with 5 home runs and 39 runs batted in. He also ran out half a dozen triples and 20 doubles—and except for one single in 12 games at the start of the following season, 1925, they were the last hits he ran out as a major league player.

On May 12 the next spring, *The New York Times*, under a headline that read, "Casey Stengel Buys The Worcester Club," reported from New Haven as follows:

> The Worcester Eastern League baseball club was sold today by A. H. Powell and G. H. Andrews of this city to Casey Stengel, the Boston National League outfielder, it was announced here tonight by J. Harmon Bronson of this city, who acted as agent for Powell. Stengel will be president of the club and playing manager, and will take charge of the Worcester organization on

Friday. He will bring with him from the Braves the following players who have been awarded to the Worcester club through sale or option: Pitchers Batchelder, Muich and Ogrodowski; Outfielders Sperber and Wilson, Infielder Thomas and Catcher Cousineau. Eddie Eayrs, present manager of the Worcester club, and 3 players are likely to be disposed of.

Actually he was taking over Worcester as an agent for Boston, the parent club, but Charles Dillon Stengel had crossed a Great Divide—a divide greater than indicated in that paragraph. Though he played ball for Worcester in 1925 and for Toledo in 1926, 1927, 1928, 1929 and 1931, he ended a chapter of his professional life that May 12 as irrevocably as he had ended one the day 15 years earlier when he had put aside his frock coat, walked out the door of Western Dental College and headed for the ball park in Kankakee, Illinois. He might be listed afterward as a "playing-manager," even a "playing-manager-president." But he was out from under the shadow of more durable outfielders like Youngs and Meusel and of more "promising" managers like Bancroft, and he graduated almost imperceptibly into the small group of wheelers and dealers who hired, fired and exchanged baseball talent.

He even made the adjustment without changing too many of his stripes.

"He looked exactly the same as he did 35 years later," recalled Ken Smith, who was then a sports writer for *The Hartford Courant* and who later became director of the Baseball Hall of Fame. "The Eastern League was a good league, too. Lou Gehrig had played for Hartford two years before, and Leo Durocher was on the club then.

"I went by the bench one day when Worcester was playing in Hartford and asked him who was pitching and catching for him that day. It happened that he was going to use two guys with alliterative names—Wentz and Woock. And he made the most of it. He looked at me, raised his eyebrows and said, 'W-W-Wentz and W-W-Woock'—rolling his W's, if you can roll a W."

Thirty years later, Smith reminded Stengel of that early meeting in both their careers, and Casey, brandishing his unusual memory for places, people and situations, recalled it in detail.

"Even his best friend might have reservations about Casey as a manager," Smith observed, analyzing the impact that Stengel began to have on the game in his new role in Worcester in 1925 and that continued for 40 years. "But he was one of those guys who mastered the details from the start. You know, one of those managers who watch the other team's batting practice. He was a marvel at manipulating player traffic."

He was also an unreconstructed marvel at getting into trouble, despite his new and presumably more dignified station in baseball life.

Just 29 days after becoming manager at Worcester, he was suspended as manager at Worcester. Not only that, but he dragged a rival manager along with him into limbo, probably setting an Eastern League record for provoking trouble. Stengel and Bill McCorry, the manager of the Albany team, were suspended, indefinitely, according to a straight-faced news report of the day from Albany, "as a result of their actions in the game here yesterday. Stengel threw a ball into the grandstand and McCorry threw a bat at a pitcher."

Still, Stengel found that even occasional frolics like this one did not relieve the tedium of playing 100 games in the outfield for Worcester, despite the rewards of a batting average of .320 plus 10 home runs; or of watching the team's 25 other games from the manager's perch in the dugout, despite the rewards of the club's third-place finish. He was simply too far from Broadway. But returning to Boston would be no solution, even if the Braves would countenance—and finance—such a move. He mulled the problem over briefly, then made a decision with characteristic mischief and, as things turned out, with characteristic results.

Reversing the unusual process that had made him president of the Boston farm club who had "hired" himself as a manager, who in turn had "hired" himself as a player, he simply released himself as an outfielder, fired himself as a manager and resigned as a president. Judge Fuchs of the parent team, observing the comic-opera scene from the club's sedate offices in Boston, was not amused. Later, though, he conceded the delicious irony of it all and joined in the applause and laughter that trailed his executive-clown as he left Boston and Worcester.

He was not between jobs very long, though his exit from the big leagues was now—temporarily—confirmed. The following spring,

1926, being a "free agent" for the first time since Larry Sutton had approached him in Aurora for the Dodgers 15 years earlier, he signed on as manager of the Toledo club of the American Association at the behest of his old friend McGraw, who owned the team and ran it as an adjunct of the Giants. Now he was back in the Middle West, he would spend six seasons in one place for the first time in his career, he would manage a baseball team to a league pennant for the first time and he would head back toward the major leagues again as an experienced field manager.

In fact, in his first season in Toledo, using players "sent down" from New York by McGraw, he made good almost immediately. He began to outdistance—outlive would be too strong a word—his reputation as a clown. He accepted "trouble" players from the major leagues. He directed them and molded them into a triple-A minor league team that for a time threatened to win a pennant in the American Association the first time around.

Bill Veeck, the imaginative genius who built the Cleveland Indians into a sensational money-maker in 18 months a generation later, and who liked to point out that his name rhymed with "wreck," was a boy of 10 when Stengel joined Toledo. Veeck's father was president of the Chicago Cubs, and Bill used to follow him around the circuit as he inspected the minor league holdings of the Cubs. "He was never necessarily the greatest of managers," Veeck Jr. said one spring day in 1966, reflecting on Stengel's career, "but any time he had a ball club that had a chance to win, he'd win."

He evidently got such a chance in his second season at Toledo, in 1927. His team won 101 games, lost 67, swept the pennant and defeated Buffalo, five games to one, in the "Little World Series," while Babe Ruth and "the greatest Yankee team" of all time, in many views, were cementing the Yankees' dominance on the major leagues—the dominance that had begun to be asserted in Stengel's final season in New York with the Giants.

Stengel the manager had arrived, so to speak; but his "colors" as a troublemaker were still flying, as *The New York Times* observed on September 7 that season when the Toledo Mudhens came pounding down the homestretch of the season. The headline said "Casey Stengel Suspended" (which may have become a stock head by then) and the story, under a Chicago dateline, said:

Casey Stengel was suspended indefinitely by President Thomas J. Hickey as a result of an attack by the fans on Umpire Derr, following the first game of the Labor Day bill in Toledo with Columbus. Stengel, whose club has been on a losing streak, was charged with having incited the fans after the umpire had rendered a close decision at first base. Several hundred spectators rushed from the stands and attacked the umpire, who was forced to retreat in the dugout, where police reserves came to his rescue.

As gaudy as this incident appeared in cold print, Stengel had an even gaudier year two seasons later, when the Mudhens had slipped from first place to sixth and were in a headlong collapse to eighth.

On May 23, 1929, it was reported from Toledo: "Casey Stengel tonight surrendered to police when he learned that a fan with whom he had an altercation in the grandstand before today's game with Indianapolis had preferred a charge of assault and battery. The spectator charged that Stengel had struck him on the jaw during an argument over a ball that had been fouled into the stand during batting practice. The spectator was excluded from the park and his admission money refunded to him. Stengel was released on his own recognizance."

On July 7, 1929, from Columbus, Ohio: "POLICE RESCUE STENGEL. A near-riot of baseball fans was precipitated today when Manager Casey Stengel of the Toledo Mudhens rushed from his dugout and knocked down Third Baseman Boone of the Columbus American Association team. Stengel claimed that Boone had held McCurdy at the plate. Police quelled the crowd and escorted Stengel to the clubhouse and later to a taxi."

On July 13, 1929, from Chicago: "Casey Stengel, manager of the Toledo team, was reinstated today by order of President Thomas Hickey of the American Association. Stengel was suspended Monday for striking Third Baseman Lute Boone of Columbus during the Toledo-Senator game Saturday."

The *pièce de résistance* was a footnote to the above report, recalling in a kind of throwaway line that Stengel and Sammy Bohns of the Minneapolis club had been suspended after a "general fight" in the Fourth of July game at St. Paul, in addition to a "general fight" in the Seventh of July game at Columbus. "Near riots resulted from both encounters," it related, as though routinely summing up all the near-riots of the weekend in which Stengel might have had a hand.

Time was running out for Casey in one respect, though, despite his seeming durability as a main-event fighter on the ball diamond: His days as an active player were nearing an end. He played in only 20 games for Toledo in 1929, none in 1930 and two final ones in 1931 (he made two doubles and a single in eight times at bat). From then on, he would be either a coach, a manager or unemployed.

Already, though, he had begun to make a reputation—to say nothing of money—as a Trader Horn who operated at the highest minor league levels with one foot in the majors and one in the sticks. He was a natural judge of potential who could size up a dubious or marginal or troublesome player in the act of falling out of major league grace; then, as a manager, he could play a leading role in rehabilitating the refugee; and finally, as a front-office man, he could resell him back to the majors for new value in cash. It worked with untried players, too, and at Worcester and Toledo it worked to the tune of three-quarters of a million dollars. Part of Stengel's share of these profits went into stocks—the kind he advised his players to buy one day in Toledo because their impending trips to the bush leagues would profit the nation's railroads so heavily.

If horse sense was emerging as the dominant Stengel trait, some of it may have rubbed off from Allie Reuben, whose securities company helped local interests in Toledo to buy the club and the ball park, Swayne Field, from McGraw and who later became the owner of the Hasty House Farms. He also became one of Stengel's closest friends, and when the ball club finally buckled in the crash and went into receivership, Reuben was appointed Receiver.

"Mrs. Reuben and I persuaded Casey and Edna to move into the Park Lane Apartment Hotel in an apartment opposite ours," Reuben recalled, "and enjoyed their company greatly. Edna was sweet and understanding and always took a constant, deep interest in looking after his personal welfare."

One of the things that Edna did during those years in the minor leagues in looking after his personal welfare was to sit in direct line of fire between disgruntled fans and her man. As the Toledo club began declining after the opening days of instant success, the line of fire became withering.

"McGraw's brother was traveling secretary of the club," Edna said, looking back on life in Toledo, "and he suggested I sit in the bleachers to get away from the booing and noise around the dugout. But it didn't faze me."

Edna had good sporting blood at ball park or race track. She did not cry over spilled milk either then or during visits to race tracks that she and Casey made during their long friendship with the Reubens, who crossed their path in Chicago, Florida and other horse ports of call around the country. However, in the late twenties, Stengel was becoming concerned about gambles of a different type than baseball flesh or horse flesh.

The stock market crash in September 1929 and in subsequent months cost him much of his embryo fortune, which had been abetted by his wife's business sense and interests. But, with a base of operations securely rooted in Glendale and with a baseball reputation more securely rooted than ever after his 5-year term as a minor league manager, he was in business to stay. After all, Trader Horn was still at the crossroads looking for talent, as *The Times* reported on April 5, 1930, from Memphis, where the Giants were ending their spring training:

> This was another off day in their exhibition schedule, but John McGraw's boys found time hanging as heavy on their hands as the pick and shovel gang trying to get some rest at an army rest camp.
> With Mr. McGraw himself presiding as athletic director, severest critic and chief grounder-slapper, the Giants used Chickasaw Park for a training grounds again today. The practice lasted longer than yesterday's and also covered more ground, since the outfield had lost its resemblance to the Louisiana muskrat marshes and the outfielders were able to range far and wide for fly balls.
> In addition to Manager McGraw and the Bancroft-Meusel coaching system, the Giants had Casey Stengel to urge them on. Casey is Toledo's manager, and his presence symbolized to the Giants Toledo, to which point Giants are sometimes shipped. Often when a Giant felt like standing still on one spot long enough for a few deep breaths, the sight of Stengel looking in his direction was enough to send him sprinting after a fly.

The "ogre" from Toledo had a sharp eye, too. Ken Smith recalled that when he and Casey visited the Giants' camp at San Antonio the following spring, Stengel walked in, sighted a player he had never seen before and said on the spot, "I'll take him right now." The player was Hal Shumacher, who was soon en route to a career as one of the Giants' best pitchers of the nineteen-thirties.

It was only a matter of time before an ogre with sharp eyes and two decades of baseball experience would be called to work in a big league park again. The time came after Stengel's Mudhens had finished third in 1930 and eighth in 1931. The franchise was collapsing in the Depression but Stengel was rounding out seven seasons as a manager in the high minor leagues after 13 seasons as a player in the major leagues. He was ready for a big plunge. And the call came, as it had come on the fateful day in Montgomery 20 years earlier, from Brooklyn.

STILL IN THE LEAGUE

Western civilization may have had more unusual organizations than the Brooklyn Dodgers, but not too many spring to mind. They won the pennant in the interloping American Association in 1889, switched to the entrenched National League in 1890 as Club No. 26 and promptly embarrassed both leagues by winning the pennant over there. So, with the pennants—or streamers—of two rival leagues flying from the masthead, the Brooklyns embarked on a career in big-time baseball that made them instantly famous, frequently hilarious and almost always poverty-stricken.

In fact, the wife of the second owner of the club, Charles H. Ebbets, was reported to have taken in the team's laundry to save money, while Mr. Ebbets sold tickets to the ball games. It was a raggedy, rickity, rollicking baseball team that changed names almost as often as it changed uniforms, and for considerably less compelling reasons.

At the turn of the century, the Dodgers were known as the Bridegrooms, because the team's sizable bachelor corps had paraded to the altar almost en masse during the off-season. They they became the Superbas because their manager, Ned Hanlon, ran a billiard academy on the side with the sensational name The Superba and he felt that if anything deserved the implied glories of such a name as the pool hall it must be the ball club. When Wilbert Robinson appeared as manager in 1914, they naturally became

the Robins, though their long-lease nickname through all these
changes had been Trolley Dodgers, in tribute to the terrifying maze
of streetcars that crisscrossed Brooklyn. And even when the club
migrated in 1957 to Los Angeles, where trolley cars presented
nowhere near the threat that speedy automobiles did, the name
Dodgers migrated along with it.

By whatever name, though, the Brooklyns developed baseball's
outstanding talent for slapstick. Where other teams may have been
accident-prone, they grew disaster-prone. It didn't matter who happened to own them—Charlie Ebbets, an amiable, worrying archi-
tect who sometimes went into bars and took a poll on who should
pitch the next afternoon, or the Brooklyn Trust Company, which
carried the club for years as a kind of irredeemable liability and
which tried to ride out the Depression years later by requiring
its board of directors to rule whenever the manager suggested
spending $6,000 to meet the waiver price on a ball player being
peddled by another club.

The Dodgers' ranks ranged from Uncle Robbie, who had worn
a handlebar mustache in the eighteen-nineties, to Stanley "Frenchie"
Bordagary 30 years later, who at various times owned a race-
horse, a small black mustache and a Van Dyke beard.

They once boasted a pitcher named Clyde Day who came from
Pea Ridge, Arkansas, delivered outstanding hog calls in public and
even dived fully clothed into the fountain pool outside the Chase
Hotel in St. Louis to win a bet.

They tended to be so bad on the playing field most seasons that
it became commonplace for one wit to ask, "How are the Dodgers
doin' today?" and for his straight man to reply, "Great, score
tied in the sixth and three men on base." To which the sage responded: "Which base?"

So, all things considered, it was a marriage of exceptionally true
minds on January 4, 1932, when Casey Stengel rejoined the
Dodgers. He had entered the major leagues in 1912 by way of
Brooklyn and, after 14 years as an active player with four teams
and seven years as a player, coach and manager in the minor leagues,
he re-entered the majors that day as a Dodger coach.

"Charles D. (Casey) Stengel, former Giants and Brooklyn star
outfielder and in his playing days one of the most colorful figures
in baseball," reported *The New York Times*, "has been engaged

by the Robins to serve as head coach and first lieutenant to Manager Max Carey for the 1932 campaign.

"Stengel returns to the Brooklyn club exactly 20 years after making his major league debut in Flatbush. A fiery fellow with ever a talent for showmanship, he soon became a popular idol in Brooklyn and played a prominent part in the Robins' capture of the National League pennant in 1916.

"Subsequently he was cast adrift, but after serving a season in Pittsburgh and another in Philadelphia, he came to the Giants in 1921 to stage a sensational comeback for John McGraw, for whom he helped to win a pennant that year, as well as in the two seasons following.

"In all, Stengel appeared in four World Series, one with Brooklyn and the other three with the Giants, his outstanding achievement being a pair of home runs with which he brought down the Yankees in two games of the 1923 series. In 1924, though traded to Boston, he indirectly won a pennant for McGraw by beating the Robins in a 10-inning battle with a single with the bases filled. That defeat put the Robins out of the race and sent the Giants on to their fourth straight pennant."

The report, having established Stengel's unusual qualifications for rejoining the Dodger circus, which he had helped to establish in his earlier days, then cast a long shadow into the future.

"In 1926," it said, "Stengel went to Toledo as manager, winning a pennant in 1927 along with the 'little World Series' title and gaining wide renown not only for his ability in developing young players but in rehabilitating veterans whose major league playing days appeared to be over."

Since Brooklyn offered the greatest opportunities in baseball for a genius at rehabilitating broken-down ball players, Stengel's appearance on the scene amounted to a remarkable instance of the office seeking the man. He lost no time analyzing the situation in appropriate terms, either, saying: "We may lose more games than anybody, but we can out-drink anybody in the league."

Casey's departure from Toledo in the American Association had been dictated by the ravages of the Depression, which collapsed the Toledo management, and his transfer to Brooklyn had been arranged by Max Carey, his old sidekick at Pittsburgh, who was "the

best base-stealer I ever saw," but who, unfortunately, could steal
no bases for his wayward Dodgers as manager in 1932.

Still, with Stengel prowling the coaching lines, Carey goaded his
club into third place that season while the Chicago Cubs won the
National League pennant and the Giants, the arch-rivals from
across the East River, finished sixth. But when the Giants shot up to
first place the following year and the Dodgers subsided to sixth,
Max Carey's hours as manager were numbered—and there in the
middle of the debris stood his old admiring sidekick.

On the morning of February 23, 1934, Stengel was summoned
to the New Yorker Hotel, stood at the bedside of J. A. Robert
Quinn, business manager of the Dodgers, who had been as sick as
the club, and, at 8 A.M., was handed a contract to replace Carey as
manager. He signed it.

"The only unexpected feature of the whole affair," wrote Roscoe
McGowen, "was the fact that Stengel was signed for two years, as
Uncle Wilbert Robinson had only a one-year contract before he
was dropped in 1931 and Carey also worked on a single-season
basis."

Stephen W. McKeever, who was president of the Dodgers and
chief keeper of the club's deficits, said that Stengel would be paid
$12,000 a season. Then Stengel, five months short of his 45th
birthday, stepped into another suite in the hotel to leave Quinn
with his worries, stood before a swarm of newspapermen for two
hours, accepted congratulations, fielded questions and basked in the
opening moments of his new career as the manager of a major
league baseball team.

He was not overpowered by the cheerless prospect of running
the Dodgers. "Maybe this means that the Dodgers have gone in for
the N.R.A.," he quipped in the best Will Rogers fashion. "You
know, 'New Riot Act.'"

A few days later, he hied his club off to spring training at Orlando. He had an undistinguished infield of Sam Leslie, Tony Cuc-
cinello, Lonnie Frey and Joe Stripp, plus one "set" outfielder,
Danny Taylor, and one pitcher of consequence, Van Lingle
Mungo. It was, as he had acknowledged, a new riot act.

The "act" had its moments. Bill Terry, the manager of the
Giants, provided one by needling Stengel in his opening days with

a question of calculated rhetoric: "Is Brooklyn still in the league?" And, sure enough, five months later Brooklyn was still in the league and, though sunken in sixth place, stood between the Giants and the St. Louis Cardinals, who went down to the final two days of the season tied for first place.

To make matters worse for Terry, the Giants had led the league by six games on Labor Day. But in the last hours of the season, they dropped six of their final seven games to the Boston Braves, Philadelphia Phillies and Dodgers—all timid souls who turned tiger at the right moment. Stengel's boys completed the rout, reaching up from sixth place to knock the hated Giants from first to second as the Cardinals, the Gashouse Gang of Frank Frisch, roared on to win the pennant.

Mungo, the madcap right-hander with the humming fast ball, was all business the first day, halting the Giants, 5 to 1. The next afternoon, the Dodgers gave Casey a day to remember by overpowering the Giants again, this time 8 to 5, and as the Giants fell from the top of the league, all hell broke loose. Hordes of Brooklyn fans had stormed the Polo Grounds on that tumultuous afternoon, as Stengel paced the dugout and the third-base coaching box, hoisting banners that taunted Terry with the words: "Yes, We're Still In The League."

And when the game, and the season, ended a few hours later, they swarmed onto the field, hoisted Stengel and Al Lopez onto their shoulders and carried them off the field like triumphant Roman proconsuls. Even when Stengel left the clubhouse later, he was besieged by his adoring public. Throngs of cheering, shouting Brooklynites jammed into the subway with him when he headed for home, trapped him jubilantly and kept him from getting off at his station, until he rode to the end of the line and fled in joy—and relief.

Yes, the New Riot Act was still in the league, but just barely so. The Dodgers carried their momentum into the following season, and struggled into fifth place, but then receded to seventh in 1936, and their principal contribution to the American Way of Life lay somewhere between the Marx Brothers and the Ringling Brothers.

One day Frenchie Bordagary, "the only player in the major leagues with a mustache," and one of the blithe spirits of the game, managed to get to second base against Chicago with Stengel's won-dering approval. The customary stance of a base-runner leading off second is a tense crouch, from which he can spring back to the safety of the base or leap toward third, if the opportunity arises. But not so Frenchie. He meandered toward third base a bit, then stood waiting for the pitcher to get back to work, all the while amiably tapping his foot in a pleasant rhythm. He promptly was picked off when the pitcher wheeled and fired the ball to the short-stop, Billy Jurges.

Stengel roared from the dugout as though shot out of a cannon and began berating the second-base umpire in spades. But Borda-gary turned to his manager and insisted with fine equanimity that, no, he actually had been tagged out. When they got back to the dugout, Stengel immediately turned his fire on Frenchie, who was sitting on the bench surveying the splendor of the afternoon. "I *saw* your foot on the bag," Casey thundered, "so how could Jurges tag you out?"

Bordagary, without a care in the world, replied pleasantly: "It was this way, Case. I'm standing near second base doing a tap dance. I guess he just tagged me out between taps."

Actually, Casey wasn't too surprised by Bordagary's unusual insouciance. In the spring of 1935, when he joined the Dodgers in Orlando for spring training, he had made an incredible splash for a rookie by trying to steal home with two outs in the ninth inning one day and the Dodgers trailing Detroit by one run. He was out, and Stengel approached him with awe after the game and asked: "Are you crazy?"

Frenchie, who evidently regarded the question as a compliment, replied: "You ain't seen nothing yet." It proved to be an under-statement.

Bordagary later went on to a distinguished career as a musician, performing on the washboard with the famous Mudcat Band of the St. Louis Cardinals alongside Bill McGee on the fiddle, Bob Weiland on the jug and Lon Warneke on the harmonica, while Pepper Martin directed the ensemble in clubhouse concerts.

"Another time," Stengel recounted later during a conversational review of life with the Dodgers, "we bought this here pitcher, George Earnshaw, for $7,500. And he was a good pitcher, but he hadn't been going so well. So the first day he was with us, I called him over and said, 'You pitch batting practice for the next 11 days.'

"Now, Earnshaw hit the ceiling, and he had pitched for Connie Mack in Philadelphia when they had Grove and were so good, and all those other guys like Cochrane and Foxx and Simmons. And he said to me, 'Batting practice for 11 days, the hell you say.' And I said, 'That's right, Mr. Earnshaw, you will pitch batting practice for 11 days. You're too good a pitcher to waste like this sitting around, and you'll see in a few days you'll be getting the ball in there.'

"So, sure enough, he commenced pitching batting practice and he was gettin' the ball over and he was so mad he could've fired it through a wall. And after he got in shape that way, I put him in one day against the St. Louis team, which had Frisch as a manager, and he struck out 11 of them. The only thing was, they got a couple of men on base and the batter hit one toward Bordagary in the outfield and he tried to catch it down here. But the ball went right under his glove and everybody scored and they won, 4 to 2.

"Earnshaw was so mad at Bordagary he chased after him in the clubhouse and wanted to beat on him, and there was hell to pay after pitchin' battin' practice for all those days, which would've turned out so well except for the guy with the mustache."

Besides Frenchie, the bane of Stengel's existence in Brooklyn was one outstandingly loud-mouthed fan who camped in the grandstand behind third base on many days and spent pleasurable afternoons raising the roof in stentorian tones, aiming a steady torrent of invective toward Stengel, who in addition to managing the team was still doubling as his own third-base coach.

"But it was all right," Casey said, sounding like Voltaire defending unto the death the right of his critics to torment him. "It was okay, he paid to get it." Still, he couldn't help marvel at the bellower's intractable view of the Stengel strategy, particularly when it involved the simple act of juggling the talents of a catcher like Babe Phelps, "which could hit the ball real good but wouldn't be too safe behind the bat as catcher until maybe the eighth or ninth inning and we were ahead."

One day, Casey started Phelps as the Dodgers' catcher and Phelps responded by hitting a home run with the bases loaded in the second inning. By the ninth inning, however, "he'd let in a bunch of runs and they caught us, so this guy behind third is hollering at me: 'If ya'd saved Phelps for the ninth, we wouldn't be in this mess.' "

Stengel, amused at the incongruity of the abuse, shook his head and marveled. "He's hollering at me," he said, "and this guy has batted in four runs already, which he forgot about by the ninth inning."

On another occasion in 1934, the famous Dean brothers—"me and Paul"—descended on Ebbets Field with the St. Louis Cardinals and throttled the Dodgers during both halves of a doubleheader. Dizzy opened the massacre by mowing down the Dodgers on exactly three hits. Then his younger brother Paul took over and mowed them down on exactly no hits.

Stengel, who had watched both games from the solitary splendor of the third-base coaching box, was walking toward the clubhouse after the Deans had finished their chores and chanced to run into Dizzy, who had dressed in his civilian clothes after the first game to watch Paul in action.

"Wasn't that something?" Diz whooped at him. But Casey just snorted and continued down the runway leading to the Dodgers' locker room. Then as the crowning indignity, the bane of his existence, the basso profundo of the grandstand, his constant heckler, leaned out of the seats along the passageway and yelled at Stengel:

"That's okay, Casey. You played a doubleheader today and didn't make one mistake."

"Yes," Casey recalled 30 years later, reviewing life with the Dodgers one rainy day in St. Petersburg, Florida, "I didn't see a base runner for 18 innings, so I *couldn't* make any mistakes."

It is true that during his tenure nobody took a telephone pole and battered their way into Ebbets Field through the center-field fence, as 500 fans had done one day in 1924 in a gallant effort to watch the heroes of Flatbush. Nor did any of Stengel's men simply disappear one night, as Boots Poffenberger did later, only to wind up in Maryland. Nor did a man perched on a window ledge of the Gotham Hotel in Manhattan reply, as one did in 1938 when urged not to jump but to spend a nice afternoon at a ball park watching the Dodgers: "I'd rather jump than watch the Dodgers."

However, the team was terrible enough for the board of directors not to want to watch it particularly, either. So, on October 3,

1936, just after the Dodgers had finished seventh and Stengel had finished his third season as a major league manager, a statement he had made three seasons before came back to haunt him: "Every one of the gentlemen directing this club wanted me to be the manager."

Now, every one of the gentlemen directing the club decided that they wanted him to be the ex-manager. So, on that October day, with the Yankees facing the Giants in the World Series, it was the Dodgers who stole the spotlight. One hour before the official announcement was distributed at World Series press headquarters at the Commodore Hotel in New York, Stengel was called into what he thought was a conference about some player exchange. But to his surprise—since his contract still had a year to run—he was advised by Jim Mulvey and Joe Gilleaudeau, two vice presidents of the Dodgers, that he was now an ex-manager.

Otto Miller, who had been a catcher on Brooklyn's last pennant-winning team in 1920, and Zach Taylor, also a catcher from the old days, were similarly released as coaches. But Casey was the only one of the trio with the remarkable distinction of being dropped and being paid for not managing a team at the height of a depression by a club that was hard pressed to pay even its people who worked.

"They told me the club hadn't done so well," he said. "It hadn't made much money. And they had decided unanimously to make a change. They didn't say who would follow me, though."

"But what I'm interested in now," he said, showing his chronic interest in the economics of any situation, "is the three-year contract into which I entered in good faith and the feeling that there was good faith on the other side. I've got a year to go on that, you know, and I'm going to be curious, not only about whether I'm to be paid off, but how."

The situation was loaded with pure Dodger irony. When Max Carey had been relieved in 1934, he still had a year to go on his contract as manager, and the Dodgers were just as penniless. But the board, fishing frantically for something that would attract paying customers, had decided to pay him for not managing while Stengel took the reins. After one season, Stengel had been called in by Steve McKeever, the club's president, and, with Mulvey and Gilleaudeau smiling their approval, had given him a new contract for three seasons—now that the club had fulfilled Max's contract and presumably had to worry about paying only one manager at a time. And McKeever had sealed the deal by saying: "Casey Stengel will manage the Brooklyn ball club as long as I have anything to say about it."

He still had something to say about it two years later, but evidently his resolve had weakened under the aimless wanderings of the club in the lower reaches of the National League and its blossoming reputation as the best horselaugh in baseball.

Again—as when the Giants of 1923 shifted to a new generation of players like Travis Jackson and when the Toledo franchise wavered in 1931, spilling Stengel into Brooklyn—Casey was being engulfed by events pretty much beyond his control. A few weeks later, a new day would begin in Brooklyn baseball with the arrival of Leo Durocher, and 15 months later a new era would begin with the arrival of Larry MacPhail. The fact was that the club was in hock, and John Drebinger summarized the situation on November 5 as follows:

> The peremptory dismissal of Casey Stengel in the middle of the recent World Series almost took the play away from the contending Yankees and Giants.
>
> The very manner in which the Dodgers ousted Stengel a month ago took the wind right out of the sails of even the supposedly best-informed chroniclers. All sorts of wild rumors followed this, the most persistent being that the club was about to be sold and the new owners wanted the decks cleared to name their own manager. Most prominent among the supposed purchasers was Colonel T. L. Huston, who was reported to be heading a syndicate which planned to install Babe Ruth as manager.
>
> Others mentioned as possible successors to Stengel include Dutch Reuther and Zach Wheat, also former Brooklyn favorites, as well as Max Carey, who in the spring of 1934 suffered a fate similar to that which befell Stengel by being dropped with a year of his contract to run.
>
> In baseball circles, however, it is being accepted as a foregone conclusion that the new pilot will be Burleigh Grimes, veteran spitball pitcher and onetime Dodger ace who closed his active major league career in 1934 and spent last summer managing the Louisville Colonels in the American Association.

He was right. Burleigh Grimes, the old spitball pitcher, did succeed Stengel as manager and chief sufferer of the Dodgers' unpredictable shenanigans on the field. However, Colonel Huston, the onetime partner of Colonel Ruppert as owner of the Yankees, did not reappear with a syndicate of purchasers. MacPhail did, and showed his class by immediately borrowing $50,000 from the harried board of directors to buy a first-baseman, Dolph Camilli of the Phillies. Babe Ruth arrived, but not as manager. He became a coach in 1938 and helped to draw attention to the "new" Dodgers, but even the Babe was overtaken by events in Flatbush. It was Durocher who became the manager after Grimes had sweated and fretted through two seasons, and then the Dodgers began to do something they had rarely done from the time that Stengel arrived as a rookie player in 1912 to the time he arrived as a rookie manager in 1934 and to the time he departed—for good —in 1936: succeed.

As Stengel left, he received the answers to the two questions that had been troubling him. He was paid, all right, for not managing in 1937; and he was paid, as before, by regular checks, which he accepted happily and put to use immediately.

With Casey gone from Brooklyn, the Dodgers fired a final salute in his direction: they showed the world that they could finish in the second division just as hopelessly without him as they had with him. They ran sixth in 1937 under Grimes, while the Giants and Yankees ground out their second straight pennants, with the Yankees emerging into their post-Ruth, or Joe DiMaggio, era.

As for Stengel, he spent 1937 in a flamboyant display of his immense talent for making the best out of a royal mess. He was in the somewhat precarious position of being out of it all, after three fairly unsuccessful seasons with a loser. Instead, though, he settled back and enjoyed himself. He commuted on a reasonably regular basis between Glendale, where he basked in the sunshine, and Brooklyn, where he would deposit himself in the grandstand of the stadium, which was mortgaged half a million dollars' worth. Then, treating himself to several bags of peanuts, and having nothing better to do, he would establish himself several rows from his successor's roost in the dugout and watch a ball game.

Some people thought Casey made his excursions to Brooklyn simply to irritate the management that had recently humiliated him. But it was more likely that he was just combining his outstanding talents: a zest for mischief; a need to be near the center of a hurricane; a longing for baseball, the only professional activity that interested him absorbingly; and an unmatched ability to land on his feet when dropped from high places.

He exhibited this last talent, as well as a remarkable Midas touch, by taking the Dodgers' $15,000 that season and, besides investing some of it in peanuts at the ball games, investing much of it in oil. It proved a deal of handsome proportions, even for someone like Stengel who was addicted to grandiose schemes.

The contact was Randy Moore, a former outfielder who had some in-laws drilling for oil near the little town of Omaha, Texas, and who let some of his old baseball cronies in on a good thing. Stengel, with Dodger money freshly in hand, lined up along with Al Lopez, his catcher and confidant; Johnny Cooney, an outfielder for the Dodgers; a pitcher named Watson Clark, and one or two other players. They literally struck oil, and so, while Stengel collected his checks during that idle summer of 1937 from a team that owed $1,200,000, his fortune was being made 2,000 miles away (though the Dodgers kept sending his salary checks by mistake to a bank in Omaha, Nebraska). And in a few years, that money in turn would be invested in California real estate, and ultimately the Valley National Bank would rise in Glendale with Edna's family in control and with a likeness of Stengel's stooped figure carved into the front doors and with his imprint all over the place.

The baseball scene that Casey surveyed from the grandstand of Ebbets Field that season, though, was changing fundamentally.

The excitement that Ruth had imparted in the early 1920's had rescued the game from a decline that was inevitable after the Black Sox scandal of 1919. Now, a generation later, baseball turned to other things to last out the Depression and to prepare itself, financially, at least, for an international crisis that was already spiraling.

Ruth hit his last home run in the major leagues in 1935, but he was in the position of an Old Master whose work survives him many times over. In 1927, at his peak, he hit 60 of the 920 home runs in the big leagues; in 1935, he hit 6 out of 1,325. A whole generation of "sluggers," as the big-batsmen were called, would be compared to the Master: Lou Gehrig, Jimmy Foxx, Hank Greenberg, Joe DiMaggio and Ted Williams in the American League, and Mel Ott, Johnny Mize and Joe Medwick in the National. Great new pitchers like Carl Hubbell, Lefty Gomez, the Dean brothers and Red Ruffing began to succeed Lefty Grove, Waite Hoyt and Dazzy Vance. Teams like the Yankees had reached the million mark in attendance in 1920 with the advent of Ruth and had played before a million or more persons in eight other seasons since then, and in 1937 were still drawing 998,148 persons at home.

The Yankees paid a lot of bills by drawing big on the road, too, but the pattern of success was irregular, and teams like the Cincinnati Reds, the original professional baseball team, drew only 411,225 in 1937. But even they were already adopting revolutionary new gimmicks to get people besides Casey Stengel out to the ball park.

In 1933, the major leagues had played their first All-Star game, asking the fans to elect the best performers, then pitting the best of the American League against the best of the National League. The inaugural game was played in Chicago in 1933, with 49,200 customers present, with the American League winning, 4 to 2, and with Ruth, naturally, hitting a home run.

In 1935, the first big league game was played at night, with Larry MacPhail throwing the switch in Crosley Field, Cincinnati, with the Pittsburgh Pirates and Reds the opposing teams and a capacity crowd of 30,000 in the seats. In 1938, MacPhail, who was by then running the show for the Dodgers, introduced night baseball to New York after buying $72,000 worth of lighting equipment from the General Electric Company—on the cuff. Undaunted by the enormity of his own thinking, he staged a carnival on the night of June 15, with the Dodgers playing his old team, the Reds, and with Jesse Owens, the Olympic sprinter, racing several ballplayers. Then, as the *pièce de résistance*, when the game finally started, the Reds' young left-hander, Johnny Vander-Meer, who had pitched a no-hit, no-run game five days earlier, pitched another.

Ladies Day was becoming a runaway success, too. It flowered most riotously, as might be expected, in Brooklyn, where two men were arrested one afternoon for trying to take advantage of the new promotional generosity by disguising themselves as women and getting by for just the tax. Another man brought suit against the Dodgers, alleging that he had been trampled in a Ladies Day rush. But in spite of diversions like these, Ladies Day began to interest wives in what was going on inside the fences of baseball parks, and when this interest was stoked by daily radio broadcasts of the games—especially when MacPhail installed Red Barber behind a microphone in Ebbets Field in 1939—Ethel Barrymore and other hard-core lady fans began to have a lot of company in the grandstand on those summer afternoons.

Things were going so well at this time, too, for Charles Dillon Stengel, the financial investor and former manager, that he even considered severing his ties to baseball to enter the oil business. But the petroleum industry was spared that revolution when Bob Quinn, who had been business manager of the Dodgers during Casey's tenure in the dugout and had gone on to Boston in 1935 as president of the Braves (or Bees, as they were called for a time), suddenly offered him the job as manager at Boston. The offer came in October, as soon as his idle season ended. It was no outstanding favor, since the Braves had been right down there with the Dodgers, running eighth, sixth and fifth the previous three years after not finishing higher than fourth in 20 years.

Casey, mercurial as ever at the age of 47, promptly accepted, ended his year in exile and headed for Boston. He succeeded his old friend, Bill McKechnie, stayed five seasons plus part of another, finished fifth one year and seventh four straight years, and was saved from the worst standing in the league only because Philadelphia ran a colossal string of five consecutive seasons in last place.

Life was not so raucous as it had been in Brooklyn, but it had flashbacks to the good old days. He owned no ballplayers with racehorses or mustaches, but he did own one who had fought a draw with a catfish.

"I got me a young first-baseman, in the hospital after a fight with a catfish," he said wonderingly.

The ball player, George Metkovich, had hooked the fish in the Manatee River in Florida, then had become absorbed in trying to extract his hook when the fish fired a parting salvo, ramming a feeler fin through his foot. For the rest of his career, notably with both the Braves and the Red Sox in Boston, Metkovich carried the nickname "Catfish" as a memento.

But the Boston years were not too amusing in most ways. Stengel had neither a batting champion, home run king, runs-batted-in leader, or pitching ace. Even after the Braves moved to Milwaukee

15 years later and to Atlanta 10 years after that, their "short history of the Braves" included these sentences: "There have been many great pitchers in the Braves' organization. Cy Young won the last of his 511 games while a member of the team, etc." Warren Spahn had not yet arrived on the scene when Stengel managed the club and, though a renaissance of sorts was just around the corner for the Braves, the Stengel administration went rapidly downhill.

In his first season, the club won 77 games and lost 75, the first time since he had become a manager in the big leagues that his team had won more games than it had lost. But if he had any fears about prosperity, they were soon dispelled. The next year, the Braves slumped from fifth place to seventh by winning only 63 games and losing 88. They improved fractionally the next year, winning 65 and losing 87. But they reversed the course again, going 62-92 and finally 59–89, with rain and postponements intervening on six days that final season, 1942, to prevent an even worse showing.

The situation was actually worse than that—just losing games; Stengel was beginning to lose money. He had invested $50,000 of his own money in the Braves, being now something of a capitalist in baseball circles and having, as usual, an insatiable craving for getting involved. But then, one night in April 1943, just after he had come north to open the season, with players beginning to disappear from baseball to enter the military services and a kind of bewilderment settling over the game, he was snatched from the stagnation of life in the second division by one of those dramatic acts of fate that popped up so often and ruled so much of his life.

He was crossing Kenmore Square in the rain and fog when he was struck by a taxicab, knocked down and hospitalized with a broken leg.

"No one but me," he said later, "could get hit by a taxi, break a leg and wind up in the maternity ward."

His admittance to the maternity ward was simply in the nature of an emergency, but Casey's pals on the ball club and on the Boston newspapers immediately barraged him with letters and messages of condolences addressed to him "care of the Psychopathic Ward." Someone who disagreed with his overall genius even sent him a citation as "the man who did the most for Boston baseball this year"—by spending the season flat on his back while the team struggled up one notch to sixth place.

At least, wrote Dave Egan in *The Boston Record,* "no one did more for Boston baseball."

Well, Boston baseball may not have done more for anyone, either. It was not just that Stengel got paid for not managing, for the second time in seven years. Nor that he and his "partners" were finally bought out by Louis R. Perini, the construction man, who eventually transferred the club to Milwaukee. Nor was it that the Stengel legs picked up another scar of battle, a knot and a limp, both of which he retained. It was, rather, that the accident in Kenmore Square put him on the sidelines in Boston for good—just before the axe fell, most insiders believed. Otherwise, he might not have shaken loose from an increasingly difficult situation, beat a retreat back to the minor leagues and been ready when the most remarkable change in his fortunes arrived five years later.

At first, though, he seriously considered getting out of baseball, as he had during his year in exile in Brooklyn. After all, he was 53 now and the war was spreading all over the world and both he and his profession were forced into some eclipse because the drain on manpower had already begun to result in spectacles like a one-armed outfielder (Pete Gray) in the major leagues and a batting average of .309 (George Stirnweiss) that was good enough to win the American League title.

In fact, some of the best baseball—and football, for that matter—was played in military camps during World War II. Maxwell Field, at Montgomery, Alabama, organized one such baseball team by an ingenuity and determination that might have made its pilot-selection boards jealous. It frequently played four night games a week in Crampton Bowl, plus Sundays, and had no difficulty finding starting pitchers for such an arduous schedule. At one time its pitching staff consisted of two professional right-handers and two professional left-handers: Mel Parnell, who became one of Stengel's irritations when he pitched for the Boston Red Sox later; Royce Lint, who became the property of the Pittsburgh Pirates; George Turbeville, who had already pitched for years under Connie Mack at Philadelphia, and Bill McCahan, who joined the Athletics after the war and pitched a no-hit game against Washington in 1947.

The Bainbridge Naval Base in Maryland once furthered its baseball fortunes by trading some water-survival equipment, which it did not need, to another base for an outfielder, which it did need.

In spite of such aberrations in the pattern of the game, though, Stengel was pried out of his "retirement" in May 1944, by Charlie Grimm, his old friend, who was managing the Milwaukee Brewers in the American Association but who wanted to accept a job managing the Chicago Cubs and needed a fill-in for himself back in Milwaukee. The season was already underway and available managers were scarce, but there was good old Casey Stengel, a manager and available. So Grimm sent an SOS to Glendale, and Casey, as a favor to his old pal, limped from the side of the swimming pool, headed back east and took over at Milwaukee.

As things turned out, he was about to be rewarded a hundredfold for doing Grimm the favor. The Milwaukee team was no patsy. It tore the league apart, winning 91 games and losing 49, and winning the American Association pennant.

Somehow now, all the tricks Stengel had acquired on the way up from Kankakee 35 years earlier began to crystallize: how to evaluate baseball talent, how to invest in a winner, how to resurrect a loser, how to buy low and sell high, how to manage a baseball team in one league and still spend time and money wheeling and dealing in another.

The Brewers were owned by Bill Veeck, who had followed his father around the Chicago Cubs' holdings 20 years before as a little boy and who had run across Stengel in his early days as a manager at Toledo in the same league. Now Veeck Jr. was an executive himself, and, more than that, he was a Marine in the Canal Zone. So he and Stengel ran the club through a brisk correspondence that, years later, Veeck said astonished even him.

One day during the 1944 season he received a letter at his post in the Canal Zone in which Casey announced that he would trade Jim Pruett, a catcher with a reputation for having an exceedingly weak throwing arm. Casey even predicted when and to whom he would sell—or peddle—Pruett. Veeck was amazed, since he saw no chance of such a deal, whether the war had weakened the will of rival club owners or not.

He was even more astonished, though, to learn five months later that Pruett had caught two games under the interested gaze of a scout for the Philadelphia Athletics, and moreover had caught five runners off base with a throwing arm that seemed like the greatest rifle since Daniel Boone. The Athletics promptly coughed up $40,000 and took Mr. Pruett and his rifle home to Philadelphia.

Stengel later let Veeck in on the machinations behind the deal, which Veeck was being advised of through communiques between Milwaukee and the Canal Zone.

"He had carefully set the stage," Veeck recalled. "He had encouraged the notion that Pruett had a weak arm, weaker than he actually had. He didn't even use him behind the bat too often, just nourished the idea that Pruett couldn't throw. Then, he got Pruett primed for the Philadelphia scout—well-rested, warmed-up and hungry as anything. He was an instant success, because he was really better than Casey had let on. But that's the way Casey had been brought up as a minor league manager: his biggest job was probably developing players to sell somewhere. And he got awfully good at it."

He got so good at it that he caught the eye of another old friend, George M. Weiss, who had been administering minor league clubs and systems for the New York Yankees since the old Eastern League days of 1925, when Stengel managed his first team. Now, in 1945, Weiss had a weak team at Kansas City in the American Association and he went to Casey with the same appeal for a favor that Grimm had floated the year before.

Stengel by this time had accepted the cheers for his whirlwind success at Milwaukee but, being an interim manager, had then resigned and bowed out after the briefest and most successful pinch-hit job of his career. He gave Weiss the same respectful ear he had given Grimm. And, where he had done Grimm the favor of taking over a pennant-bound team the year before, he now did Weiss the favor of taking over a cellar-bound team—but a cellar-bound team owned by the Yankees. Besides, he was back home with a Kansas City team for the first time in 35 years. The team, the Blues, plunged into seventh place, but Stengel had now made contact with the organization that was to change his life. All he had to do was wait.

The wait lasted three years, and he spent them in the Pacific Coast League as manager of another Triple-A team, the Oakland Acorns. The league was no pushover, listing among its managers, in addition to Stengel, such professionals as Paul Richards, who later had several careers as a manager and executive in the majors; Lopez, who later achieved the best career record of games won and lost as manager of the Cleveland Indians and Chicago White Sox; Bobby Bragan, later the manager at Pittsburgh, Milwaukee and Atlanta; and Bill Kelly, later a superscout for Stengel when both labored for the New York Mets.

The Acorns had so many veteran players that they were called "the nine old men," in the manner of Franklin D. Roosevelt's Supreme Court. The old men did splendidly for their 56-year-old manager, who was making his debut on the Pacific Coast in a league that included Los Angeles and Hollywood and that made it easy for Edna Stengel, for once, to keep her man within a reasonably short radius. In the long season made possible by the weather on the Coast, they won 111 games and lost 72, in 1946, finishing second. In 1947, they won 96, lost 90 and ran fourth. But in 1948, they dominated the league, winning 114, losing 74 and taking the pennant for Oakland and Stengel.

Casey had now managed at Worcester, Toledo, Milwaukee, Kansas City and Oakland for 12 seasons in the Eastern League, American Association and Pacific Coast League, 11 of the 12 seasons being in the highest category below the majors. He had managed at Brooklyn and Boston for nine seasons in the National League. His minor league teams had won 1,037 games and lost 924. He had won two pennants 20 years apart in two Triple-A leagues.

It was a good place to stay, to ease into retirement. But now, without warning, Stengel's world turned upside down.

The New York Yankees had dropped from first place in the American League to third that season. The 16-year reign of Joe McCarthy had ended, and in one season the club had played under McCarthy, Bill Dickey and Johnny Neun before Bucky Harris took over for 1947 and 1948. Postwar attendance zoomed to 2,373,901, and the Yankees' position of dominance, established with Ruth three decades before, was now being challenged before the largest crowds in sports history.

The Yankee scouts on the West Coast, Bill Essick in Los Angeles and Joe Devine in San Francisco, passed the word to New York, where George Weiss had been installed as resident director of the Yankees' empire by Dan Topping and Del Webb, who had recently bought control of the club after a public row with their partner,

MacPhail. Webb, moreover, played plenty of golf with Brick Laws, owner of the Oakland club, and heard much about the glory of the nine old men and their ringleader. Then, Gene Bearden, one of the *young* men developed at Oakland, began to pitch his way to considerable fame as the star of the Cleveland Indians' dramatic playoff victory for the American League pennant.

So, it was the "tenth old man" of Oakland who got the call from the Yankees on Sunday, October 10, 1948, and who, the next day, more solemn than usual, boarded an airliner and headed for New York.

THE YEAR THE YANKEES WON THE PENNANT

On May 11, 1944, *The Sporting News*, the weekly journal of baseball, reported the results of a poll of 151 newspaper writers on the subject: the "most" in major league managers. Leo Durocher, for example, was voted the most pugnacious. Connie Mack was voted the best-liked. Bill McKechnie the most studious. And Casey Stengel, who that season was not even in the major leagues, was voted the "funniest."

He received four times as many votes as the runner-up, Jimmy Dykes, and six times as many as the No. 3 man, Charlie Grimm, who played the banjo and was considered exceptionally funny even by Stengel. Still, no one came close to Stengel, the onetime bow-legged outfielder for the Dodgers, Pirates, Phillies and Giants, the brawler and practical joker who later cemented his reputation as a clubhouse comic by directing the exceedingly funny—and spectacularly unsuccessful—Brooklyn Dodgers.

Consequently, it came as a distinct shock to most persons when Stengel appeared suddenly in New York in October 1948, and was introduced as the new manager of the New York Yankees, the most exceedingly unfunny—and spectacularly successful—baseball team in history.

It was as though the State Department had borrowed Emmett Kelly from Ringling Brothers and introduced him as the government's new Chief of Protocol. It was universally regarded as an interim step between Yankee dynasties, as when John XXIII was elected Pope a dozen years later and was considered by most persons a "transition Pope." And the results in Stengel's case were almost as surprising.

For one thing, the Yankees, like Old Man River, had just kept rolling along, winning 15 American League pennants and 11 world championships, principally under two of the more strait-laced managers in the game, Miller Huggins and Joe McCarthy. But then, adjusting to the lean days of World War II, and later emerging from them, the Yankees slipped. They finished third in 1944 after winning three straight pennants, then dropped to fourth in 1945, edged back to third in 1946, went all the way back to first in 1947, but then sank again to third in 1948 under Stanley R. (Bucky) Harris, who had been installed as manager by Larry MacPhail. Finally, after a sensational brawl in public, MacPhail had been bought out for $2,000,000 by his partners, Dan Topping and Del Webb, and Harris had abruptly lost his patron.

So the Yankees were struggling to recapture their equanimity and Rock-of-Gibraltar quality in the fall of 1948, when Stengel flew to New York in response to an invitation from the new owners of the Yankees. He arrived on Sunday night, October 10.

Everybody's attention in baseball at that hour was fastened on the World Series, which was being played between the Boston Braves and the Cleveland Indians. The Indians in 1948 had enjoyed a remarkable renaissance under Bill Veeck, the promotional wizard who once sent a midget named Eddie Gaedel to bat when he owned the St. Louis Browns (Gaedel walked on four straight pitches) and who later had stormed Cleveland with so many stunts that the team performed before an average of more than 40,000 persons every time it appeared in Municipal Stadium in 1948.

The Indians' magic touch lasted right up to the final hours of the season, which found the club in a tie with the Boston Red Sox. Finally, after winning a tumultuous playoff for the American League title, the Indians swept into the World Series and, on the day after Stengel arrived in New York, edged out the Braves, 4 to 3, before 40,103 persons in Boston and brought the championship back to Cleveland.

It was a gaudy finish to a gaudy season. Lou Boudreau, the boy manager and shortstop, led the Indians to their first championship since Tris Speaker's team had defeated Wilbert Robinson's Brooklyn Dodgers 28 years earlier. Joe Gordon, "the sterling second-sacker whom the Yankees cast adrift in 1946," according to one report of the final game, hit a home run in the sixth inning. And Gene Bearden, the young left-hander developed by Stengel at Oakland in the Pacific Coast League, saved the game while Cleveland routed Boston's pitcher, Bill Voiselle, with the great young left-hander Warren Spahn pitching in relief for the Braves.

It was a difficult act to follow. But the next day, October 12, the Yankees followed it with Casey Stengel.

It was a cloudy, rainy day, and the World Series was still dominating the front pages, though Allison Danzig wrote in *The New York Times* that "now that the World Series has come to an end, football holds the center of the stage for a run through November." Columbia, it seemed, was preparing to open a long home stand that Saturday against the University of Pennsylvania, and "New York hasn't seen any bigtime football for some time."

At the St. James Theatre off Times Square, Ray Bolger had just opened in "Where's Charley?" and Brooks Atkinson noted that the dancer made "a mediocre show seem thoroughly enjoyable." Tony Pastor and his orchestra were holding the fort at the Paramount, with a new singing star, Vic Damone. Vito Marcantonio was running for a seventh term in the House of Representatives from his district in East Harlem and *The Times* asked in an editorial whether the electorate would "vote Russian or vote American."

Harry S. Truman was whistle-stopping his way across the country against Thomas E. Dewey, while George C. Marshall headed for the opening of the United Nations General Assembly meeting in Paris, saying the country was "completely united" in foreign policy—though the Presidential campaign indicated otherwise. And Great Britain at that hour was asking for a censure of the Soviet Union over Andrei Y. Vishinsky's disarmament proposals, charging that Vishinsky actually was obstructing disarmament.

The Alger Hiss-Whittaker Chambers controversy was at its height, too. And stylists were reporting that Persian lamb collars on women's coats were about to make a solid "bow" for the fall season. It was Columbus Day. Yom Kippur began solemnly at sundown. And at the 21 Club, one of the toniest nooks in town, Dan

Topping stood before a phalanx of microphones in the glare of spotlights raised by swarms of photographers and television cameramen and introduced the new manager of the New York Yankees.

"Meet the new manager of the Yankees," wrote John Drebinger in *The Times*. "Charles Dillon (Casey) Stengel, onetime hard-hitting outfielder, manager of both major and minor league clubs, sage, wit, raconteur as glib with the wisecrack as the late Johnny Walker."

True, but the man brought 2,700 miles to take over the American League's most successful team had never played, coached or managed for a single inning in the American League. And, to compound his innocence, he had been flown to New York, had been taken directly to the Waldorf-Astoria that night, had signed a two-year contract and now, 36 hours later, had been put on display like one of the wonders of the world in the broad, artificial daylight of a high-toned nightspot.

To present a united front for such an incongruous occasion, the Yankees also put Joe DiMaggio on display alongside Stengel. The great centerfielder was going on 36, had suffered a painful charley horse in his frequently bruised legs during the closing weeks of the season, had almost single-handed salvaged something better for the Yankees as they finished third behind Cleveland and Boston, and now was explaining that he planned to visit Johns Hopkins for a medical checkup to determine whether an operation would be required on his right heel to remove a bone spur similar to the one that had been removed from his left heel two years earlier.

That was symbolic enough, and bad enough: that the central figure in the Yankee dynasty on the field appeared to be in fading health. But his presence was intended to allay a worse suspicion: namely, that DiMaggio regarded the appearance of Stengel as a menace to his own ambition to manage the Yankees. But the Yankee Clipper, as he was called, smiled broadly, engagingly and convincingly as he stood shoulder to shoulder with Stengel. No, he said, he had no managerial ambitions.

"You know me, boys," he said. "I'm just a ball player with one ambition, and that is to give all I've got to help my ball club win. I've never played any other way."

Clarence (Brick) Laws, owner of the Oakland team in the Pacific

Coast League and Stengel's most recent employer, also stood in the front ranks in another show of force and unity. He had released Stengel from his obligations at Oakland so that he could accept the Yankees' offer, which Casey said had not been made until that Sunday despite the fact that he had been reading speculation about it on the Coast for nearly a month.

One other Stengel "connection" with the Yankees was suggested. Precisely 25 years earlier, to the day, he had hit the home run for John McGraw's Giants off Sad Sam Jones to defeat the Yankees, 1 to 0, and tighten the 1923 World Series, just two days after his inside-the-park home run had won the opening game. The Yankees eventually took the series, four games to two, but the implication now was that, a quarter of a century later, the Yankees had decided that if they could not beat Stengel, they might as well join him.

None of this symbolism overcame the fact that the Yankees in reality had reached out into left field, so to speak, for a celebrated comic as their field leader in a strange new context for both, and not even Stengel could find the words to dispel the misgivings that had settled over the party at "21."

In fact, with the first words he uttered to acknowledge his accession to power, he fell on his face verbally. With tape recorders, microphones and cameras all switched on from a common cue, the man of the hour said: "I want first of all to thank Mr. Bob Topping for this opportunity." That was all right, except that Mr. Dan Topping should have been thanked for this opportunity instead of his brother Mr. Bob Topping, whose marital difficulties with Arlene Judge, the film actress, formerly Dan's wife, had put both Toppings in headlines even before Stengel had arrived.

Cries of "Cut!" and "Hold it!" drowned out whatever else the Yankees' new manager had in mind for his opening sentence. Then, after everybody had rewound the equipment, Casey took another cue and made another start.

"This is a big job, fellows," he said, with no trace of his usual plunges into slapstick, "and I barely have had time to study it. In fact, I scarcely know where I am at."

Then, turning to the Yankee "situation," he delved into generalities and said: "There'll likely be some changes. But it's a good club and I think we'll do all right. We'll go slow because you can tear down a club a lot quicker than you can build it up."

The performance of all concerned was not entirely convincing.

"Most observers," recalled Drebinger, "always kindly disposed toward the engaging Stengel, were viewing his forthcoming assignment with some misgivings. Casey's rows with umpires stand as classics, one of his most brilliant performances having occurred one day when he strode to the plate, bowed to the arbiter and doffed his cap, from which a sparrow escaped. Just what he plans to spring out of his cap for the Yankees next spring is a matter which gives much food for speculation."

The next day, Casey made his first move as manager of the Yankees: he signed Jim Turner, a onetime milkman, pitcher for the Boston Braves and manager at Portland in the Pacific Coast League, as a coach, his first appointment. He made two moves, actually, as *The Times* noted, and the second became a much more characteristic one:

"Last night Casey went into a huddle with George M. Weiss, general manager of the Yankees. It is a fair guess that there will be many such sessions in the next few weeks, for all interested parties realize there is much work to be done before the Yankees can ever hope to reclaim their baseball leadership."

Ben Epstein wrote in the New York *Mirror*: "One can get better odds naming the Yankees' opening-day lineup than the 1949 opening-day manager. Such a smart-alecky attitude is sneered at as right unneighborly by the ownership. Yet Casey Stengel will be the fifth candidate to have stabbed at this morning glory since 1946."

Sure enough, the 1949 season became an unending series of huddles between Stengel, Weiss, Topping and a platoon of physicians and surgeons who were summoned in a struggle to rescue the Yankees from an epidemic of breakdowns—while their new manager, a 59-year-old man, struggled to put nine sound young men on the field.

Joe DiMaggio missed the first 65 games because of the bone spur on his heel, then missed two more weeks in September because of a virus infection that weakened him right through the final inning of the season. The back-up sluggers were hobbled, too—Tommy Henrich (wrenched knee, three broken vertebrae), Charley Keller (chronic back ailment) and Yogi Berra (broken finger). Seven men played first base at one time or another—Henrich, Johnny Mize, Dick Kryhoski, John Phillipps, Billy Johnson,

Fenton Mole and Joe Collins. Third base was shared by Johnson, a part-time first-baseman, and Bobby Brown, a part-time medical student, who, it was suggested, might have helped the team more with scalpel and bandage than with bat and glove. Two accomplished midgets played shortstop and second base—Phil Rizzuto and George Stirnweiss—with support from Jerry Coleman, a Marine Corps Reserve pilot who shuttled between the Yankees and the Marines for years. Berra, an outfielder, was made a catcher. And Johnny Lindell, a pitcher, was made an outfielder.

Every day when he arrived at the stadium, Stengel would check with the team's trainer, August R. Mauch, to determine the number of able-bodied men before putting nine names down on his lineup card, which he then would sign in his mid-Victorian script with flowing letters as though it were a historical document. He put down the names of the three "middle" batters—Henrich, DiMaggio and Berra—supposedly the anchor of the lineup, only 17 times as a unit in 154 games.

Ten years later, Stengel started 100 different lineups to get through a schedule of 154 games, and was both hailed as a Merlin among managers and criticized as a meddler. But he had been "platooned" himself as an outfielder 40 years earlier, and whatever his excesses as a juggler of men later, he platooned players as a manager that first year of the epidemic with the Yankees out of dire necessity.

Mauch, a trim man who wore white slacks and tennis sneakers, held degrees as a Doctor of Naturopathy and as a Doctor of Chiropractics, had treated professional baseball players, college swimmers, football players at all levels, George M. Cohan, Jimmy Durante and even George Bernard Shaw, and played a calculated hand of contract bridge, besides.

He was the trainer for the football Giants in New York for 17 seasons, the football Yankees for 4, the baseball Yankees for 16, New York University for 6 and Manhattan College for 12. He eventually trained eleven baseball pennant winners, eight World Series winners, two National Football League champions, six American League All-Star teams, one National League All-Star team and one All-Star team each in the N.F.L. and the All-America Football Conference.

He once helped keep Cohan dancing on stage for weeks while

the entertainer was suffering with a sprained ankle, a pulled hamstring muscle and a case of influenza. Shaw visited him at the McAlpin Hotel's roof club in 1926 for massages. Durante called on him for help during his Copacabana appearances in 1940. And Admiral Richard E. Byrd—who "looked a little pale when he came back from the North Pole"—was a fairly regular patient starting in 1927.

But Mauch said without hesitation that the busiest year in his career was 1949.

"Every day I'd walk into Stengel's office," he recalled, "and I'd say, 'Your star outfielder is hurt and can't play.' And he'd say, 'Thank you, doctor.' He never blinked an eye. He grew tougher later, but that year he was gentle. If the team was on a winning streak, he might howl and shout, but he was mild when we were losing or when we were hurting."

The Yankees grew so accident-prone that even Mauch became a casualty in a far-fetched way. The team was in Boston near the end of the season and Charley Silvera, a second-string catcher, was in a doughnut shop when he noticed Mauch walking by. So Silvera picked up two doughnuts, put them over his eyes, peered out through the holes and rapped on the window. Gus was so amused by the spectacle that he began to laugh—and walked into a parking meter, breaking two ribs.

"Joe DiMaggio had a pain in his heel like the pain of a hundred carpet tacks," Mauch said. "He had a flock of tiny calcium deposits that had to solidify into one before the pain would stop. We could have filled a Fibber McGee closet with all the contraptions that shoe companies sent us to correct the problem. They sent shoes with half-soles in the front and iron bars in the rear to act as a cradle for Joe's foot. People who had had bone spurs sent advice and even medicine."

One day DiMaggio stepped out of bed and discovered that the pain in his right heel had gone. It was already late in June and the Yankees were struggling to keep pace with the Boston Red Sox of Ted Williams, Bobby Doerr, Dominic DiMaggio, Ellis Kinder and Mel Parnell, a talented bunch who played under the stern hand of Joe McCarthy, who had led the Yankees in their heyday. The Yankees had an exhibition game on June 27 against the Giants, and DiMaggio walked into Stengel's office while Casey was fiddling with his lineup card and said without warning: "I think I'll give it a whirl tonight, Case."

"Great," Casey croaked, "you can play as long as you want. Just let me know when you're ready to quit."

Instead of taking a "mild workout," as expected, DiMaggio played the whole game. The next night, against the Red Sox in Boston, he got back into the regular lineup, hit a single his first time up and a home run the second, then hit two home runs the next day and another the day after that.

Before the last one, he had hit a long foul ball that just missed being a home run, and McCarthy had shot out of the dugout waving his arm and scowling toward the pitcher's mound. He was growing weary of DiMaggio's theatrical comeback. He retreated into the dugout, and just had time to sit down before Joe rocked the next pitch even farther, and this time there was no doubt that it was a fair ball—or that the Yankees had started to revive.

Still, few sane persons would have gambled on the Yankees' health or luck or ability to survive. "If Casey pulls this one out," said Bill Dickey, the onetime catcher who was then a coach, "he's a Houdini.'

"It was hard to believe," Mauch said, "but Casey would take a guy out of the lineup and the substitute would do better than the original. He moved players around, he switched positions, he did everything, and everything seemed to work."

Berra, a 23-year-old who had been paid $90 a month when he signed with Norfolk in 1943 and who later became celebrated as "Mr. Berra, which is my assistant manager," hit 20 home runs and batted in 91 runs. Allie Reynolds, the part-Cherokee "Chief" from Oklahoma who later struck oil, had been acquired from Cleveland in exchange for Joe Gordon after the management had consulted DiMaggio on the league's toughest pitchers; he won 17 games for Stengel and lost 6—though he finished only four. But a young left-hander with great speed, Joe Page, finished what Reynolds started most times, appeared in 60 games and won 13 as one of the new breed of heavy-duty relief-pitching specialists.

Somehow, with emergency performances like these and with heavy reliance on intuition and Gus Mauch's wizardry in the trainer's room, Stengel brought the Yankees home on September 26 in a tie for first place with the Red Sox and with one week to go in the season.

When the Yankees arrived in Grand Central Terminal that Sunday night, they were astonished to find a crowd of 7,000 persons jamming the station waiting for them, including Mrs. Johnny Mize, the wife of the veteran first-baseman the club had bought from the Giants (who was injured, of course), and Mrs. Babe Ruth. A detail of policemen had to escort the players out through side exits through the cheering mob, and as they did, Stengel said above the noise: "We're still up. Tomorrow we'll have them on our home ground, and tomorrow's a big one."

It was a big one, all right. Before 66,156 persons in Yankee Stadium, the Red Sox took the league lead by scoring four runs in the eighth inning and beating the Yankees, 7 to 6. The game ended in a monstrous argument when Johnny Pesky slid across home plate on Bobby Doerr's squeeze bunt as Ralph Houk lunged to tag him out and the home-plate umpire, Bill Grieve, called him safe.

The Yankees lost the game, the league lead and $500 in fines on one play—$150 each for Houk and Stengel and $200 for Cliff Mapes, an outfielder who wasn't even in the game but who was tactless enough to ask Grieve as the players and umpires headed for the dressing rooms: "How much did you bet on the game?"

Four days later, after the Yankees had played three games against the Philadelphia Athletics, the Red Sox still clung to a one-game lead with two to go—two to go against the Yankees in New York. And as the teams staggered toward the climax of an improbable season, *The New York Times* paused in its coverage of the world scene to say, in an editorial titled "Days of Anguish":

> In times like these, we customarily repair to the classics for what calm we can discover. We like the soothing cadence, marching though it does to doom, of the Ernest Thayer lines:
>
> > Oh, somewhere in this favored land
> > The sun is shining bright.
> > The band is playing somewhere, and
> > Somewhere hearts are light.
> > And somewhere men are laughing, and
> > Somewhere children shout . . .
>
> Charity and the fear of laying a hex on Casey Stengel lead us to draw a veil, temporarily, over the last line of this masterpiece. We will not believe that our Casey has struck out until the baseball mathematicians say the Yankees are impossible.

The Yankees were almost impossible from the first inning on the fateful day, Saturday, October 1. It was "Joe DiMaggio Day," and close to $50,000 worth of gifts were showered on the Yankee centerfielder, who was still pale and drawn from his siege of virus infection. But as 69,551 persons crammed Yankee Stadium, with the Red Sox needing one victory to win the pennant and the Yankees needing one defeat to lose the pennant, Stengel sat in the dugout before the game and said: "I think we've got 'em. I feel it in my bones."

But the Yankees, who felt fatigue and pain in their bones, fell into all kinds of trouble at the start when Allie Reynolds lost his control and gave up four runs in the first three innings. But somehow, six innings from losing it all, they scraped together enough hits here and there to survive, as though having been through hell every day of the season, why be panicked now? And when Lindell hit a home run in the eighth inning, they went ahead, 5 to 4, with Page pitching in relief and saying later that he kept looking out to center field to his dog-tired idol, DiMaggio, and thinking: "If he can play the way he feels, I can pitch forever."

"And so, it develops," John Drebinger wrote after the game, "that those battered Bombers with their countless aches and bruises, weren't ready to be rolled into a boneyard after all. At least, on this final day of the American League championship season, they are still standing as well as their formidable rivals, the hale and hearty Bosox."

And, on the final day, 68,055 persons filled the stadium as the teams met in the final game of the season—winner take all. It was 1 to 0, Yankees, until the last half of the eighth inning, with Vic Raschi pitching for New York, and, after each team had fired a kind of spasmatic parting shot in its last turn at bat, it was 5 to 3, Yankees.

"We had had 72 injuries that season," recalled Gus Mauch, whose ribs were still taped following his collision with the parking meter in Boston. "I mean, 72 injuries that kept a man out of the lineup. And when Henrich caught the foul ball that ended that last game and gave us the pennant, Bill Dickey jumped up in the dugout and cracked his head on the roof. That made 73."

"That was the most fighting team I ever saw," Mauch said. Stengel, said many people, "did it with mirrors." It was, said Henrich, "a team of destiny."

The "team of destiny," though, still had to get through the
World Series, and the National League was providing an opponent
with almost as pronounced a flair for melodramatics and "destiny."
The St. Louis Cardinals had already begun selling and distributing
tickets for the series, then lost four straight games to the sixth-
place Pittsburgh Pirates and the eighth-place Chicago Cubs. That
gave the Brooklyn Dodgers a last-minute chance, and while the
Yankees were squeaking past the Red Sox on the last day of the
season in New York, the Dodgers were squeaking past the Phillies, 9 to 7, in 10 innings on the last day in Philadelphia.

What would they all do for an encore? On October 5, the first
day of the World Series, 66,224 persons packed Yankee Stadium
to watch Don Newcombe allow the Yankees five hits and strike
out 11. But Reynolds allowed the Dodgers two hits and struck
out nine. They were scoreless until Henrich led off the last half
of the ninth inning, with Newcombe keeping one eye on Joe
DiMaggio in the batter's circle and letting the count on Henrich
slip away to two balls and no strikes. He got the next pitch over
and Henrich hit it into the right-field seats.

The next day, Preacher Roe, a left-handed country boy, allowed the Yankees six hits while the Dodgers made seven off Raschi
and Page. Brooklyn won this time, 1 to 0, before 70,053 persons.

In the third game, they were still tied, 1 to 1, after eight innings in Ebbets Field before 32,778 fans. Then the Yankees scored
three times in the visitors' half of the ninth; the Dodgers scored
twice on two home runs in their half and lost, 4 to 3.

In the fourth game, the Yankees rushed to a lead of 6 to 0
inside five innings, then gave back four runs and Stengel had to call
in Reynolds to protect what was left of his lead. Reynolds did,
striking out four of the seven batters he faced.

Finally, in the fifth game, the Yankees treated Stengel—after an
unholy season of one suspense after another—to the luxury of a
nine-run lead. Gil Hodges, who once received the prayers of an
entire congregation in Brooklyn during a batting slump, hit a three-
run home run in the seventh, and Stengel, his season not yet over,
wearily signaled Page into the game. Page stopped the Dodgers,
the Yankees won their 12th World Series, the triumvirate of
Topping, Webb and Weiss won its first—and Casey Stengel completed his tumultuous debut in the American League.

What had Houdini wrought? Had he done it, as so many people

believed, with mirrors? Had the Yankees simply revived after a dormant period? Had justice triumphed? Had tomfoolery triumphed? Had Gus Mauch conquered adversity with Band-Aid and rubbing alcohol?

"It was," said Arthur E. (Red) Patterson, 17 years later, "part of the greatest rebuilding job in baseball. Between 1948 and 1953, Topping and Webb gave Weiss the authority and the money, and Weiss rebuilt an organization. Stengel had been hired with the complete respect of all three. They didn't think he was a clown or a buffoon. They knew that he had a record in the minor leagues that maybe nobody else could match—making out with old players, new players, finished players, professional players. And they brought him to the Yankees with their eyes wide open. He was no diversion to keep the public amused enough to forget the club's collapse."

Patterson, looking back on the year that the Yankees won the pennant between surgical operations, puffed on a cigar in a handsome office on the fifth "level" of Dodger Stadium, the only ball park in the major leagues with Sandy Koufax on the pitcher's mound and palm trees rising over the bullpen fences. He had preceded Stengel by three years with the Yankees, as public relations director and road secretary from 1946 until midway through the 1954 season, then had switched to the Dodgers and jumped the continent with them in 1957 to Los Angeles, where Stengel lived 15 miles from the new home of his old rivals of the 1949 World Series.

"Stengel," Patterson went on, "took a few veteran ball players who required special treatment, like Joe DiMaggio, Charley Keller and Tommy Henrich. Kids who needed encouragement and experience, both at the same time, like Gil McDougald, Whitey Ford, Billy Martin, Mickey Mantle. Several established stars whom Weiss bought when things got rough, like Johnny Mize, Johnny Hopp and Enos Slaughter.

"How do you get all these elements to work together, to succeed together? His minor league background made him a natural. Hank Bauer, for example: Casey played him only against left-handed pitchers early in his career until Bauer became established, and then played him against all kinds of pitching.

"I think he was the father of the two-platoon system. And he was criticized for it. But in defense of the platoon system, he'd say: 'If I still had DiMaggio, Keller and Henrich at their prime, I wouldn't platoon. But I don't.'

"And the 73 famous injuries. It would be like this: During one doubleheader in July of 1949, just after Weiss had bought Mize from the Giants for $40,000, Mize played first base, so Henrich was bumped to right field. In the first game, Henrich crashed into the wall and broke three vertebrae. He was carried out on a stretcher. In the second game, Mize dived to make a tag, threw his shoulder out, and for the rest of the year all he could do was pinch-hit. So now, both first-basemen were out.

"Not only did Stengel make changes that paid off in situations like that, but he made the Yankees more popular, more likeable than they ever had been. They always won everything but love. But then, when they were hurt, they won the public, too."

And if the sleight-of-hand had not worked out, would Stengel's wandering road from Kankakee have ended 40 years later in New York?

"They would have forgiven him, I think, considering all the injuries, because he did a good job of rebuilding," Patterson said, "and they would have given him the next season to finish the job."

Still, Edna Stengel kept 1949 apart in its importance to his career, which at least won a reprieve of sorts by the margin of one game. When, 19 years later, he was elected to the Hall of Fame chiefly because of his success with the Yankees, she wiped tears from her face in St. Petersburg and said: "I can't get over it. This is greater even than winning the World Series in 1949."

Stengel, hard-nosed in financial, economic and "career" matters despite his insouciance in most other things, regarded 1949 as a milestone for good reason. He entered his 60th year during that difficult season; he was operating in a new league in an unforgiving city; he had an unbroken record as a manager of losing baseball teams in the major leagues; and he was on the brink of seeing the great opportunity of his lifetime obscured by his firm reputation as a fair major league player, an accomplished minor league manager and an outstanding practitioner of horseplay at all levels. He was, as *The Sporting News* had reported, the "funniest" manager in the game. And, until 1949, that stood as his most enduring claim to fame.

"No skipper," wrote Arthur Daley, "was ever handed a more formidable task than the Ol' Perfessor. The Bronx Bombers just didn't have the ball players they once had in profusion. But for 148 of the 154 games they were in the lead. There is no escaping the fact that the major part of the credit for this astonishing performance has to go to Stengel."

"Watching Professor Stengel manage a pennant-contender club for the first time in his career," he observed on another occasion, "seems to reveal talents few believed he possessed. Yet, he must have had them all along . . . Certain it is that he didn't learn it all overnight when they named him to lead the Yankees."

The talents that Stengel brought with him to New York had one outstanding thing going for them: George Weiss, general manager of the Yankees and their prime minister for almost a quarter of a century, had implicit faith in his old friend from the Eastern League days. And he gave the Stengel talents wide room in which to maneuver.

Weiss, after conferring with Stengel during the earliest days of their joint stewardship, mailed more than 30 contracts just before the 1949 spring training season, indicating some new directions the Yankees would take. Raises were awarded to several players who had endured the team's defeat in 1948 with some distinction, like Berra, Henrich and Bob Porterfield, the young pitcher who had won his letter almost as soon as he had been elevated from the minor leagues. But most of the other players received "conditional" contracts. That is, a certain sum was to be withheld, every month, its payment remaining optional with the manager—Stengel. The option was exercised if the player hustled, kept himself in good physical shape and went all-out—in the opinion of Stengel.

With this much control of the situation in his hands, Stengel had less trouble surmounting any dugout opinions that he was chiefly a theatrical personality. Money was one thing that the ball players didn't think was funny. The only rub, though, was that the platoon system made it difficult for some players to play steadily enough to please Stengel without the strain of being injected into the line-up in pressure situations.

Once the contracts had been mailed, and returned, Stengel shifted his command of the personnel onto the field from the opening day of spring training. He instituted double practice sessions

—two a day—and organized Yankee workouts on what was called "the most elaborate scale since the days of Miller Huggins."

Having lashed himself to the mast, so to speak, Stengel made certain that he could not escape the Yankees' fate in 1949: the club had his stamp, required his approval, played his type of game. By the margin of that one game, it survived the plagues that visited it during the season and he survived with it.

"If we had lost," he said, after "we" had won, "I would have offered to resign in case the club wanted to get somebody else. You know, I am getting along in years, and this was a pretty rough season for a man of my age."

He also acknowledged the mutual dependence he and the players had shared, and would share for the next dozen years, when he said:

"This is the greatest ball club a man could manage. We've been one happy family from the time spring training started. There has never been a sour note in the clubhouse, on the bench, or on the field. A really great bunch of fellows, and I am indebted to them for the way they came through for me. They won it. Not me."

After a riotous celebration at the Biltmore Hotel, and with the World Series victory behind them, the "greatest ball club" dispersed for the winter. John Drebinger, surveying 1949 in sports, wrote:

"In the first few postwar years, such sports as baseball and racing soared to fantastic heights, chiefly because, aided by prevailing conditions, they were better equipped to break away from the barrier. Folks went to ball games because there wasn't much else to do and they plunged on the horses in staggering amounts because there wasn't much else to do with their money, it still being something of a trick to buy an automobile, a refrigerator or even an extra pair of shoes. With the fourth postwar year, however, the final leveling-off resulted.

"Outstanding in achieving the totally unexpected were the Yankees, who, making a mockery of the baseball experts' forecasts and flashing an utter disregard for an unprecedented total of injuries, swept to a pennant and world championship as well. The Bombers started the year with a manager, Casey Stengel, who never spent a day in the American League and closed it monarchs of all they surveyed."

As the monarchs of all they surveyed headed home for the winter, their manager and his wife flew from New York to California, then stepped down at Glendale to find a cheering crowd whooping it up on the steps of the City Hall. They were driven in an open car strewn with flowers through the downtown business district, passing under a banner that stretched across the street reading: "Glendale, Calif., is proud of Casey Stengel."

It was one year almost to the day since he had left the job at Oakland for New York. And now the "healthy" Yankee returned, stood in front of his cheering townsfolk and neighbors and Edna Stengel's relatives and, when the noise had quieted down, told the throng in vintage Stengel understatement:

"I'm tired. I've been pretty busy."

8

THE 12 MOST SPLENDID YEARS

When Babe Ruth died on August 16, 1948, the United States reacted as though a great American institution had fallen, as indeed it had. It was not just that Ruth had dominated an industry for most of his 22 years in it; nor that he had played in 2,503 major league baseball games, gone to bat 8,399 times, made 2,873 hits, scored 2,174 runs and batted .342. Nor that he had excelled as a pitcher before becoming a great hitter. Nor that he had rescued the professional game from its decline after the Black Sox scandal of the 1919 World Series; nor that he had "built" Yankee Stadium and the modern Yankees.

But, by hitting 714 home runs and revolutionizing the image of baseball, he had elevated the game itself, raised the sights and salaries of all players along with his own, increased the revenue of all clubs and captured the public's imagination to an incredible degree.

So it seemed fitting when he died to signal the passing of an institution, not simply the passing of a man. The *St. Louis Post-Dispatch* caught the mood and the significance of the moment in a remarkable editorial that did not lament his death nor even mention his name, but that simply symbolized—almost photographed —his meaning to the national life. It was titled "Bambino" and it said:

There he stood, a great tall inverted pyramid at the plate. At the top were two of the broadest, most powerful shoulders the bleachers had ever seen. His slender legs hugged each other and his feet came together like the dot of an exclamation point. He was not fussy. No nervous swinging of the bat. No uneasy kicking of his shoes. No bending over. No straightening up. Just a deliberate getting set. Maybe a little motion at the wrists—that and a death watch on the man on the mound.

Then the first pitch. Low and outside. Everybody tense except the inverted pyramid. Another pitch—low and away. Were they going to walk him? With two on and the winning run at bat, a walk was the play. Then a third pitch. The pyramid gathers himself, steps into the ball and swings—all in one motion. Before the crack of the blow reaches ears in the stands, the ball is lofting away on wings. It rises right of second, arches higher and higher over right field and drops into a sea of upraised hands for another home run. The Babe is jogging around the bags, two runs scoring ahead of him.

Another game won for the New York Yankees, another game nearer the American League pennant and still another World Series. Jogging on, around second, up to third as the din rises, now spikes down on the plate and home again—home for all time.

Two months after Ruth died, the passing of the "institution" was followed by the passing of the Yankees into the era of Casey Stengel, the "funniest manager in baseball" and something less than an institution at the time. And the transition was accompanied by widespread misgivings. In fact, few baseball seasons marked the end of an era more graphically than the next one, 1949, when the Yankees under Stengel played without any "big" man for their first 65 games until Joe DiMaggio recovered from an operation, then juggled lineups perilously until they squeezed out the pennant on the final day of the season.

The team had moved from institution to improvisation. And, after recovering his breath, his calm and his poise, such as they were, during the winter of 1949–50, Professor Stengel headed for St. Petersburg, Florida, in February of 1950 feeling like a man who had won a reprieve—but who was not certain how long it would last.

"Our improvement for 1950," he said, lapsing into the double-talk that had become a kind of institution itself, "will be the strength we added to what was our strongest department: the bench. There, too, lies our material for trades. Any club offering us a starting pitcher will find us willing to deal."

A few days later, in a fine display of the second-guessing that had been forced upon him during the hectic 1949 season, when every new day offered a new emergency, he reflected:

"Everybody we talked trade with wanted Johnson"—Don Johnson, a promising 23-year-old right-handed pitcher—"and this prompted me to take another look at him myself. He must be good, and if he is, we can use him."

The fact was that Casey could have used anybody with sound health and effective major league experience to prevent a recurrence of the panic of 1949. He looked enviously at pitchers like Bob Kuzava of the Chicago White Sox and Rae Scarborough of the Washington Senators as possible additions to his Big Three of Allie Reynolds, Vic Raschi and Ed Lopat. But, meanwhile, he was beginning to experience the kind of trouble that descends on all teams when they win, before they can start worrying about losing.

Yogi Berra, the young catcher who had led the club in runs batted in, with 91, had been offered a slight raise over his salary of $14,000, but wanted more. Bobby Brown, Tommy Byrne and Raschi wanted more, too. Eventually, Berra signed for $20,000 and Raschi for $30,000, and everybody else got into line. Then, shortly after all hands were present and accounted for in spring training, the inseparable Joes—Page and DiMaggio—were shaken up in an automobile accident on the causeway leading to St. Petersburg Beach.

The holdouts and minor scrapes were not defeats in themselves, of course; but Stengel was trying to regroup a team that had survived 73 "out-of-the-lineup" injuries the season before. So the health and conduct of the troops at spring training assumed exaggerated importance.

He briefly considered imposing a curfew to protect the players from themselves, but then reached back in his memory for precedents and discarded the idea.

"Uncle Robbie even put in a curfew," he said, reflecting on the rough-and-tumble days of Wilbert Robinson and the Brooklyn Dodgers of 35 seasons before. "But he soon called if off. A curfew may be all right when you had a lot of good ball players like

McGraw had on the Giants, Robbie would say, but with this bunch it just won't work."

Stengel's problems continued at a galloping pace right through his second season as manager of the Yankees, a team that for two decades during the Ruth-Gehrig era had presented a calm, unruffled, imperturbable face to the world but that now, despite its dramatic salvaging job the season before, was still picked to finish second behind Boston.

Joe Page suddenly lost his effectiveness and George Weiss, the power behind the shaky throne, had to go shopping for an experienced relief pitcher; he got one, Tom Ferrick, from the St. Louis Browns. Tommy Henrich added a battered knee to the club's medical log and was out most of the season; Weiss bought Johnny Hopp from Pittsburgh in September to take his place.

But the move that paid off the best—and for the longest time—was the elevation of a 21-year-old left-handed pitcher from the Yankee farm at Kansas City in midseason to Yankee Stadium: Edward Charles Ford. He was a short, fresh-faced New York City boy who had attended Manhattan Aviation High School, played sandlot ball with the Police Athletic League and the Kiwanis League, and had started his professional career at Butler in the boondocks leagues in 1947 by winning 13 games and losing 4. By the time the Yankees brought him up two and a half years later, he was about to enter military service for two years—but before he did, he pitched in 20 games for them, started 12, won 9, lost one, completed 7 and wound up with an earned-run average of 2.81.

He still autographed baseballs "Ed Ford," but he was already beginning to be called Whitey Ford and, having helped stabilize the situation in a few months in 1950, he went off to the Army. When he returned in 1953, he won 18 games, lost 6 and resumed a career under Stengel that never included a losing season.

When the trading, promoting, and wheeling and dealing were finished in 1950, the Yankees somehow were leading the league again at the end of the final day, with Detroit, Boston and Cleveland in that order behind them. In the National League, the Philadelphia Phillies—who had won only one pennant in 81 years—held a seven-game lead on September 23 and seemed in no danger of not winning their second in 82 years. But they won it the hard way. They lost 9 of their final 13 games, let their lead dissolve to one game, then had to play 10 innings on the final day of the season at Ebbets Field before defeating the Dodgers on a home run by Dick Sisler, with a young right-handed pitcher named Robin Roberts outlasting Don Newcombe.

There were extenuating circumstances, apart from the fact that the Phillies had finished last in the league more than half the time in the previous 30 years. They had lost two bright young pitchers, Bubba Church and Bob Miller, to injuries and had lost their 21-year-old left-handed pitching star, Curt Simmons, to the Army. Simmons, in fact, was inducted during the pennant run in September and got back to watch the World Series by special dispensation. And what he watched was a massacre of sorts in which the Yankees extracted maximum value out of the World Series debut of Ford, who ironically entered the Army just after the series instead of just before it.

The Phillies, living up to the descriptive cliché, the "Whiz Kids," engineered a surprise as the series opened, and nearly got away with it. Their manager, Eddie Sawyer, started Jim Konstanty —more elegantly known as Casimer James Konstanty—against Stengel's choice, Vic Raschi, in the opening game. Konstanty had set a major league record by pitching in 74 games that season, winning 16, losing 7 and starting none, and, in fact, he had never started a game for the Phillies.

Konstanty not only started, but almost finished, this one. He allowed four hits until he left for a pinch-hitter in the eighth inning, after coming close to one of the great coups of baseball history. But Stengel had horses, too. Raschi allowed the Phillies only two hits and won the game, 1 to 0.

The next day, Roberts tangled with Reynolds for 10 innings until Joe DiMaggio, after six straight pop-ups, popped one into the upper grandstand in left-center field in Philadelphia.

The third game, in Yankee Stadium, went to the Yankees by a score of 3 to 2, and not only put the Phillies three games behind but also marked the seventh straight time they had lost a series game by one run—having lost the final four of the 1915 series to the Red Sox by one run.

They finally managed to break that streak the next day against Ford. Instead of losing by one run, they lost by three. The score was 5 to 2, the Phillies also lost the series and now suddenly "the funniest manager in baseball" had taken two consecutive world championships and was beginning to build a new "institution" for the Yankees.

However, institutions like the old Yankees needed titans like the old Yankees. Nine members of the club had made the All-Star team that season—Byrne, Raschi, Reynolds, DiMaggio, Coleman, Henrich, Rizzuto, Berra and Stengel; even Dickey and Crosetti were there as coaches, and Turner pitched batting practice. But in spite of this saturation of talent, the American League had lost the game, 4 to 3, in 14 innings and, far more important, none of the army of Yankees on hand seemed to represent a new link in the line of titans that had stretched from Ruth to Gehrig to DiMaggio, who was nearing the end of his career.

Nevertheless, Stengel pitched his camp early the following February in Phoenix, Arizona, occupying the training base of the Giants, who had switched with the Yankees that year and who were now advancing on St. Petersburg. It was the Yankees' first penetration of the Far West, and they not only found gold there but also brought gold there. Phil Rizzuto, the smallest member of the club, who had once received milk money of 20 cents during a tryout with the Yankees, arrived with a contract worth $50,000, the third highest in the team's history after Ruth's $80,000 and DiMaggio's $100,000. The feeling was that Rizzuto may not have been precisely a titan but that he was worth it. He had played in all 155 games in 1950, had hit .324 and had made exactly 200 hits.

Stengel, always sensitive to the bread-and-butter factors of baseball, arrived with a new two-year contract himself. It was worth $65,000 plus bonuses and it made him the highest-paid manager in history. He was 60 years old, though, and was still impressed by that fact as much as anybody else.

"The only question," he said after the 1950 season, "concerns my health. I was sick during the spring but I feel fine now. I will pass up most of the winter dinners and hope to be ready for 1951. If my health does not hold up, there's a clause in my contract permitting me to step down."

He had talked of retiring after winning in 1949 and again after winning in 1950, but had not been taken too seriously; a few years later, though, when he talked of retiring after *losing*, he was to find "sympathizers" in the Yankee hierarchy.

Nevertheless, he made it to Phoenix in 1951 in fine fettle and was on hand on February 21 when the advance guard of the Yankees descended on Arizona. It was a four-man delegation consisting of four pitchers—Raschi, Porterfield, Spec Shea and Tom Ferrick—with Dan Topping in command. The caravan had set out by railroad from New York on a Sunday night, detoured for a party in the Cameo Club in Chicago, basked in the warmth of an outpouring of admirers at Tucumcari, New Mexico, and pulled into Phoenix to a full-blast welcome from the mayor, natives in cowboy regalia, a hillbilly band and Casey Stengel.

The manager had been on the scene since February 15 with Dickey, Crosetti, Turner, Henrich and Johnny Neun, "inspecting rookies." In particular, they were inspecting a short, brutally strong blond from Oklahoma, who looked many days like the missing candidate for the institutional lines of succession.

"Mickey Mantle," wrote James P. Dawson in *The New York Times*, "rookie from Commerce, Oklahoma, will be the subject of an extensive experiment in the Yankee training campaign. No less an authority than Manager Casey Stengel revealed this information today, one of those rare days when rain dampened activities in the Valley of the Sun.

"Stengel said he would work the 20-year-old Mantle in center field, and immediately speculation arose over whether the Yanks regarded the rookie as the eventual successor to the great Joe DiMaggio."

The great Joe DiMaggio added a bit of urgency to the situation by declaring that he intended to retire after the 1951 season. That gave Stengel one season to groom a replacement, and if the replacement was to be Mantle, who had played at Independence, Kansas, in 1949 and at Joplin, Missouri, in 1950, then the grooming process suddenly became a quandary.

"The husky blond," according to one flowing report, grasping the problem well, "has the speed of a deer, the swinging power of a seasoned hitter and the throwing arm that compares with anything in camp right now. But he is both a delight and a problem. Should Casey play him or let him ride the bench after a jump from Class C at Joplin, Missouri?"

Mantle had a problem, too. He had osteomyelitis in his left ankle and, in fact, was 4-F in the military draft. He was not in the lineup, in any event, when Stengel shepherded his team west for a 21-day, 12-game swing through his home state of California, a cavalcade that started with this batting order: Rizzuto, shortstop; Coleman, second base; Berra, catcher; DiMaggio, center field; Bauer, right field; Mize, first base; Gene Woodling, left field; Billy Johnson, third base, and Reynolds, pitcher.

It was a great show, except that Stengel's affinity for catastrophe flashed on, even while the team was playing games before Governor Earl Warren, Hollywood stars like Max Baer and Hollywood stars unlike Max Baer, huge, glittering crowds—and ambitious, tough teams from the Pacific Coast League. DiMaggio repeated his announcement about quitting. Mantle, in spite of his osteomyelitis and 4-F rating, was notified by a draft board in Oklahoma to report for an examination. Reynolds developed sinovitis in his elbow on the opening day of the tour. And the Yankees, after winning six games, immediately lost four straight to minor league teams.

Somehow, they made it north for the start of the regular season at Yankee Stadium, then went to Washington for the ceremonial opening, which had been rained out and which now, consequently, had been rescheduled as a doubleheader. President Truman, a southpaw, wearing an infielder's mitt on his right hand, threw out the first pitch; Reynolds caught it on the bounce, and the Yankees lost both games to the Senators, 5 to 3 and 8 to 4.

Mantle appeared in 96 games for the Yankees and 40 for their farm team at Kansas City that season, and was still being groomed, so most of the burden fell on the "old pros" behind DiMaggio. The "old pros," though, were a little frayed around the edges. Berra led the club in runs batted in, with 88 (Gehrig had batted in 175 in 1927), and a rookie infielder named Gil McDougald was the only .300 hitter on the roster. But the Yankees had so much momentum that they rolled right through the Cleveland Indians (15 times in 22 games) and the Boxton Red Sox (7 times in 8 games in September alone) and won their third straight American League pennant.

The high spots were a pair of no-hit games pitched by Reynolds: against Cleveland on July 12, by a score of 1 to 0, and against Boston on September 28, by 8 to 0. The games had one thing in common: Reynolds's catcher was Yogi Berra, the short, blunt St. Louis boy who was growing side by side with Stengel in Yankee folklore, and who was becoming a national character as Casey's "assistant" in later seasons and who was to follow him into high places during the next 15 years.

Stengel instinctively liked the primitive nature-boy qualities of Berra, who became a kind of hero lovably caricatured as "Yogi Bear" and who was constructed along such lines of fireplug simplicity that baseball writers sometimes sent waiters to his table in restaurants with notes addressed to Yogi's dinner partner, saying: "Who's your ugly friend?" He even displayed a Stengelese flair for philosophy couched in doubletalk, remarking on one occasion during a discussion of baseball sagacity: "You can observe a lot just by watching."

But Berra had flourished artistically and financially, rising from $90 a month at Norfolk in 1942 to $5,000 a month a dozen years later. One season he caught 151 games out of 154 played by the Yankees and Stengel usually wrote "Berra" first on his unpredictable lineup cards the way the First Lord of the Admiralty might write "Gibraltar" first on a list of things-to-count-on during the threatened dissolution of the Empire.

DiMaggio was about to leave the Yankees' empire, and Mantle had not yet established his place in it, but there was Berra anchoring things and winning a place in Stengel's affections that no other ball player ever quite matched. On the day that Reynolds pitched his second no-hitter, though, Yogi unaccountably gave Stengel and the rest of the Yankees, to say nothing of Reynolds, a moment of runaway excitement. With two outs in the ninth inning and Reynolds one out from baseball history, Ted Willliams swung and lifted a towering foul ball off to the side of home plate. Yogi drew a bead on the ball, carefully tossed his mask out of the way, waited —and dropped the ball. Now Reynolds was still one out from baseball history but, with Williams still "alive," he also was one pitch away from seeing the ball disappear toward right field.

If Yogi's error was astonishing, what happened next was incredible. While Reynolds, Stengel, Berra and everybody else held their breath, Williams lifted an identical foul ball off to the side of home plate. But this time Berra clutched it to preserve Reynolds's no-hitter.

"I thought Reynolds was gonna catch that one himself," Stengel said, shaking his head over the incident years later.

"I called for the same pitch the second time," Yogi recalled, reviewing the technicalities. "Fastball across the letters and tight. And Reynolds pitched it right there."

"I'll tell you where Berra was pretty good as a ball player," Stengel said. "People don't understand it. He put time in on the sport; he knew everything about different sports. He'd like to sit and watch. Berra was pretty good, too, watching pitching. He was very good when he saw them careless. Berra was pretty good making them do it. I though he was wonderful in jacking up Raschi. He was very good in doing the same thing to, you might say, Reynolds. I thought he was one of the best catchers. When he started, he couldn't do it. He couldn't go out and pick up a bunt. Now, in the World Series he's proved it. He's quick, he could get out—he looks awkward to get a bunt—he knows, its a suspicion, if you watch the hitter, whether the man's gonna bunt or isn't gonna bunt."

If that analysis wasn't entirely clear, Stengel's reliance on Berra was, especially since the Yankees' chances of winning a third straight World Series were blocked by the Giants, who got into the series through a succession of feats that many persons regarded as the most improbable in the history of baseball. The Giants lost 11 games in a row as the season started and were still 13 ½ games behind in mid-August. But, under the goading of Leo Durocher, they caught and tied the Dodgers on the final day of the season, then defeated them in the third and final game of a playoff series when Bobby Thomson hit his famous three-run home run off Ralph Branca in the last half of the ninth inning.

The World Series started the next day and was a bit of an anti-climax, though the Giants won the opening game and appeared en route to certifying their nickname of "Cinderella Team" once and for all. But the Yankees, by now old hands at the perils of the "short series," made it three straight championships by winning four of the next five games.

Three things transcended even the fact that Stengel had gone 3-for-3 as a Yankee manager: A rookie named Willie Mays played center field for the Giants in the series; he was flanked by Henry Thompson and Monte Irvin, giving the Giants the first Negro outfield in the major leagues, and on October 10, the day the

Yankees won the series, Joe DiMaggio played his last game. Two months later, on December 11, DiMaggio went by the Yankee office on Fifth Avenue and wrote this valedictory message to Weiss:

"Mr. George Weiss—They will come and they will go, but with you at the helm there will always be Yankee pennants."

It wasn't a bad prediction, even though the Yankees were still being troubled by the fact that DiMaggio's successor, Mantle, was being plagued by two chronic weaknesses: He was prone to knee and leg injuries and he was prone to strikeouts.

In fact, during the following season, 1952, Mantle's first as the "big man" of the club, he set a record by striking out 111 times. However, Berra set a record by hitting 30 home runs, the most ever hit by a catcher, and the Yankees individually and collectively set or tied 33 records, hit 129 home runs, won the club's 19th pennant and Stengel's fourth straight, and equaled Joe McCarthy's streak of four titles from 1936 through 1939.

But some distant shadows were already falling across the Yankees. They were forced to seven games in order to defeat the Dodgers in the series, then had to win the final two games to do it, which they did by scores of 3 to 2 and 4 to 2. Duke Snider hit four home runs for Brooklyn, and Peewee Reese and Jackie Robinson demonstrated the advantages of "old-fashioned" baseball by pulling a double steal and otherwise running aggressively against the Yankees for Charlie Dressen. Stengel, though, still had the horses to pull him through the thickening competition. Berra and Mantle each hit two home runs; Mize got off the bench after three games to hit three. And Billy Martin, a graceless youngster with few classic talents but all kinds of brass, hit, ran, fielded and plain pestered the Dodgers into submission.

Martin, a scrawny 165-pounder who had enthralled Stengel at Oakland, scrambled back into Casey's affections in 1953, too. He hit .257 while the Yankees were winning their fifth consecutive pennant, a record for one club and for one manager. Then, in the World Series against Brooklyn, Martin hit a cool .500; Carl Erskine struck out 14 Yankees in the third game; Ford made his first World Series start in the fourth game after two years in the Army, and lost; Mantle hit a home run with the bases loaded in the fifth game, and the Yankees won it all when Martin singled over second base in the last half of the ninth inning in the sixth game.

The series, noted Frederick G. Lieb, came close to being the first $3,000,000 series in history, and Ford C. Frick, the Indiana farm boy, sportswriter, broadcaster and president of the National League who had succeeded Happy Chandler as commissioner in 1951, commented in a rousing understatement: "Receipts of $2,979,269 aren't hay." Television fees, already becoming a significant part of baseball revenue, totaled $925,000; radio brought in $200,000; a pre-game TV program was worth $100,000; each Dodger got $6,178 for losing, and each Yankee, including Stengel, got $8,280 for winning.

However, it was temporarily the last winning share for each Yankee after an unparalleled string of five years in which regulars like Berra collected $30,000 apiece in World Series checks alone; in which the Yankees had somehow made the transition from the McCarthy-DiMaggio era to the Stengel-Berra-Mantle era, and in which Stengel had parlayed his wits and Yankee depth in players into the most successful span in baseball history.

The Professor also had blossomed, during this rush of prosperity, into a more indulgent type himself—less primitive than in his earlier years, less imperious than in his later years.

Even the image of "Casey the Clown" was being soft-pedaled to some extent. When one of the most famous trick pictures of his career was taken, showing him as a Swami peering wide-eyed into a crystal ball, his old friend and boss Weiss was not particularly amused. He still did not want the Stengel image to be presented in ludicrous terms.

When Mantle started the 1953 season in Washington by hitting a fastball thrown by Chuck Stobbs over the bleachers in Griffith Stadium, Red Patterson rushed outside the park with a tape measure. He found a boy who had chased the ball into the yard of a house across the street, brought it back, paced off the distance back to the 50-foot-high bleacher wall, added 69 feet for the depth of the bleachers and 391 feet to home plate, and calculated that the ball had traveled 565 feet. The ball and bat later were enshrined in Yankee Stadium, were stolen and were eventually returned. But Patterson's principal memory of the incident was Stengel's admonition to him to promote all possibilities, saying of Mantle: "I want to make that boy some money."

When the Yankees got into an extra-inning game in Philadelphia one night, missed their train and went instead by chartered bus to the Broad Street Station, the old man saw that all the seats on the bus were taken and croaked: "You fellas played hard and you're tired." So he stood alongside Gus Mauch, holding onto the vertical metal pole. His concern for his troops took an odd turn. The bus driver tried to go through a tunnel that was too low, the top of the bus struck the roof of the tunnel and, in the grinding crash that followed, the metal pole broke and fell on Mauch, with the 62-year-old manager still gripping it.

He carried his compassion a step too far, perhaps, in the spring of 1954 when he declared, as the Yankees opened spring training in search of an improbable sixth straight pennant: "If the Yankees don't win the pennant, the owners should discharge me."

Having crawled that far out on the limb, he analyzed the situation further: "Perhaps I should be worried, but I'm going to tell you why I'm not worried. I still hear the other clubs moaning that we keep coming up with new players. Well, why wouldn't they moan? I would, too, if I were in their shoes. We have come up with three tremendous youngsters this spring—Bill Skowron, Bob Cerv and the young pitcher, Bob Grim. I would say as of now all three have definitely established themselves with the club.

"Right now I would have to say my infield has been shaky, the pitching, especially the left side, has been wild and a lot of the regulars, excepting Yogi Berra, have yet to start hitting."

Having thus switched from the pitchers of the left side to the hitters of the left side without punctuation in mid-sentence, Casey then led his club into the training exhibition season, in which they proceeded to win 8 games and lose 16. Now it was Topping's turn not to be worried.

"I don't think there's any reason to become unduly alarmed just yet," the Yankees' owner commented, sounding duly alarmed. "Casey doesn't seem too greatly disturbed, so I don't see why I should be."

Nevertheless, there was cause for at least curiosity, if not concern. Mantle's right knee was troubling him again, and the Yankees had begun to resort to the hit-and-run, the bunt and opposite-field hitting, all old-fashioned remedies, to neutralize the ailments that had begun to creep into their pattern of play. On the opening day of the season, April 13, a golfing enthusiast named Dwight D.

Eisenhower threw out the first ball, Bucky Harris presided over the Senators' dugout and his successor in the Yankees' dugout, Dr. Stengel, platooned 19 players like a football coach. However, in the 10th inning, the Senators' 36-year-old first-baseman, Mickey Vernon, hit a home run to beat the Yankees, 5 to 3. Eisenhower, who had a golfing date in Augusta the next day, stuck it out to the end, called Vernon to the Presidential box and shook the hand that shook the Yankees.

The 27,160 persons at the game in Griffith Stadium had seen the beginning of the end. Five months later, Casey got around to acknowedging his position on the limb, too.

"I got a shock this morning when I looked at the standings," he admitted. "We could have been 4½ games out. Instead, we're 8½. That frightens me. It should frighten the owners, too. Something will have to be done or the Yankees will not be the Yankees."

The optimism of his view in the spring had now shifted to pessimism in September, and not just because the Yankees were losing for the first time in six seasons. Now he was grumping about the long-range view and was intimating that the "owners" had better start becoming alarmed, as he was. But they were the same owners who had relied on his *not* being alarmed a few months earlier. So a tug of war was setting in, one that would intensify gradually during the next seven years—the second "half" of the Weiss-Stengel administration—as the club inevitably meandered in the one direction open to a club at the top: down.

Would he be back as manager the next year?

"I won't talk about that because I don't have to talk about that," Casey replied, sounding a bit crotchety, and giving an answer that he would repeat almost annually (and petulantly) for the rest of his career.

Yet, a week later, on September 19, the Yankees won their 100th game—the first time they had won 100 under Stengel and the first time in 40 years that a team had won 100 games and still lost the American League pennant. They lost it, all right, as the Cleveland Indians won 111 games behind the remarkable pitching of Bob Lemon, Early Wynn, Mike Garcia, Bob Feller and Art Houtteman. The Indians' remarkable pitching, though, did not prevent an even more remarkable upset in the World Series, which the Giants swept in four games.

But the lasting significance of the 1954 season was that, after five years, the Yankees' dominance was broken. The next seven years would produce five more pennants but only two more World Series victories, and already the competition was gathering as the Yankees' rivals began to spend big money for bonuses to entice young ball players who formerly had wanted only to wear the magic pinstripes.

The Yankees still had flair, though, and on September 23, one week before the season ended, instead of sawing off the limb that Casey had crawled out onto in the spring, they awarded him a new two-year contract for 1955 and 1956 at $80,000 a season. It was his fourth contract with the Yankees, and as it was tendered everybody naturally recalled his admonition that "if the Yankees don't win the pennant, the owners should discharge me."

"I meant what I said then, and I still feel that way," he said, pocketing the contract.

"We talked him out of it," Topping said.

"We were beaten in a good fair way by Cleveland," Casey went on, summing up the decline and fall of his heroes. "They had the pitching, the power, the bench. My job now is to better the Yankees. The Yankees are not gone. We'll have to change our methods somewhat."

As things turned out, the Yankees changed their methods somewhat less rapidly than their ex-victims changed theirs. Perhaps the Yankees had less reason to change, considering their record of success. Perhaps they had grown too attached to the methods that had bred such success. Perhaps they were just growing older together. Whatever the reason, fundamental changes were taking place in baseball outside their sphere of influence. The Boston Braves moved to Milwaukee and the St. Louis Browns were reincarnated in Baltimore in 1953; the Philadelphia Athletics became the Kansas City Athletics in 1954; the Brooklyn Dodgers migrated west to Los Angeles and the New York Giants to San Francisco late in 1957. Yet, Yankee attendance, which had reached 2,281,676 in Stengel's first year, went down with only minor adjustments to 1,428,438 in 1958, then crept up to 1,627,349 in 1960—but still totaled 600,000 below Casey's first season, in spite of the fact that the Dodgers and Giants had left town and the Mets had not yet arrived.

Outwardly, the Yankees were still one big, mostly happy family and the patriarch was still the old man in uniform No. 37. He still, as his fortunes began to ebb slightly, showed a soft spot for the younger players, who were inheriting the "situation."

Whitey Ford, who was maturing into a prosperous Long Island suburbanite and one of the most effective pitchers in the club's history, named his pet poodle "Casey." Mantle allowed that Casey "used to get mad at me sometimes" but rated him one of the smartest baseball men ever, and "about the funniest person I've known." Bobby Richardson noted that Stengel used to twit him when he first came up to the Yankees by saying: "Look at him. He doesn't drink, doesn't smoke and he still can't hit .250." But when the dedicated young Baptist from South Carolina was about to earn his letter a few seasons later and got a hit in the final game of the season, Stengel telephoned the club statistician from the dugout, ascertained that Richardson's average had reached .301 and took him out of the game to preserve it.

Bill Veeck recalled that whenever the Yankees played in Cleveland, he and Casey would have breakfast together, and one morning Stengel said over the toast: "I blew a ball game last night."

"How so?" Veeck asked.

"Well," Stengel said, "out kid shortstop, Kubek, slipped on the wet ground chasing a line drive in the ninth and two runs scored and they beat us, 3 to 2."

"How was that your fault?" Veeck persisted, and he was surprised when Stengel said:

"Yeah, well, after the game I said to the kid, let me see your spikes, and he showed them to me. They was the same ones he used in high school, all worn down and no spikes left to run on. So it was my fault, I should've asked sooner."

Ten years later, Veeck added that he had learned that Stengel then had told Kubek to get a pair of new shoes at once and charge them to him—$26.

Another day the young left-hander Bob Kuzava found himself sitting alone in the dugout with the manager, who had squirmed the night before while Kuzava was giving up the winning run in the last inning.

"What did you throw that fella?" Stengel asked.

"A curve ball," Kuzava said.

And where did it break?

"Right across here," the pitcher said, motioning across the waist and over the plate.

"If it breaks over the plate," Stengel said, delivering one of his briefest lessons on the art of pitching, "it ain't a curve."

One day in St. Petersburg, Casey enacted one of his more memorable performances at the behest of a group of New York writers who enlisted him in a practical joke. The victim was John Drebinger of *The Times*, an accomplished extrovert who relished and perpetrated many pranks himself despite the fact that he was hard of hearing and, in fact, wore a hearing aid that became a prop in clubhouse horseplay. Casey was headed across the outfield at Huggins Field—later renamed Huggins-Stengel Field in tribute to his 12 splendid years with the Yankees—and it was decided to conduct the daily press conference in pantomime without advising Drebbie. Casey gave a virtuoso performance. He pointed, roared silently, waved his arms and mouthed exaggerated imprecations—while his old friend bent his head, shook his earphone, frantically cranked the control knob on his chest and finally removed the "faulty" equipment, trying to tune in the great man.

Another day, Harry Harris, first-string photograper for *The Associated Press*, dropped by the dugout at Huggins-Stengel Field and found the old manager sitting alone. Harry had heard that it was wise to avoid Casey on days when he wore Mexican sandals in the dugout; it meant he was probably suffering a "morning-after" grouch. So, spotting the sandals, he began to beat a strategic retreat. But Casey shouted after him and summoned him back, saying he felt lonely and wanted to talk.

"You look grim," Harris said tentatively. "Did you lose your best friend?"

"I sat up all night," Stengel said. "One of my relatives died."

"Close?"

Casey took a deep breath, sighed remorsefully and replied with a wink: "Old Grand-Dad."

Stengel's understanding of the aberrations of human nature had frequent opportunity to develop on the Yankees, who were such a clamorous lot off the field despite their cool efficiency on it that the management once hired private eyes to shadow the ringleaders. That was Keystone Comedy stuff out of Stengel's own days as a mischief-maker 40 years earlier and, although he was instinctively against such surveillance, he went through the motions of enforcing the club's will, especially when off-duty pranks were followed by on-duty setbacks.

One such setback came in 1955, the year after the Yankees lost the pennant. This time, they won seven fewer games but out-distanced Cleveland in a difficult race and went into the World Series with Mantle and Hank Bauer hobbled by injuries. The Dodgers, who had led the National League by 13½ games, swaggered into the series under their second-year manager, Walter Alston, lost the first two games, but made history by winning four of the last five, principally on the stout pitching of Johnny Podres, and won their first series after eight defeats and their first against the Yankees after six.

Having dropped a pennant and a World Series now in successive years, Stengel recouped some of his losses in 1956. Mantle had his strongest year, winning the so-called Triple Crown by leading the league in batting average (.358), home runs (52) and runs batted in (130). But in the World Series, the last to be played by the Dodgers in Brooklyn, the Yankees lost the two opening games, then had to go the full seven again before winning—for the first time in three years.

The redeeming feature, apart from the victory itself, was the comeback of Don Larson, a man who, in Stengel's words, "liked to drink beer" and a man who had run his car into a tree one night in St. Petersburg that spring. Casey sized up his man and played down the incident but told Larsen that the next time it would cost him a bundle of money. Larsen got the message. He won 11 games and lost 5 that season, then on October 8, with the World Series tied at two games apiece, the 27-year-old right-hander from Michigan City, Indiana, paid Stengel back before 64,519 persons in Yankee Stadium.

Twenty-seven Dodgers went to bat and Larsen, pitching mostly fastballs to Berra, got all 27 out for the first perfect game in World Series history. His 96th pitch was a shoulder-high fastball that Dale Mitchell, a pinch-hitter, looked at and that Babe Pinelli, the home-plate umpire, called Strike 3. That ended the game and Pinelli's career as a balls-and-strikes umpire, since he retired after the series. The box score read like this:

October 8, 1956

BROOKLYN (N.L.)						NEW YORK (A.L.)					
	ab	r	h	o	a		ab	r	h	o	a
Gilliam, 2b	3	0	0	2	0	Bauer, rf	4	0	1	4	0
Reese, ss	3	0	0	4	2	Collins, 1b	4	0	1	7	0
Snider, cf	3	0	0	1	0	Mantle, cf	3	1	1	4	0
Robinson, 3b	3	0	0	2	4	Berra, c	3	0	0	7	0
Hodges, 1b	3	0	0	5	1	Slaughter, lf	2	0	0	1	0
Amoros, lf	3	0	0	3	0	Martin, 2b	3	0	1	3	4
Furillo, rf	3	0	0	0	0	McDougald, ss	2	0	0	0	2
Campanella, c	3	0	0	7	2	Carey, 3b	3	1	1	1	1
Maglie, p	2	0	0	0	1	Larsen, p	2	0	0	0	1
a-Mitchell	1	0	0	0	0						
							26	2	5	27	8
	27	0	0	24	10						

a-Called out on strikes for Maglie in ninth.

Brooklyn .... 000 000 000 — 0
New York .... 000 101 00x — 2

Errors–none. Runs batted in–Mantle, Bauer. Home Run–Mantle. Sacrifices–
Larsen. Double plays–Reese and Hodges; Hodges, Campanella, Robinson;
Campanella and Robinson. Left on base–Dodgers 0, Yankees 3. Bases on
balls–Maglie, 2. Struck out–Larsen, 7; Maglie, 5. Umpires–Pinelli (N), Soar
(A), Boggess (N), Napp (A), Gorman (N), Runge (A). Time–2:06. At-
tendance–64,519.

The jubilation caused by Larsen's perfect game was still loud
seven months later, on May 15, when Mantle, Bauer, Johnny
Kucks, Ford and Berra gathered with their wives at the Copacabana in Manhattan to celebrate Billy Martin's birthday. The party
broke up after a fight in the men's washroom, in which a Yankee
non-fan was the loser and in which nobody claimed to be the
winner. Accordingly, the Yankee management levied equal fines
of $1,000 each ($500 on Kucks, who was less affluent), and a few
weeks later, Casey's boy, Martin, the guest of honor and room-
mate of Mantle, was traded. The gang was beginning to break up.

Two seasons later, Casey was to criticize "cut-ups" on the team
publicly, the day of indulgence having ended with Larsen in the
spring of 1956. But before the gulf began to widen, Stengel and
his young adults went through more rough-and-tumble days.

For the second straight year, in 1957, they were carried to the
full seven games in the World Series, after winning the pennant
by eight games. Their opponents were the Milwaukee Braves,

who won their first pennant since being transplanted from Boston four years earlier. The series was exciting, almost hysterical, with Lew Burdette pitching three victories for Milwaukee and Ford, Larsen and Turley one each for New York. Spahn also pitched one for the Braves, and now the Yankees had gone four years with only one World Series success and were, by their own standards, at least, wavering.

They were still wavering in 1958, winning only 92 games, but the rest of the league was wavering worse. After two months, nobody was playing .500 ball except the Yankees, who played little better than that the rest of the way and who, as the World Series opened in Milwaukee, were described by Lieb as "still in their slump" and frequently acting "like a team in a trance."

Becalmed as they were, they lost three of the first four games to Spahn (twice) and Burdette. But somehow, they pulled it out, with Turley pitching in all three remaining games and winning two of them for a team that batted .210. It was a bittersweet victory—the third straight series in which they had been extended to the limit, and the last they would ever win for Stengel.

In fact, his job wavered with the club that season and even though the club won, the wear and tear was beginning to tell. For five years, Stengel's teams had won five straight pennants and championships; for the next five, they won four pennants but only two series. And the worst was yet to come. In 1959, they not only wavered but also collapsed, winning 79 games and losing 75 for a playing percentage of .513, the lowest for a Yankee team in 34 seasons. The Chicago White Sox filled the vacuum by beating out Cleveland for the pennant and later George Weiss looked back and analyzed the debacle:

"It was the only year we lost decisively in 12 years of operation. Criticism went on all year and, as a sensitive man, I think that Casey would have quit if it hadn't been for his great desire to beat McGraw's managerial record. Most of the criticism was against his two-platooning, but the fact is that we lost that year because of constant injuries to key players like Bill Skowron, Gil McDougald and Andy Carey. Stengel had his first-string lineup intact for less than a month. That was the sole reason we lost."

Maybe Weiss knew that was the sole reason and maybe Stengel felt it; but more and more, they were holding a minority position in the Yankee scheme of things. For the first time, Weiss recalled, he even met resistance in a manpower matter. He suggested trying to acquire Ned Garver from Kansas City, but nobody in the front-office superstructure would second the nomination. The handwriting was on the wall, and even Stengel, whose eyes would be 70 years old the following season, could read the message.

The Yankees of 1960—Stengel's 12th and last Yankee team—were built around old pros like Mantle, Ford and Berra; new young players like Richardson, Clete Boyer and Elston Howard, who had been the Most Valuable Player in the International League in 1954 and who became the Yankees' first Negro player; and Roger Maris, the left-handed-hitting outfielder who had just been acquired from Kansas City. Stengel was still brooding over the front office's critical appraisal of the previous season when the team fell two games behind Baltimore in September, but the boys rallied round the flag with a 15-game winning streak that won the pennant—No. 10 in 12 years.

Casey opened the door to second-guessing by starting Art Ditmar in the World Series against the Pittsburgh Pirates instead of Ford, who was 32 years old now and who had won only 12 games and lost 9 in a disappointing season. Ditmar lost. But then the Yankees scored—"wasted" might be a better word—26 runs to win the next two games before losing the two after that.

So, Pittsburgh held a lead of 3 games to 2 on October 12 when the action shifted back to Forbes Field. Ford, who pitched better with four or even five days of rest, had had only three; but he assured Stengel that morning that he felt all right. The Yankees had backed him in his previous game with 10 runs and now, before 38,580 persons, they backed him with 12 as he pitched his second shutout and evened the series, 3-all.

After the game, Mayor Robert F. Wagner sent a telegram to Stengel saying: "Our city solidly behind you and hope that you will stay with the Yankees and win the series next year."

Casey also received a petition from the New York newspaper writers—"my writers"—asking him to remain as manager as long as his health would permit. He replied:

"I've been here 12 years and when a feller stays as long in one place he gets a lot of people mad at him and he gets mad at a lot of people when they blame him for blowing the tight games."

The tightest of tight games was still ahead of him, unfortunately.

The fateful day was October 13, with 36,683 persons sitting and standing in the Pirates' old stadium. Pittsburgh scored four runs in the first two innings, routing Stafford and Turley, who had started and who threw only 20 pitches, the 14th of which was hit for a two-run home run by Rocky Nelson. But in the fifth inning Skowron hit a home run and in the sixth "my assistant, Mr. Berra," hit a three-run home run, and the Yankees scored four times, chasing Vernon Law and Elroy Face. And now the Professor had a one-run lead in a series in which 72 runs had already been scored, with more to come.

But as cheap as life seemed in Forbes Field that afternoon, nothing could have prepared Stengel for what happened in the final two innings.

First, the Yankees added two runs in the top of the eighth, making it 7 to 4. But in the home half, Gino Cimoli singled and Bill Virdon hit a double-play grounder toward Tony Kubek, the long, strong Wisconsin boy who "threw like a girl" but who, in Stengel's description, "made the play."

Tony never had a chance to make this play, though, and for want of a good bounce a grounder was lost and, a few moments later, for want of a grounder, a series was lost. Virdon's grounder took one final hop off the hard Pittsburgh infield—one of the hardest in the major leagues—and struck Kubek in the Adam's apple, then bounced away for a hit. He was rushed to a hospital, while the Pirates rushed to one of the most unlikely climaxes imaginable. Dick Groat singled; Jim Coates replaced Bobby Shantz for Stengel on the pitcher's mound; Nelson flied out; Roberto Clemente hit a grounder right of the mound for the "third out," but Coates failed to cover first base and Cimoli scored the second run of the inning.

Then Hal Smith, a onetime Yankee prospect, knocked the ball over the left-field fence and it was suddenly 9 to 7, Pittsburgh.

Things would have been bad enough if the game had ended there, but Stengel's nightmare was just beginning. Richardson opened the ninth inning with a single, Dale Long pinch-hit a single and Harvey Haddix replaced Bob Friend as the pirates' pitcher. Maris fouled out to the catcher, but Mantle singled to right, scoring Richardson and sending Long to third, and it was 9 to 8.

Suddenly, it almost ended when Berra hit a rifle shot down the

Far from the madding throng, the Old Man would take fungo bat and practice ball in hand and show $100,000 rookies the left-hand swing that made Ethel Barrymore gasp.

The United States Senate had heard Daniel Webster and Henry Clay but not Casey Stengel—until July 9, 1958, when the Professor testified on baseball as a business. Mickey Mantle and Ted Williams were solemn. Estes Kefauver, the committee chairman, was mystified.

What so proudly we hailed.

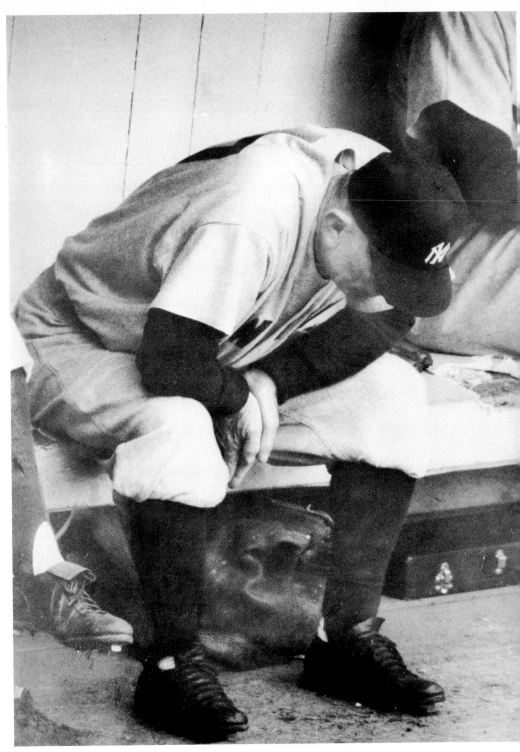

Even with the Yankees, these are the times that try men's souls.

July 27, 1960: The Yankees defeated the Cleveland Indians in the first game of a doubleheader and now Casey, strictly informal, is threatening to make a clean sweep of things. Ralph Houk is slightly amused.

He could read the small print in contracts without eyeglasses, but by 1960 he found
he could focus his attention on the Yankees better this way—like Mr. Chips.

July 30, 1960: Would you believe 70 years old? The family exchanges a madcap toast 70 seasons after Kansas City, 50 after Kankakee, 36 after they met at a ball game at the Polo Grounds.

Like the Marx Brothers, he was a tough act to follow—as Ralph Houk discovered in 1961 after Casey had been ringleader of the Yankees for 12 years and as Wes Westrum learned in 1965 upon stepping into the Great Man's shoes with the Mets.

Why would Uncle Robbie suspect that the great velocity experiment of Daytona Beach in the spring of 1915, featuring a biplane and a grapefruit, was the handiwork of Charles Dillon Stengel?

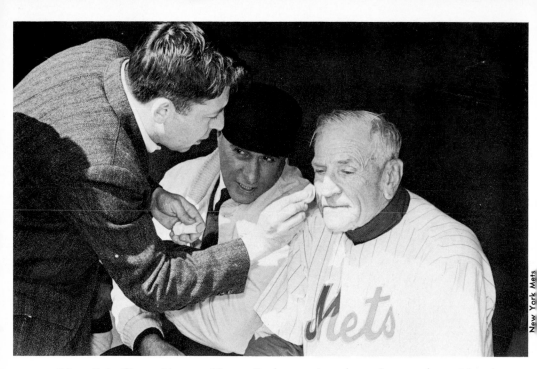

It's a little like making up Mount Rushmore, but the makeup artist tackles the supreme test, invades the dugout and prepares the Professor for television. The other half of the problem was preparing television for the Professor.

No. 37 confers with No. 1, Joan W. Payson, the matron of Manhasset, the mistress of the Greentree Stable, the mother of the Mets, the amazin', splendid, rich, last-place Mets.

"He can talk all day and all night, on any kind of track, wet or dry" . . . "He's one one of the smartest men in baseball, in business, in anything he'd try" . . . "You have to see him in action to appreciate him."

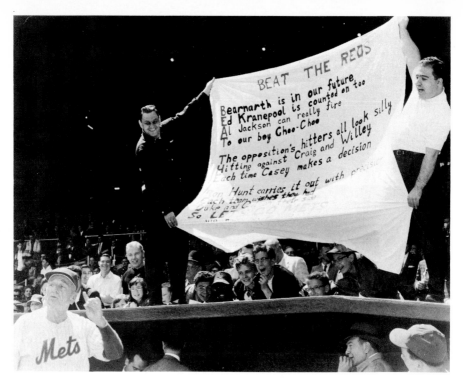

Every day was a Banner Day at Shea Stadium: The Professor and his fans are impressed by a Beat the Reds poster and a paean to Met heroes Larry Bearnarth, Ed Kranepool, Roger Craig, Carlton Willey, Choo-Choo Coleman—and somebody named Casey.

If you, the manager of the Mets, can keep your head when all about you are losing theirs and blaming it on you. . . .

Sunken Gardens, Florida, 1965: Berra and Stengel, after 14 years together on the Yankees and the Mets, a pair of blooming geniuses with no place left to hide.

August 30, 1965: After 55 years in a baseball suit, Casey fell, fractured his left hip, was forced to end a career that had started in Kankakee, Illinois, in 1910, retired at an emotional ceremony—and was consoled by the woman in his life.

September 2, 1965: "I got $2,100 a year when I started in the big league, and they get more money now. . . . And Grover Cleveland Alexander pitched in a bandbox in those days and still won 30 games. . . . And there was Walter Johnson, who could pitch for a second-division club. . . . I chased the balls that Babe Ruth hit."

March, 1966: The Socrates of the dugout presides at a seminar on the grass in St. Petersburg, Florida, for young Mets like Ron Swoboda and Greg Goossen and old Mets like Ken Boyer, Chuck Hiller, Ed Kranepool and Whitey Herzog.

The bats, the balls, the cartoons, the plaques, the trophies, the mementoes, the souvenirs, the spoils of war, the den in Glendale, the bar—and the Professor.

The plaques read:

THEODORE SAMUEL WILLIAMS
"TED"
BOSTON RED SOX A.L. 1939-1960

CHARLES DILLON STENGEL
"CASEY"

July 25, 1966: Theodore Samuel Williams becomes No. 103 in the Hall of Fame and Charles Dillon Stengel No. 104, in the little country town of Cooperstown, New York, where Abner Doubleday may have started it all a century and a quarter before.

first-base line that Nelson somehow grabbed, almost doubling Mantle off the bag. But Mickey dived back in ahead of the tag, while McDougald, running for Long, scored the tying run.

Yogi Berra's son Larry was watching on television back home in New Jersey when Bill Mazeroski, a 24-year-old West Virginian, led off the Pittsburgh half of the ninth with the score tied, 9 to 9. He saw Ralph Terry throw one ball, then he saw Mazeroski hit the next pitch toward the wall in left field and, Larry said, "I thought, if only my father could catch it." But Yogi was watching it, too, as it sailed over the wall for a home run, abruptly making the score 10 to 9, giving Pittsburgh its first World Series victory in 35 years, giving the Yankees their seventh defeat after 18 victories, and giving Casey Stengel, who had won seven World Series in 12 seasons, his third defeat—and his last.

"I can't believe it," said Yogi in the stunned clubhouse.

"I'll never believe it," said Dale Long.

9

COMMENCE BEIN' AMAZIN'

When Harry S. Truman's Secretary of Defense, Louis A. Johnson, was enduring heavy criticism during the early days of the Korean War, he likened his position to that of another national figure. "I am reminded," Johnson said, in a thrust at his critics, "of the bleacher fans at the Yankee Stadium who credited the victories of the team to the players and always blamed Casey Stengel for temporary setbacks. So it has often been with me."

Having thus phrased his defense in terms that would be unmistakable to the nation, Johnson stood his ground until replaced at the Pentagon on September 12, 1950. His allusion, however, grew increasingly more accurate as the years went by. One decade and one month later, while the bleacher fans at Yankee Stadium were still talking about the bizarre climax to the World Series of 1960, in which the Pittsburgh Pirates nipped the New York Yankees by one run in the last half of the last inning of the last game, Johnson's fate befell the man he had selected to illustrate the slings and arrows of outrageous fortune.

The Yankees assembled their highest echelons of executives at the Savoy-Hilton Hotel on Fifth Avenue in New York—all except Del Webb, co-owner of the club with Dan Topping, who was in Los Angeles, where Casey Stengel had started his trip East in 1948 to become manager. In 12 years, the Yankees had survived the postwar transition on the most lavish scale ever known in pro-

fessional baseball. They had won five consecutive world championships, they had won ten American League pennants in 12 seasons,
they had won seven World Series. But most of their success had
come during the first half of the Stengel administration; the club
had not won a series since 1958; it had just lost one to a team
rated far below it in man-to-man ability, and Professor Stengel, now
presiding over a less serene dugout, had just turned 70 years old.

Topping, puffing somewhat nervously on a cigarette, opened the
momentous meeting by reading a prepared statement that was considered a model of diplomatic, euphemistic language that the denizens of Washington might have envied.

Two years earlier, he said, Stengel had "quite reluctantly signed
a new two-year contract with the understanding that after the first
year he could retire if he desired to do so. Keeping in mind his
possible retirement, the Yankees set out to develop a program for
the eventual replacement of Casey."

Under the club's profit-sharing plan, he added, Casey would be
relieved of his burdens with "an amount exceeding $160,000 to
his credit to do with as he pleased."

As for reports that Stengel's retirement signaled a wholesale
shakeup that would also hasten the retirement of George Weiss as
general manager at the age of 65 and that would hasten the ascen-
sion of Ralph Houk as manager at 41, Topping parried the pitch.
He said merely: "We decided to let this be Casey's day."

It wasn't exactly Casey's idea of a "day," however. With evident agitation and anger, the Old Man faced the turbulent gathering of writers, broadcasters and photographers who were recording
the milestone and left no doubt that the owners had given him no
choice on forestalling "his day."

"I was told that my services no longer were desired," he said,
breaking the pattern of minced words. "Yes, sir, Mr. Topping and
Mr. Webb paid me off in full and told me my services were no
longer desired because they want to put in a youth program as an
advance way of keeping the club going. That was their excuse—the
best they've got."

He insisted that the first he had known of the impending "eventual retirement" was three days earlier, when he had met Topping
and Weiss just after the World Series had ended in Pittsburgh. Now

it was October 18, and now the "understandings" reached in the preceding 72 hours were being rapidly obscured in recriminations. The three men, according to some front-office people, had shaken hands on the timetable. But then, it was intimated, Edna Stengel had raised the family hackles and goaded Casey into resisting. In any event, he was resisting as flamboyantly as he had done everything else since arriving in the major leagues as a rookie outfielder in 1912.

"If I had been offered a new contract," he said, "I would have wanted certain changes made. I would have wanted to have known who was the boss. When Weiss was the boss, I wanted a player and he would go get him for me. They say they need a new manager for a new system and a new organization. They don't want the old way. Mr. Webb is letting Mr. Topping run the ball club. I don't want to return to an organization where I don't have the authority.

"I want to run the players on the field. I want to discharge the players and tell them who to get rid of. I want to play the players I want and not the players they want. If I manage, I must manage with full authority."

Was he suggesting that the front office had interfered with his authority?

"Just once," he replied, in a mild non sequitur. "They got rid of one player, but they got him back for me."

The inference was that the "once" involved Ralph Terry, the young right-handed pitcher who had been traded to Kansas City in 1957 but who then had been reacquired two years later—and who subsequently was traded again to Kansas City.

"When I heard their demands about this new program they were trying to build," he went on, oscillating unhappily between chagrin and righteous indignation, "I told them, 'If that's your program, gentlemen, don't worry about Mr. Stengel. He can take care of himself.' "

Could a man of 70 direct a big league team effectively?

"It depends," he said, "on what you can instill into a ball club and how you run the club. The results—a pennant in 1960—prove it."

He softened at that point to speak warmly of the team, which won the pennant by taking 15 games in a row in September just after he had returned from a brief illness. But then he bristled, noted that he would be under contract for 13 days more, until November 1, and said: "I never will return to the Yankees."

That made it unanimous. It was a little like the night the Titanic sank, since Stengel and his old idol, mentor and boss John J. McGraw had dominated—or, at least—embroiled New York baseball for 40 years since the turn of the century. And like the iceberg that punctured the Titanic, only a fraction of the penetrating mass was visible above the surface. Lurking beneath the turbulence of Casey's departure were powerful personalities—one going and one coming.

The one going was Weiss, who had helped direct Yankee affairs for a quarter of a century and who, with Stengel, had dictated them for half that time. The one coming was Ralph Houk, 41 years old and a generation younger than the Old Guard, the man whose personality was to dominate Yankee affairs on the field and in the front office in the era that was starting the day the Weiss-Stengel era was ending.

Houk was a Kansas farm boy who had entered professional baseball in 1939 in the lowest minor leagues as a catcher. Three years later he entered the Army as a private, served with great distinction for four years in the "Recon" penetration units of the Rangers, emerged as a major in 1946 and stepped up to the Yankees' highest affiliate, Kansas City. He was a competitor, but not overly productive as a batter, hitting no home runs in his major league career, and in fact going to bat only 158 times.

Later, when he failed to select Dick Stuart to the American League All-Star squad, Stuart upbraided him as a "third-string catcher." Stuart was being caustic, though his appraisal was realistic enough, since Houk lived in the shadow of the man the newspapers called "the incomparable Yogi Berra." That was true enough, too, since both had arrived on the Yankee scene at about the same time after the war. But Berra made the "big team" and stayed with it throughout the Stengel years—the only player who did so—while Houk went up and down between the Yankees and their minor league teams three times.

"My annual job," recalled Red Patterson, who was road secretary of the Yankees after the war, "was sending Ralph back to

Kansas City. Once, though, he refused to go back down unless the Yankees gave him some incentive for not quitting altogether. And he told me, 'If you think I'm kidding, here's my airline ticket home.' Sure enough, he showed me one. So the club gave him a $500 raise, and he went to Kansas City. But he came that close to leaving for good."

It was ironic, since 10 years later Houk was waiting in the wings while Stengel and Weiss, the men who had sent him "down," were going through their final acts as Yankee headliners. It became even more ironic, after he had first succeeded Stengel as manager and later Weiss as general manager, that he elevated Berra to the manager's job in 1964 and, one season later, deposed him in favor of Johnny Keane of the St. Louis Cardinals. Then, when Keane was deposed a season and a fraction later, Houk returned as field manager.

Houk's strength through all these fluctuations, obviously, was not his ability with a baseball bat or catcher's mitt, though he was respected as a player. It was, rather, his qualities of leadership, the same qualities that had made him a war hero. He was rough, blunt, decisive and sound in tactics. When the Yankees sent him to manage their club at Denver in 1955, he guided the team to third place, then to second place two years in a row, and he went on in 1957 to win the American Association playoffs and the "Little World Series" against the pennant-winner of the International League.

He came back to the Yankees in 1958 as a coach, but his reputation as a successful manager was already established. Moreover, at Denver he had managed the young Yankee prospects like Bobby Richardson and Tony Kubek, who began to struggle a bit under Stengel's demanding style of managing in the late fifties. To make the conflict decisive, Houk was receiving offers to manage other major league clubs—and was, with justification, exerting an upward pressure on the patriarch of the dugout.

The other protagonist in the situation was Weiss, who had brought Stengel to the Yankees late in 1948 and who had shielded him from pressures of this kind, especially in the later years, like 1958, when the pressures seemed to be growing irresistible. Like Houk, Weiss was a man to be reckoned with, except that he had been a man to be reckoned with for more than 40 years, since becoming the impresario of baseball in New Haven, Connecticut.

Damon Runyon, upon contemplating the memorable features of covering a Yale football game, once wrote:

> New Haven—what fond memories the name conjures—
> Elms.
> The Campus.
> More elms.
> George Weiss.

It was no exaggeration. Weiss had fashioned a career in the business side of baseball as powerfully as Stengel had fashioned his career in the artistic side of baseball, and at about the same time. He was the son of a "fancy-grocer" in New Haven and got his first job as a "front-office" man while student manager of the New Haven High School baseball team in 1912. Five years later, while still studying at Yale, he became manager and master of the New Haven Colonials, a semipro team that promptly began to make life difficult for the professional team in town, which played in the Eastern League—but never on Sunday, because of regulations on organized sports.

Weiss immediately filled the vacuum by scheduling such Sunday attractions for the Colonials as an All-Chinese team, a Bloomer Girls team, and a team led by the great Ty Cobb, who insisted on a $350 guarantee to make the side trip to New Haven from either Boston or New York, where his Detroit Tigers were similarly kept idle on Sundays. When Weiss forked over $800, Ty was impressed and came back often—with no written guarantee.

His Colonials became studded with famous athletes like Charlie Brickley and Eddie Mahan, the Harvard football heroes, and Wally Pipp, Walter Johnson and Cobb from the big leagues. Once they even defeated the Boston Red Sox, 4 to 3, with Babe Ruth playing first base for Boston in "the greatest baseball attraction ever offered New Haven fans." That was in 1916, the year Boston won the World Series, and in another exhibition Ruth pitched for the Red Sox while Cobb, playing for Weiss, nicked him for a single and double and the Colonials tied the world champions, 3 to 3. After that, evidently to forestall such spectacles—a "semipro" team defeating the best in the major leagues—the National Commission of baseball ruled that only three members of a championship team could participate in post-season exhibitions.

"In 1919," Weiss said, "the New Haven club apparently decided to stop fighting us, too. They came to me and said, 'You want to buy the club for $5,000?' I had to borrow the $5,000, but I did."

Ten years later, he moved up to the International League as general manager at Baltimore, succeeding Jack Dunn, who had died after falling from a horse. Weiss arrived in Baltimore with the Depression, and cash was becoming tight, but he sold eight players to the major leagues in three years (while Stengel was selling players to the majors from the American Association). Then, in 1932, the telephone rang and Jacob Ruppert invited him to join the Yankees.

He rose from farm director to secretary to general manager and vice president. He was voted "major league executive of the year" 10 times. He brought his old friend from the Eastern League days, Stengel, back from the Pacific Coast in 1948 to manage the Yankees. He was the power behind the greatest throne in baseball.

But now, in October 1960, the throne behind which Weiss stood was tottering. Why?

"The Yankees," commented Frank Lane, a baseball impressario himself, though a dedicated critic of the Establishment, "had one great thing during the Weiss and Stengel years: players. They had been hunted up by great scouts like Joe Devine, Bill Essick and Paul Krichell. They had built a great farm system with teams at Newark and Kansas City and Denver that were almost of big league caliber.

"But, by the nineteen-fifties, the competition was beginning to increase. The other clubs, with the postwar attendance boom and all that going, began to spend big money for young players. I was chairman of the major leagues' bonus committee in the early fifties, and we put through two bonus rules—the idea being to require a free-spending team to keep a boy who got, say, $6,000 for signing. They had to keep him on the varsity roster. But the rich teams like the Yankees weren't the ones who did the big spending. Weiss just did not believe in big bonuses.

"The Yankees had always been in a strong position with young players, anyway, and the young players would flock to the Yankee farm teams. But now the minor leagues were beginning to fade, with television cutting into their attendance, so it became harder to maintain strong minor league systems. Even then, the Yankees were slower with bonus money than the others—they simply didn't meet the competition for talent.

"To be fair about it, the Yankees not only wouldn't spend big money for bonus players, they couldn't. They couldn't afford to carry a first-year man on the roster because their roster was already loaded with professionals. The less successful teams, having less to lose than the Yankees, obviously would suffer less if they carried a few extra rookies. A few years later, when the rookies had matured, their teams wouldn't suffer at all—while the Yankees' professionals would be that much older.

"When the player draft was set up in 1964, giving the lowest teams first pick of talent, the Yankees were against that, too. But by then they had lost their monopoly on players. It's unlikely that any club will ever again dominate the game the way the Yankees did for those 12 years. They were spoiled by success."

Still, nothing succeeded like success on the playing field, and for the first half of the Weiss-Stengel term of office, the Yankees succeeded. The second half was different. Casey grew older, for one thing, and his competition was growing smarter, for another. Then he tended to become more arbitrary with younger, inexperienced players—the kind he had doted on during the first years. Then his platooning, born of necessity, had become almost a compulsion— partly because he was an all-out manager of the McGraw school and partly because he was driven to even heavier platooning as his teams inevitably lost their absolute, five-for-five touch.

Phil Rizzuto looked back years later and confessed that he "did not enjoy" playing for Stengel particularly.

"He had two tempers," the little shortstop said. "One for the public and writers, and one for the players under him. The players were frequently dressed down in the dugout and clubhouse. He could charm the shoes off you, if he wanted to, but he could also be rough. And after the first couple of seasons, he began to believe he had as much 'magic' as the newspapers said he did."

"In later years," recalled Tony Kubek, "Casey's platooning probably became rougher on the young players. He was more difficult with them then. I played five different positions before settling at shortstop, but even then I figured he platooned me less than some of the others."

Richardson described how, after his arrival from Denver in 1955, "I had my first taste of real platooning, Casey Stengel's specialty. If I started in a game, I'd be pulled out almost immediately as a pinch-hitter was sent to the plate in my stead. If I did get to bat once in a game, I was so tense that I tried too hard." Two years later, Bobby was so discouraged that he considered quitting baseball, but "Ralph Houk talked me out of it."

John Blanchard became another case of frustration, appearing in one game in 1955 (his fifth year in professional baseball), then waiting four more years before getting back to the Yankees, then playing less than a third of a season until 1961—when Houk, another frustrated catcher, became manager.

In one World Series game, Clete Boyer was removed for a pinch-hitter the first time he went to bat.

The outstanding "angry young man," though, was probably Norm Siebern, an outfielder and later a first-baseman who had led the American Association in eight categories, batting .349 with 24 home runs, before "sticking" with the Yankees in 1958. Stengel, though, tended to describe him in somewhat neutral terms —coolly, some thought—and appeared dubious of Siebern's talents. When Bob Turley went into the ninth inning one day with a no-hitter, Julio Becquer of the Washington Senators looped a fly into short left field and it fell in front of Siebern for a single. Should he have caught the ball? the manager was asked later. "Shouldn't anyone?" he asked in return. Siebern wept at the criticism. After two years on the Yankees, he was traded to Kansas City.

The ultimate in second-guessing the manager occurred after the World Series of 1960, when Stengel started Art Ditmar, who lost, instead of Whitey Ford, who later won twice—both times by shutouts. The Old Man's critics had a field day speculating on the results if Ford had been rotated into three starting assignments instead of two, and they were still speculating a week later when the 12 most splendid years came to an end at the Savoy-Hilton.

It was evident that day that even the most carping criticism could not by itself have shaken down the castle that Weiss and Stengel had built. After all, they *had* won ten pennants and seven World Series in a dozen years. But Casey *was* 70, his contract *was* expiring, the club *had* slipped a bit on the field and the Yankees *were* in danger of losing their heir apparent, Houk, to another club.

"I guess this means they fired me," Stengel said as his "day" drew to a close. "I'll never make the mistake again of being 70 years old."

"The first person to call Casey after the Yankees let him go," Edna Stengel recalled later, "was Bill Veeck, saying, 'Don't do anything until you check with me.'"

Casey did nothing, all right, despite the interest shown by Veeck, by the Kansas City Athletics, the San Francisco Giants and other baseball people. He just said, when he had calmed down, "My own plans are indefinite." Then he headed for Glendale, the swimming pool, the hacienda with its Japanese bed and Chinese room and orange bushes and tennis court out back—and the Valley National Bank.

A couple of weeks later, the decline and fall of the empire was complete. Weiss followed him into "retirement," headed for his country home in Greenwich, Connecticut, and figured he would never make the mistake of being 66 years old again, either.

So, there they sat, a continent apart. Weiss puttered around the house on Round Hill Road, made a pass or two at his hobby of handicapping horses, "played a little golf," and got in Hazel Weiss's way until she complained one day to a friend: "I married him for better or for worse, but not for lunch."

Stengel, meanwhile, was puttering around the house on Grandview Avenue, resuming his mild duties as vice president of the bank, sitting in the sun and getting in Edna's way.

"How did we pass the time?" Edna mused five years later when the question was put to her as the lady of the house. "Casey started out on January 6th with a broken back that took place in Toluca Lake while watching the completion of our second bank. It was finished the end of January, and Casey spent most of his days just watching and waiting to move into his new quarters. Then on May 4th my back also went out, a disc condition, that lasted for months all through 1961 and more. I for one spent the entire year in pain, giving baseball little thought. Matter of fact, when he turned down Detroit and other offers to manage in the majors, I was sure he would not take another baseball position."

Casey, though, was not so sure. At least, he hedged his bets, saying at the time:

"By the time the season's over, I'll know what's going to happen to myself in baseball or whether I don't want to go back into baseball. Right now, I can't tell you just what I'm going to do. I don't think I'll become an actor, although I will be interested naturally in watching baseball games. I can't just take baseball and cast it away. No, I can never do that."

George Weiss's recollection lay somewhere in between. "He couldn't make up his mind," he said later, reconstructing the mood. "My impression was that his wife was encouraging him not to return."

In February, the telephone rang in Weiss's home and he heard the voice of a New York stockbroker named Donald Grant. He had an invitation that would add a chapter to the professional life of the team of Weiss & Stengel. He was calling for Mrs. Charles Shipman Payson, nee Joan Whitney, the sister of John Hay Whitney and the matron of Manhasset, Long Island, the mistress of the Greentree Stable and a longtime, incurable New York Giant fan.

Joan Payson had been put on a collision course with Grant, Weiss and Stengel almost as soon as Walter O'Malley took the Brooklyn Dodgers west to Los Angeles and Horace C. Stoneham took the New York Giants west to San Francisco in the fall of 1957. Mayor Robert F. Wagner had decided on the spot that it was unthinkable for New York not to have a team in the National League, and he had asked his friend, William A. Shea, an energetic and successful lawyer, to start thinking about the unthinkable.

Shea tried to inveigle the Cincinnati Reds, Pittsburgh Pirates and Philadelphia Phillies to take up residence in New York. Then he enlisted Branch Rickey, the old Deacon of baseball in St. Louis, Brooklyn and Pittsburgh, to join him in forming a "third league," the Continental League.

Dwight Davis, the New York financier, had checkbook in hand as a potential angel for New York's entry in the Continental League, and he, Rickey and Shea all converged on Joan Payson as a possible partner, too. Mrs. Payson's resistance, which was not too high anyway where baseball was concerned, gave way completely when the American and National Leagues voted late in 1960 to expand from eight to ten teams each—the American League adding Minnesota and Los Angeles, and the National League adding Houston and New York.

Two strategic jobs had to be filled before New York's new

National League team could take shape: general manager and manager. For a while, Rickey himself was a prime contender for the former, and his prime candidate for the latter was Casey Stengel. However, Rickey was holding out for substantial authority to buy players by spending in the neighborhood of $5,000,000— no strings attached. Mrs. Payson, by now the grande dame of the enterprise, was dissuaded by her advisers from being too free with blank checks, so Rickey backed off—and George Weiss marched in. He had a prime candidate for manager, too, one who "drove the World Series off the front page," he said later.

"We arrived in New York," Edna Stengel related, "and were driven from the airport in a Rolls-Royce. Casey wondered about it, so I said to him: 'You're returning to baseball in New York, Casey. We might as well go first class.' "

It was the fifth time in nearly 50 years that Stengel had marched on New York: In 1912, eagerly, to join the Dodgers; in 1921, jubilantly, to become a Giant; in 1932, gratefully, to coach the Dodgers; in 1948, solemnly, to take over the Yankees, and now in October 1961, apprehensively, to direct the Mets.

The Meadowlarks, Joan Payson preferred. But the Mets they were, and by any name they would strike apprehension into the heart of even a battle-scarred manager like C.D. Stengel. The reason became clear on October 10, when the "expansion teams" stocked their rosters by selecting players from the rosters of the eight regular clubs—from the unprotected, or nonexempt, portions of their rosters, in any event. And the nonexempt players available to the Mets resembled "bargains" at a rummage sale—Hobie Landrith, a 31-year-old catcher from San Francisco was No. 1. Then things went from bad to worse. For the established fixed price of $125,000 for "outstanding" talent, the Mets selected such outstandingly mediocre players as Jay Hook, an electrical engineer, from the Cincinnati Reds; Bob Miller from the St. Louis Cardinals, Don Zimmer from the Chicago Cubs and Lee Walls from the Philadelphia Phillies.

For $75,000 apiece, they added Landrith and 15 others, mostly retreads, and for $50,000 they picked up a pitcher named Sherman (Roadblock) Jones from Cincinnati and a minor league outfielder named Jim Hickman, who had hit .249 at Portland.

The total tab was $1,800,000, an overprice of the wildest sort. And it was as something less than a conquering hero that Stengel returned to New York to take charge of the ragamuffins, Rolls-Royce or no Rolls-Royce—especially since the Yankees, under young Houk, had just made a smooth transition into the post-Stengel era by winning the smashing total of 109 games, losing only 53, winning the World Series and capturing the attention of the nation for weeks by the stirring home-run rampages of Roger Maris (61) and Mickey Mantle (54).

Stengel's mission with the Mets lay precisely astride that obvious fissure in New York baseball. On the one side, the Yankees were lords of all they surveyed—and any new team in town would inevitably live in their shadow for years, maybe decades, maybe forever. On the other side, the Mets were as inept a baseball team as the United States had ever seen—"the worst club in baseball history," said Veeck, whose credentials were unassailable, since he had once owned the St. Louis Browns.

That was the "artistic" situation, and Weiss and Stengel did not have to strain their genius to decide that they could not rival the Yankees on the field for a long time. But they could also sense the golden opportunity beyond: namely, that New York held an immense reservoir of National League interest, and that the Yankees could never draw on that reservoir, nor replace it. The year after the Dodgers and Giants left town, Yankee attendance had actually dropped—from 1,497,134 to 1,428,438. Then Maris and Mantle helped revive it in 1961, up to 1,747,736—but that was the high-water mark, and it was still half a million below the immediate postwar years.

That was the "commercial situation," and Weiss and Stengel did not have to strain their genius to decide that they *could* rival the Yankees there. And they did. They made no pretense to glory on the playing field; in fact, they made the Mets a "mirror image" of the Yankees, and they proceeded to capitalize on the image.

Where the Yankees were successful as ball players, the Mets became monumentally unsuccessful. Where the Yankees were cool cats, the Mets grew up as warm ugly ducklings. Where the Yankees were institutional, the Mets lunged into the public domain. The Yankees, on top, had everything to lose; the Mets, on bottom, had everything to gain. And they set out to gain it with those Yankee renegades, Weiss and Stengel, who discovered now that the same public that had criticized them in the later Yankee years was clamoring to adopt them in their new roles, to idolize them—to support them at the box office.

Weiss gave full credit for this support to two things: "The latent interest in the National League after the Dodgers and Giants left, and the energies and personalities of people like Casey Stengel and Mrs. Joan Payson."

Two years later, Weiss would add a third asset to this list, Shea Stadium. But for the first two years of their existence, the Mets were forced to play in the old Polo Grounds, where Stengel had played two generations earlier to the cheers of Ethel Barrymore and Al Jolson and where demolition men were waiting, along with the Mets, for the ball club to vacate the premises so that a housing development could rise on John J. McGraw's sacred acres.

The idea was that the Mets would entertain the public with a kind of Circus Maximus. The aim: to keep the people docile until times grew better. The ringleader: Casey Stengel, who would run the show by doing what had come naturally since his days of mischief-making at Western Dental College.

"Yes sir," he said, as he took charge, capturing the mood to the letter, "come see my amazin' Mets, which in some cases have played only semi-pro ball."

The Mets responded nobly. Their opening game, April 10, 1962, was a night game in St. Louis; it was rained out. As things turned out, that was the Mets' finest hour. The next night it did not rain, unfortunately, and in the first inning Roger Craig, the Mets' first starting pitcher, committed a balk with Bill White on third base and they were behind, 1 to 0, before they had even struck a blow in their own defense. Stan Musial, who was 41 and the nearest thing in age to Stengel on either team, got three hits; the Mets made three errors, the Cardinals stole three bases and scored 11 runs, and the Mets scored 4. A whole new concept in losing baseball games was unfolding before the eyes of the man who had tried to keep his sanity running the old Brooklyn Dodgers.

Then Casey packed everybody off to New York to give the big city its first look at its new baseball team. It was, appropriately, Friday the 13th. It had rained and the field was muddy. Only 12,447 people paid their way into the Polo Grounds, and after

Mayor Wagner had hoisted the first pitch toward the wet infield, the Mets unwaveringly pursued their destiny.

In the second inning, on a ground ball by Smokey Burgess of the Pittsburgh Pirates, Charley Neal made a spectacular stop at short-stop, then slipped in the mud. Don Hoak doubled to right and Bill Mazeroski hit a fly to right-center. Gus Bell crabbed to his right toward the ball, Richie Ashburn drifted to his left. Bell waved him off, Ashburn stopped short, Bell stopped short and the ball fell for a triple. Three wild pitches let in two more runs later, and the Mets lost the game, 4 to 3.

In fact, they lost nine straight and Casey began to wonder. "This sets up the possibility," he said, "of losing 162 games, which would probably be a new record, in the National League, at least." The chance for "a new record," evaporated, though, on April 23. The Mets finally won one, beating Pittsburgh, 9 to 1, and cele-brated in the clubhouse as though they had won the World Series, amidst shouts of "break up the Mets."

"We didn't start with the idea that we were going to be as bad as we were," Weiss said in July of 1966, when the team had become one of the wonders of the baseball world by climbing into ninth place after four seasons of almost unbroken tenancy of tenth place.

One reason for his chagrin was that nobody started with the idea that any team could be that bad. The Mets scored runs, all right. Ashburn hit .306 and Frank Thomas hit 34 home runs, batted in 94 runs and was struck by pitches eight times—giving him undis-puted possession of first place in offensive departments of all kinds. But the nine other teams in the league scored runs against the Mets in lavish numbers. Craig lost 24 games, allowed 35 home runs, gave up 261 hits; Alvin Jackson "led" the club in earned-run average, allowing 4.4 runs a game. The Mets won 40 games, lost 120, played before 922,530 customers at home (876,780 on the road) and began to be called "my amazin' Mets" by Stengel, who meant that he, at least, was amazed.

He may have been amazed most by the commercial success of the club despite its spectacular lack of artistic success. For, after drawing 922,530 persons in the Polo Grounds the first year, the Mets vaulted over the million mark in attendance, toward two million, and stayed there.

As Branch Rickey diagnosed the situation, the "perfect link" between the ball club and the public was Stengel.

Everything he did for the Mets, he did with fanfare. Every picture he posed for, he posed for with gusto and expressiveness. Every speech he made, he delivered with vivid "image." He emphasized the fact that the Yankees had "fired" him and that he now had been reincarnated as the Great White Father of the Amazing Mets, who were everything the Yankees weren't—warm, lovable, comically unpredictable, splendidly unsuccessful Sad Sacks.

Now, in a stunning postscript to his professional career, he returned to tie up all the loose ends of his rambling life in baseball. He brought to the Mets his sense of humor and sense of histrionics from the earliest days of his playing career, days of umbrellas, flashlights, birds-under-hats, manhole covers, grapefruit dropped from biplanes, the works. He brought his playing sense, as taught by Robinson and McGraw. He contributed his business sense from the wheeling-and-dealing days in the minor leagues. He excelled in the arts of distracting the public, arts he had polished to a dazzling shine in Brooklyn and Boston a generation earlier. The only phase of his career that went slightly against the grain was the Yankee era. But he even borrowed from that—the strategy of mass platooning and the awareness of Yankee haughtiness that now, with the Mets, became the most obvious and effective foil of all.

From the start, he skillfully blended all these strands of his life into one towering Met mountain. All roads led to my amazin' Mets. Even the name helped forge the link to the public: it was chosen in a public contest, and when Joan Payson decided that the best name submitted by the public was "Mets," somebody said, "Let's go, Mets." When a banner day was held to translate this spirit into slogans, one bright banner-maker paraded around the Polo Grounds with a lace-curtain version that said: "Let us proceed, Metropolitans."

When Stengel was placed before the public as the spirit behind this spirit, he demonstrated again the great characteristic of his 50 years in the shifting fortunes of baseball: his adaptability to disaster or success, depending on the roll of the dice. He had adapted to success with the Yankees; then to runaway disaster with the Mets. Now he was to go full cycle and convert disaster into success, or at least to make people forget about the disaster long enough for success of a sort to crystallize. He was bugged by only two things during this great public relations campaign: his age, which was a mixed blessing, and the fact that the Yankees had "fired" him after his proudest achievements. But even here, he could exploit the axiom that two minuses make a plus.

When the Mets unveiled him as their first manager, they staged the great event with a tragedian's sense of drama. They hired the same hall the Yankees had hired to dismiss him, Le Salon Bleu of the Savoy-Hilton. The date was October 2, 1961, almost a calendar year since the Yankees gave him his "day." Now the Mets were giving him another "day," and they rang up the curtain with theatrical splendor: After everybody had been seated, the Old Man entered to a standing ovation. Score: Mets-1, Yankees-0.

"My health," said the Professor, exorcising one of the chief demons at the start, and also betraying his own concern over the subject that had concerned the Yankee brass a year earlier, "my health is good enough above the shoulders, and I didn't say I'd stay fifty years or five years.

"Most people are dead at my age, and you could look it up."

Now he had sounded an echo of his parting shot at the Yankees, which had been: "I commended winning pennants when I came here but I didn't commence getting any younger."

And to demonstrate that, a year later at the age of 71, he had commenced getting younger indeed. He parlayed his unveiling on October 2 into a triumphal ride down Broadway on Thanksgiving Day in the 30-degree cold of Macy's annual parade, waving his arms to the throngs on the sidewalks as though he wished Glendale were only this splendidly warm and calling everybody to "come out and see my own amazin' Mets."

Besides Hippodrome showmanship of this personal sort, Stengel showed an incisive knowledge of the mechanics of newspaper production, and he used this knowledge to cultivate "my writers," who welcomed him with open arms as the man who had resurrected their own spirits after the Dodgers and Giants had traduced the public by leaving town.

On days when his amazing Mets were, for some reason, amazing, he simply sat back and let the writers swarm over the heroes of the diamond. On days when the Mets were less than amazing—and there were many more days like that—he stepped into the vacuum and diverted the writers' attention, and typewriters, to his own flamboyance. Then he would hold forth at interminable length with stories, anecdotes of half a century before, Uncle Robbie, McGraw and you could look it up, all in highly quotable and lovable Stengelese.

He even scheduled daily press conferences at 12 noon in spring training in order to provide sparkling copy before his team had had a chance to boot a few in practice. And he carefully distinguished between morning newspapers and evening newspapers, with the precision of the dean of the Columbia Graduate School of Journalism. He knew their various writers, requirements, even deadlines. When *The New York Times* switched its Yankee and Met writers in the middle of spring training, an event that might have gone unnoticed for at least a day or so in the commotion of the training camp, he gave it sly notice during dinner in the Fort Lauderdale airport restaurant while both groups of writers were gathered following a Yankee-Met game.

"I made a mistake there in the seventh inning," he said, with exaggerated sincerity, "and it cost us the ball game. But you see, I was upset at the time and simply blew the play. I was sitting there thinking that Mr. Durso was going to leave us after the game and Mr. Koppett was going to switch over from the Yankees, and I just forgot to give the sign for the play."

So, the perfect link to the public was formed, and it grew stronger as the team grew zanier. True, the Stengel style caused irritations in the clubhouse, as it had on the Yankees. After all, if Bobby Richardson felt nervous about making a mistake, how nervous would, say, a Marv Throneberry feel about making a mistake, especially since he had earned the nickname "Marvelous Marv" through sensational mistakes at first base? Or Charley Neal, who pounced on the first grounder of 1963 and threw it over first base for an error while Curt Flood of the Cardinals circled all the way to third base and the Mets launched an eight-game losing streak at the start of their second season? Or Roger Craig, who looked like Slim Summerville and even pitched a little like him, losing 18 straight games? Or the whole ball club, which lost 22 in a row on the road before winning?

But if the Stengel manner kept some players on edge—in the lineup one day, out the next—it also covered a multitude of sins, and that was his great service during the Mets' formative years. By the time the boys played, and lost, the final home game of 1963, the final game ever played in the Polo Grounds, they had exhibited their antics before 2,002,638 cash customers in two years and they had already succeeded the Yankees as the toast of New York.

The irritations slackened as this type of success increased, and as Stengel realized that he was managing a team with screaming limitations. At first he had expected the sophisticated maneuvers that separated the men from the boys in baseball. Then, he began to appreciate the fact that the main problem was not so much in executing the finesse as in just catching the ball. So he relented. He still platooned players wildly, but chiefly because he had to do so in order to muster the isolated talents available to him.

"You didn't see them sending up a left-handed hitter for Hornsby, did you?" he would shout during the long evenings of bourbon and soda with his writers.

He was amazed, all right, having spent 12 years with Yankee players who were Old Masters compared with his New Breed. But he grew tolerant as the hopelessness of the player situation sank in.

"He knows," said one observer, "that the kids are giving 100 per cent, but that their 100 per cent just isn't enough. So he has stopped trying to beat more out of them."

He showed one outstanding flash of his old petulance—not over an inept play in the field, but over a flip remark about his years with the Yankees. The remark was dropped during a team dinner in spring training by Duke Carmel, one of the less inept Met players, a player, in fact, with a breezy personality and a promising future as a left-handed-hitting first-baseman and outfielder. But his future with the Mets ended when he tweaked Stengel about the Yankees and how anybody could win with a team like that, right? He may have been right, but he was wrong about Casey's reaction. A few days later Carmel was shipped to the minor leagues, and although Stengel tried to rationalize the move on base-ball terms, few people in the Mets' camp doubted that Carmel had lucklessly gibed in one of the Old Man's unforgiving areas.

The Mets, meanwhile, moved from one trivial success to another. Losing eight straight games at the start of 1963, for example, was better than losing nine straight in 1962. Winning 51 games and losing 111 was better than winning 40 and losing 120. Winning four games on a 14-game road trip was better than winning three; in fact, it was a club record. Ten victories for a pitcher was better than eight, and it, too, was a club record. For a new team, of course, everything is a club record. But with Stengel providing the translation, even the molehills began to look like mountains.

So convincing was the Met mystique, and so willing to back it with cash were the customers, that the Yankees even broke tradition in 1964 in a wild attempt to counteract their new crosstown rivals. They named Yogi Berra manager, replacing Houk, who in turn was elevated to the front office as general manager. Yogi, after all, was cut from the same cloth as Stengel. He had been Casey's "assistant" manager; he was a lovable Met type, despite his great ability as a ball player; he was warm. He even won the pennant for the Yankees in the final weekend of the season, but he proved— to nobody's surprise but the Yankees'—to be no Stengel when it came to saying, doing or creating funny things, not even when reprimanding Phil Linz for playing the harmonica on the team bus. He was simply Yogi Berra. And Yankee attendance, which had dropped from 1,747,736 the year before the Mets were organized, dipped to 1,493,574 the year they took the field, and to 1,305,638 the year Yogi was installed as the "counter-agent."

The Mets, meanwhile, had moved into their resplendent new stadium that spring—Shea Stadium, just north of the World's Fair and just south of LaGuardia Airport in the parkway-studded section of Flushing, Queens. They even lost their opening game as gloriously as they had lost their previous openers. The date was April 17, 1964; the score was 4 to 3, Pittsburgh; the attendance was 50,312. And in addition to the new stadium, "which has moving stairs for the people," in Stengel's description, the Mets also had a legion of other assets and conversation pieces that far overshadowed the Yankees' best efforts at matching them.

They had one All-Star player, Ron Hunt. They had a future All-Star player, perhaps, in Ron Swoboda, a muscleman from Baltimore with the build of Li'l Abner and a Chinese step-grandfather. They had a teen-aged pitcher named Jerry Hinsley, who drank milkshakes, had never seen New York before, had thrown only to his twin brother in high school and who was instructed by his teammates to "knock down" Willie Mays the first time he ever faced the great man. Hinsley did so, sending Mays sprawling with a head-high fastball; but when Willie rocketed the next pitch off the fence in right-center for a triple, the rookie analyzed the problem like a true Met and explained: "They didn't tell me what to throw him on the *second* pitch."

They also had extra added attractions like the Astrodome in Houston, which the Mets visited three times a summer for nine games and which boasted a plastic roof 208 feet high at its apex behind second base. Stengel saw it for the first time in May 1964, as he stepped down from the Mets' bus outside the huge, circular white structure. He was impressed, having come a long way from the wooden stands in Washington Park, Brooklyn, but he also was manager of the Mets, who were in the throes of an epidemic of sky-high, futile pop flies. "Hell," he said, upon being advised that there was no danger any fly ball could reach the dome, "I got four guys on this club right now who could pop it straight up to the roof."

The Mets also had the added attraction of a National League pennant race that was even more sensational than the American League race that Berra was winning, and they were soon to play prominent roles in it. Six teams all had shots at winning, even though the Philadelphia Phillies held a 7½-game lead with only two weeks to go and then began printing World Series tickets. In fact, they distributed the first batch after losing two straight to Cincinnati in the next-to-last week of the season. That evening they made it three straight. Then Cincinnati went to New York and knocked over the Mets five times in one weekend while the Phillies kept losing to Milwaukee.

By the time the Mets had reached St. Louis a week later, with three games to go, the Cardinals, Phillies and Reds were tangled in a free-for-all, and while the Reds were playing the Phillies in Cincinnati that weekend, the Cards were host to the Mets.

Johnny Keane, who was then manager of the Cardinals but who was about to switch to the Yankees right after the World Series in a spectacular rotation of managers, watched Al Jackson shackle his Cardinals, 1 to 0, that first night, defeating the Cardinal ace Bob Gibson.

"In the runway under the grandstand after the game," Keane recalled, "I ran into Casey. We had two games left to play, and the pennant was at stake. He shook his head at me, and just said: 'You've got a job to do.' "

The Mets won the next day, too, and were leading as late as the fifth inning of the final game of the season on Sunday, October 4. Then the tide receded, the Cardinals rallied, the Reds ironically blew their game in Cincinnati to the Phillies (who had lost 10 straight while blowing the pennant themselves) and St. Louis snatched the pennant.

But hours later, the Old Man, his hair neatly combed to the side, sat in the lobby of the Chase Hotel in St. Louis, surrounded by well-wishers who had just seen him nearly score the coup of the decade. He sat politely charming a circle of nuns who gathered round him on a stone bench, presenting autograph books on behalf of their school children back home, giggling "Oh, Mr. Stengel," at his tall tales and beaming as he orated with complete satisfaction on the feats of "my amazin' Mets."

The amazin' Mets, despite all their heroics in St. Louis, still finished last—for the third straight year. But they were the most successful last-place team in baseball history, and the "perfect link" to their public was secure.

"Since Khrushchev was fired," wrote Russell Baker on the editorial page of *The New York Times*, borrowing the "perfect link" to dramatize a point in geopolitics, "the Reds have had the same problem the New York Yankees had after firing Casey Stengel. Fan interest has sagged, and the players seem more interested in playing the harmonica than in helping the Reds win the moon and the World Series."

10

KANKAKEE TO COOPERSTOWN

Jesse Owens ran, Yogi Berra batted and Warren Spahn threw baseballs in the bright sunshine of February 27 in St. Petersburg, Florida, as the New York Mets opened their fourth spring training circus while Charles Dillon Stengel stood like a ringmaster behind home plate bellowing: "Yes sir, come see the amazin' Mets."

There was something for everybody as Stengel started his 55th —and last—year in a baseball uniform that resplendent day in 1965. And it was difficult to tell who was more impressed by the staff of celebrities crowded around the Old Man in baseball knickers with "New York" embroidered across the chest and "37" across the back of the shirt—the 1,000 persons who crowded the small, wooden grandstand of Huggins-Stengel Field or the 21 young pitchers and catchers who staged the first workout of the season.

They all followed the all-star coaching staff through three hours of exercise and batting practice on a magnificently sunny day with the temperature rising to 65 degrees and a light wind blowing across Crescent Lake beyond the palm trees past the centerfield fence.

No banners were unfurled. But wild ovations greeted Professor Stengel as he crossed the infield to open the festivities. And cheers were sounded when Berra, deposed as manager of the Yankees four months earlier, opened his career with the Mets by donning a catcher's mitt to warm up a 19-year-old pitcher.

172

The 26 players on hand ranged from Mike Buist, who was 17 years old and 57 years younger than Stengel, to Spahn, who was 43 and who had won 108 games in the major leagues before Buist went to kindergarten.

Stengel started the day with an administrative announcement: After conducting two workouts a day all during his career, he would hold just one a day for the 1965 Mets. His reasons were appropriately vague.

"We had a meeting," he said, "and Mr. Spahn was for one workout, and we had two men who had amazing records with the Yankees and one of them preferred one workout and the other two. I was for one or two."

"And the consensus," he added in one of the charging non sequiturs that had made him pre-eminent as a 20th century logician, "was for one."

When this matter had been settled, Casey turned his New Breed over to Owens, who was 51 years old, who weighed 14 pounds more than his Olympic weight of 165 and who was listed on the roster as "track coach" but who described himself as "the Drillmaster."

Promptly at 10 A.M. the great sprinter took his post at the head of Stengel's young army, wearing white sneakers and a gray sweatshirt with "Ohio State Athletic Department" printed in bright red letters across the front. Then, just 29 years after he had won four track-and-field gold medals in the Olympics, he led the Mets, who had never won anything but wealth and fame, through one lap around the field. He finished a solid first.

This was followed by "bicycle" leg exercises, body bends, push-ups and sprints, and Jesse, who ran the 100-yard dash in high school in 9.4 seconds, commented that he would be pleased if his charges ran it in 11 seconds or less. "They enjoyed it very much," he said, without confirmation, after 25 minutes. "I even had old Spahn running."

He then turned the squad back to Stengel, who watched every pitcher throw five minutes of batting practice while the deputies on the Professor's staff conducted fielding, pitching and bunting drills around the fringes of the field to the delight of the fans, who feasted on a kaleidoscope of celebrity baseball. On one practice field they could see Berra, who a year earlier had been managing the lordly Yankees, still wearing his familiar No. 8; Spahn, the greatest left-handed pitcher of modern times, his $70,000 contract still unsigned but nevertheless flashing his famous No. 21; Eddie Stanky, No. 54, the onetime "brat" of the old Giants, living up to his new title of director of player development by directing his players in the art of stopping ground balls. And, at the center of the whirlwind stood Casey Stengel, who had first gone south for training one spring when William Howard Taft lived in the White House.

Now, he was starting his last spring training, though none of the people watching, nor his celebrated coaches, nor the teen-aged Mets realized it. For that matter, *any* season in the previous 30 might have been the "last," a decision being dictated by the lure of oil money, wayward taxicabs in Boston, the pressure of life with the Yankees, or simply old age. But constitutionally, emotionally, compulsively, like Sarah Bernhardt, he had resisted. And while each season might have been "the last," each season seemed to lead into yet another.

The previous September, Edna Stengel had shown friends through her house full of treasures in Glendale, the rows of tumblers and old-fashioned glasses inscribed with the red, white and blue Yankee emblem and top hat, the gilded World Series Louisville Slugger bats, the pennant rings and championship ash trays, the ceremonial sword bestowed by Dan Topping. And she had said, in a kind of whisper: "Whether this is the last year or we go on, it's been worth it."

A few days later, Casey popped up at a press conference to announce that he had signed for another year as manager of the Mets at an increase in pay and, dressed brilliantly in a suit of expensive Italian silk, said slyly: "I have a one-year contract, as I've always had with the Mets, and an increase in pay which makes me very happy that they would want to give it to me. It was a very splendid raise. I believe I can use it—this suit's a little old. I might get a new wardrobe."

Then he hopped off to the airport, climbed aboard a jet bound for Milwaukee and rejoined his players for the final week of the season, while Branch Rickey was saying in St. Louis that here was the perfect link between the club and the public.

Stengel at 74 ranked somewhere between the Pied Piper and Santa Claus, and once shorn of the pressures and second-guesses of the Yankee years, the public followed him almost blindly as the Mets bungled along magnificently.

He somehow made everybody identify with the human failings exhibited so relentlessly by the Mets. There but for the grace of God go I. Everybody a frustrated shortstop, like the Mets' shortstop; or a catcher who could not catch the Dodgers when they ran the bases. Everybody a ringmaster, a grandstand manager —even as everybody in St. Louis had been, during Veeck's promotional bomb bursts in the early fifties, when the St. Louis Browns followed strategy dictated by a whole grandstand full of managers. "Grandstand managers' day," it was called, and decisions would be made according to the response of the crowd to large signs hoisted at critical moments during the game, asking: "Infield in—or out?" and "Should we walk him?" The crowd would signify its choice by applause, while a municipal judge sat on the dugout roof in a rocking chair to determine the mob's wishes and old Connie Mack sat grandly in the stands to lend dignity to the occasion.

True, one of Veeck's pitchers, Ned Garver, refused once to pitch with the infield drawn in, as the mass strategy had dictated, but Veeck's assistant, Bob Fishel, got busy on a megaphone and influenced the crowd to reverse its signals. The Browns won the game, 1 to 0, and grandstand managing never had a more glorious day—until Stengel forged the link between the customers and his floundering Mets a decade later.

Casey had the spear-carriers for such an Everyman drama, too.

Take Choo-Choo Coleman, a stumpy, silent, friendly little sign-painter whose real name was Clarence, which may account for the Choo-Choo. He would peer out of the team bus as it wound through Florida's back roads during spring training, recall that he had been paid $1.50 an hour for lettering signs by hand, point triumphantly out the window at a roadside sign advertising a nearby beanery and shout: "There's one, there's one." Ever since the Mets had paid Philadelphia $75,000 for Choo-Choo in the expansion draft, he had astonished people by his lack of any other classical abilities, except maybe his ability to hug the ground lower than any catcher in baseball, crouching close to the dirt behind the bat, diving into the dust to trap balls and in general just making the play by fighting it into the ground. He spent most of his time in the minor leagues, despite his splendidly childlike disposition and an occasional home run—both of which made him a conquering hero to the Mets' public—and then one day, more in wonder than in anger, said: "Mr. Murphy said he was sending me to Buffalo to get in shape." But, added Choo-Choo a trifle impatiently, "that was two years ago."

Boy, was he in shape. Another spear-carrier in the cast was Danny Napoleon, a rookie outfielder who shuttled between New York and way stations like Buffalo while Johnny Murphy, vice president of the Mets, tried to assemble 25 able bodies for Professor Stengel's roster. One day Napoleon ended a long cat-and-mouse chase between the Mets and San Francisco Giants by pinch-hitting a triple that won the game. Stengel led the parade of Mets into the clubhouse, threw his hands straight up into the air and shouted, in praise of Danny Napoleon: "Vive la France!" Then, having astonished everyone by even this meager burst of French, he rendered a typically far-fetched association by adding quickly: "We been giving him so much publicity, De Gaulle oughta give us a free trip to Paris."

When Shea Stadium opened on Friday, April 17, 1964, Stengel sat at the center of his whirlwind as usual, basking in his new diggings, amazed that 50,312 persons had joined in the great occasion, impressed that the Traffic Commissioner of New York, Henry A. Barnes, was circling the field in a helicopter trying to untangle the traffic swarms, pleased that an immense horseshoe of flowers had been delivered to the dugout before the game, distressed that the first hit in the new ball park was a home run by Wilver Dornel Stargell of Earlsboro, Oklahoma, better known as Willie Stargell of the Pittsburgh Pirates—and depleted by the fact that the first game in the new stadium was lost by his Mets, 4 to 3, in the ninth inning.

Casey had now had key roles in opening Ebbets Field, Yankee Stadium and Shea Stadium and in closing the Polo Grounds. But could any of that have prepared him for the home stretch—improbable days like May 27, 1964, when the amazing Mets amazed even him?

They shook off the inhibitions of two years in the cellar of the National League and 20 straight scoreless innings, rattled the ivy-covered walls of Wrigley Field with 17 singles, three doubles, two triples and one home run and disintegrated the Chicago Cubs, 19 to 1.

Nor could it have prepared him for what happened the following day, when Cinderella turned into a pumpkin and the Cubs disintegrated the Mets, 7 to 1.

Nor could any of the preceding have prepared him and his public for what happened three days later back in Shea Stadium: a 10-hour, 23-minute doubleheader with San Francisco that included one nine-inning game and one 23-inning game that required 7 hours and 23 minutes to decide. No major league teams had ever played more baseball in one day in history (Gaylord Perry of the Giants pitched 10 straight innings in relief). The Mets even made a triple play but, having kept their 74-year-old manager on the bench from 1 P.M. until 11:25, to say nothing of stragglers in the crowd of 57,037, they not only set endurance records but also set futility records. They lost both games.

Nor could it have prepared him for the remarkable fact that one of his troops, Ed Kranepool, had played both halves of a doubleheader for the Mets' farm club at Buffalo the day before, then, having been summoned to rejoin the parent team, played both halves of the doubleheader against the Giants—50 innings in two days, at the age of 20.

Nor could it have prepared him for the day his boys led the St. Louis Cardinals by five runs going into the ninth and trailed them by one run going out of the ninth. Nor for the day his pitcher, catcher and third-baseman carefully followed a bunt up the third-base line, watching to see if it would roll foul (it didn't) while Maury Wills, who had been on third base, raced past the dedicated group and crossed the unprotected plate. Nor for the day his pitcher had only one man to get out in the ninth inning to defeat the San Francisco Giants, but that man was Willie Mays, who hit a home run, and then the game didn't end until the 16th—when Jim Davenport hit another home run to win it for San Francisco.

A man made of less stern stuff might have quit the whole farce to tend his ulcers or avocados, or might have slashed his wrists or simply flipped his lid. No 37 did none of these things. But he began to show, as his 75th birthday approached, a susceptibility to other disasters than the ones perpetrated by his amazing Mets.

On May 10, 1965, he shepherded his wards to the United States Military Academy for an exhibition game against Army, and before the day was over West Point became Phase I of the Old Man's Waterloo. He was walking down a ramp from the cadet gymnasium to enter the team bus for the trip to the playing field when his feet slipped out from under him and he slid heavily along the cement. His right wrist was broken.

However, he returned to the dugout a few days later, wrist in sling, and resumed his role in the eye of the hurricane. Then, on Sunday afternoon, July 25, five days before his 75th birthday, came the deluge.

The sound of 39,288 voices singing "Happy birthday, dear Casey," wafted over Shea Stadium that sunny day as the Mets and Philadelphia Phillies gathered to salute the Professor's diamond jubilee and, almost incidentally, to play a doubleheader. The Phillies were in fifth place, six and a half games out of first place; the Mets were in last place, 24 games out of first place. The guest of honor was in Roosevelt Hospital with a fractured left hip, facing an operation and three weeks of hospitalization, and watching on television as the crowd roared its birthday tribute in a ceremony marked by a message from President Johnson, 35,000 small birthday cakes, one 250-pound cake shaped like the stadium and a serenade by a 60-piece band.

He had arrived in front of the hospital television set by a circuitous route that had started in the Essex House the evening before.

He had gone south seven blocks to Toots Shor's emporium, had joined 38 "old-timers" from the New York Giants and Brooklyn Dodgers for one of the midsummer Old-Timers Day frolics, had had the time of his life jousting with Frank Frisch and other cronies from the good old days, had slipped in the washroom as the clock slipped past midnight, had been trundled into a car and had been driven to a house at 112 Malba Drive in Whitestone, Queens. The car and the house belonged to Joseph J. DeGregorio, controller of the Mets, and the logic behind the drive just after 2 A.M. had been this: Though the Essex House was only a few minutes from Shor's, Casey would be alone there in his suite (Edna being in Glendale), and he would be in better position to make his own birthday party if he spent what was left of the night at DeGregorio's, eight minutes from Shea Stadium.

If the logic was a bit twisted, it became apparent early in the morning that so was Casey's left hip. He awoke about 8 A.M. and complained of severe pains. The call went out to Gus Mauch, who also lived in Queens, and the onetime masseur and therapist to George Bernard Shaw and Admiral Richard E. Byrd took one look at his old friend and decided he had a problem.

"I'd never seen Casey in such pain in all the years I'd been with him," the trainer said. "I knew it was more than just a muscle spasm."

He telephoned the Mets' surgeon, Dr. Peter LaMotte, who piloted his Lincoln Continental at a low altitude from his home in New Rochelle, across the Whitestone Bridge, and who made a preliminary diagnosis of a "twisted left hip." He then called for an ambulance from Roosevelt Hospital, and while they were waiting, a statement was drafted for the 39,288 birthday guests eight minutes away in Shea Stadium. It was signed by Casey and it said:

"I know I can't make it to the stadium today. I do feel sorry for all those people who went to all that trouble for my birthday."

When the first bulletin relating his accident was flashed on the electric scoreboard in right field during the second inning of the first game, all those people groaned. They were kept posted by electric messages as the X-ray report and later diagnosis were relayed from Dr. LaMotte, and the twisted left hip became a fractured left hip.

There was a bit of a scramble behind the scenes to account for the debacle in reasonably solemn, yet honorable terms. After all, some people would raise an eyebrow over that old-timers' party. Others would suspect a heart condition or stroke, considering the patient's age and the references to pain along his left side. But whatever, any time a 75th birthday party is stood up because the guest of honor has broken his hip, it's an occasion that can't be glossed over.

Accordingly, the word was duly passed after the kind of pause that precedes unhappy news in, say, the Kremlin, that Casey had twisted his hip getting out of the car at DeGregorio's home. The medical relationship between that slip and the one in Shor's has never been established, but either one might have fractured the hip of an ordinary 75-year-old and it did not seem unusual that it would require two such falls to break the hip of an extraordinary 75-year-old.

In any event, with a broken right wrist and a broken left hip within 10 weeks' time, it was becoming evident that baseball had become a hazardous profession for the Old Man—especially since he went up and down those dugout steps so many times a day just to change pitchers.

President Johnson, who had drawn his message of greeting before the great fall, had nevertheless framed it in words that could have held up under almost any set of circumstances, and they did. "I want to join with your thousands of friends," he said, "in celebrating Casey Stengel Day and commemorating your 75th birthday. Your recent accomplishments have been a source of admiration to all and you have been a living example to citizens of all ages of human vitality and achievement."

Three of Casey's lieutenants accepted the honors for him—Yogi Berra, Don Heffner and Wes Westrum, who was designated "acting manager." Miss St. Petersburg of 1965 presented a plaque. Everybody stood and sang "Happy birthday, dear Casey." George Weiss reported, after visiting the hospital, that Casey seemed "fairly alert and reconciled to the situation, and he thought something was wrong after stepping out of the car." The Mets won the first game, 8 to 1, with the help of an error, then lost the second game, 3 to 1, after returning the favor by contributing an error at a critical moment. And then they prepared to leave for Chicago without the familiar stooped figure wearing uniform No. 37 whom they had followed around like the children of Hamelin following the Pied Piper since they were organized four years earlier.

The next day, Westrum was named "interim manager," the "interim" referring respectfully to the interim between Casey's accident and the day of decision on his future. The club went west and promptly lost a game in the 12th inning when Ron Santo of the Cubs hit a home run minutes after the umpires had announced that the 12th inning was to be the last inning, win, lose or draw. So the Mets, at least, were not rocking the boat.

That night Edna flew in from California, and when I met her at Kennedy Airport she was tired, tense and concerned. She had not been feeling well herself because of an eye infection, but now she postponed her own aches and pains and went straight to the hospital, where Casey already was under heavy sedation. The flood of fan mail that she tackled every day was about to be multiplied, as thousands of messages poured into the room on the 11th floor where the former king of the Grumblers lay with a broken hip.

Early the following morning, July 27, "more nervous" than Edna had ever seen him, Casey was wheeled into the operating room, where Dr. LaMotte led a four-man team through a 45-minute operation termed a ball prothesis. A metal ball, about the size of a plum, was fixed on top of the femur, or thigh bone, at the point where the femur fits into the socket of the pelvis. Then the femur was supposed to perform its customary ball-and-socket movements.

"Knowing the kind of guy Casey is," Dr. LaMotte said, "he'll probably want to be up and around as quickly as possible, and in consideration of his age, I thought this was the best procedure."

"Does he have all his bones?" Edna asked. Then she followed the caravan to his room, noting that he was still drowsy from the anesthesia, cooing softly to him to "go to sleep," and being somewhat surprised when he opened his eyes and said firmly: "Bring me some toothpaste."

Eleven days later, the Mets were careening along under Westrum, a onetime catcher for the Giants whose only managing experience in 25 years of baseball had been with an Army disciplinary barracks at Greenhaven, New York, during the war—tough-to-handle cases, ideal experience for a future manager of the amazing Mets.

Stengel, that day, tastefully dressed in a yellow kimono, held his first post-operative press conference and demonstrated that his fractured hip and fractured English were almost as good as new. In the course of a 45-minute session at the hospital, now 75 years and one week old, he made several things exceptionally clear—for him. He said that he expected to leave the hospital in four or five days, that he did not know if he would return to the dugout that season and that he would not know about the following season until after the current one had ended. "I am the manager of this ball club," he said, a bit testily, as though insuring his franchise, as he had during the late Yankee years, too.

He also made several things exceptionally unclear, but that was interpreted as a sign that he was rapidly returning to normal. He started by unlimbering his favorite adjectives, like "terrific" and "extraordinary." Then, alluding to the platform, blackboard, lectern, overhead lights and "briefing" atmosphere of the conference room, he said: "I thought this was the space program here."

He demonstrated how he maneuvered around the hospital corridors leaning on a tubular stroller known as a walkerette. He even lifted his kimono daintily and showed the 22 stitches in his left hip. He did not dispute a suggestion that they formed a "crescent," though it also was suggested that a more appropriate Met description might be a "boomerang."

He agreed that with the aid of the walkerette he might make it from the dugout to the mound to relieve a pitcher, but when asked if he could do without the stroller, he replied with flawless logic: "If I walk without that thing, I wouldn't need it."

He expressed astonishment at the medical technique used in his operation, saying: "I found out that there's more people alive than me with a steel ball in their leg. Why, I'll walk down the street with that wheel in there. The wheel's working, too."

Then Casey, who was still being called "Doctor" by his close friends in spite of the fact that he now was the patient, also made the following declarations, again displaying his short temper with suggestions that 75 might be a ripe old age for a baseball manager:

• Would he return to managing the Mets that season? "I couldn't tell you," he said flatly.

• Would he be back in 1966? "I always sign a one-year contract with Mr. Weiss, and when the season is over I'll go in and talk with him."

• Had he been watching the Mets' games on television? "Every one of them. Last night it gave me a pain, though. I thought the club was very well run down there in Philadelphia. I thought five or six of them looked very alert."

• What was wrong with the team? "The trouble is, how can you get it better offensively and how can you get it better defensively. I don't know how they're going to straighten it out. I would like somebody to find out how many men were claimed by this ball club and we didn't get them. I'd say outside of two men, we didn't get them. And they say we need you nice fellows to stay in business."

That was a thrust at other teams in the league who had foiled the Mets just when they had been about to claim or draft players, and at the other teams' pious protestations that they needed the Mets and other new clubs to stay in business. He was taking maximum advantage of his convalescence to assume a pose of righteous outrage, and he fired a parting shot when asked whether he had been consulted about sending Danny Napoleon to the minor leagues earlier in the week.

"They've talked to me ever since I've been in this job," he said, irritated. "I'm still the manager of this club."

Three weeks later, that statement stopped being true. Flanked by Joan Payson, Donald Grant, George Weiss, Wes Westrum and Edna, he stepped before microphones on a small dais in the Essex House and said: "If I can't run out there and take a pitcher out, I'm not capable of continuing as manager." And so he formally handed the reins over to Westrum, ended 55 years in a baseball uniform, accepted the title of vice president of the Mets for West Coast operations and became, in Arthur Koestler's words describing a more profound passing, a shrug on the wave of eternity.

But he became a shrug that threatened to outlast the wave of eternity. He had been psyched and brain-washed and almost conned into accepting retirement as a medical necessity, when the Mets' upper echelons prevailed upon the one man, perhaps, who could make such a decision stick—Dr. LaMotte. Now, Dr. LaMotte happened to believe professionally that Casey could no longer manage a baseball team because of the hardships of airplane travel and the movement around stadiums, to say nothing of going out to the mound to change pitchers, as Casey himself had described the hardship in bread-and-butter terms. But he still believed that transmitting this belief to a man as rock-solid as Casey Stengel was not going to be child's play. In a sense, as unfortunate as the whole incident was, it probably spared the Mets' directors a scene with at least some of the rancor that the Yankee directors had provoked five years earlier. Sooner or later, someone would have to decide that Bernhardt had taken her last bow and that somebody had better work up the gumption to notify Bernhardt. Now the issue was transcended by a fractured hip, and the "somebody" was an orthopedic surgeon whom Casey respected. The deed was done.

That still left Casey in complete command of his vocal and theatrical gifts, even if he would have to find a new platform for displaying them. But that was the least of his problems.

On September 2, he made his farewell to the troops at Shea Stadium. He walked out to the pitcher's mound, looked around at the empty seats, posed for numerous pictures, hobbled on a crooked black cane that he had adopted, followed Edna inside as she carried his No. 37 uniform shirt to be enclosed in a glass case in the stadium ("like a mummy," he decided), and made a valedictory to the players in which he told them that "if you keep on, you can be here four or ten years."

Then, on behalf of the players, Galen Cisco mixed a couple of metaphors as neatly as the Old Man, saying he hoped some of the manager's greatness had rubbed off on the team and that "you got us off the ground and I think we can go on."

"I'd like to say one thing," Casey said later, slightly astonished at the phrasing. "That Cisco from Ohio State University seems to have picked up some Stengelese along the way."

Then, he was gone. He faded from the scene of some of his greatest triumphs and some of the Mets' greatest failures, and left. And even in the simple act of leaving town, he went fiction one better. He stopped off in Kansas City for a few days to visit and commiserate with his sister Louise, who was 78 years old and who had just fallen and broken her hip, too.

There were some who predicted that Stengel would wither on the vine in retirement, like some great Prometheus bound to a swimming pool and silent rows of orange and lemon trees after half a century in the front trenches. But five months later, he returned to New York for the first time since his swan song and he could not have created a bigger splash if he had waded ashore at the Battery.

In one sweeping return to form, he re-anointed his successor, Westrum; promised not to haunt Shea Stadium as a second-guesser; expressed doubt that the Mets were on the verge of amazing success; supported the idea of switching Mickey Mantle to first base from the outfield; disclosed that the Yankees and Boston Red Sox once had considered swapping Joe DiMaggio for Ted Williams, and agreed that the worst thing about baseball was that the games were too long. On the last point, he agreed that he had been one of the chief offenders. But, laying aside his two stainless-steel crutches and his one black night-time cane ("which I wear to black-tie affairs"), he noted the following extenuating circumstances:

"You have to have relief pitchers nowadays, and sometimes the other club'd get five runs on us with two outs. So I'd have to go out a couple of times in one inning to change pitchers, and how many guys can pitch nine innings today, anyway?"

Having clarified that point, the Professor rambled on for two hours from "the year I won 103 games with the Yankees and still blew the pennant" to Jim Hickman's chances of playing center field for the Mets in 1966. Casey conducted his rambling tour of baseball in the living room of his suite at the Essex House. He did not ramble far on foot, however, because he had been over-exerting himself and his recovery had been somewhat slowed. But he was clearly beginning to enjoy his new role as elder statesman, though it was still a subject of speculation how well he would adjust a month later when spring training would begin to stir the juices.

Anyway, he still had enough of the old Stengel range to fly East for four sports dinners that week and then to head back to the Coast with Edna to open the new building for the Valley National Bank, C.D. Stengel, vice president.

"Don't let anybody say I'm going to manage the club," he said, nodding toward Westrum, who sat alongside, trying to make a gracious adjustment of his own. "I don't want anybody in this city to think I'm going to come in here and tell this man, 'I told you so.' If he asks me for some advice, I'll give it to him."

Then, he flashed his old form as master of the shattered syntax, using Larry Bearnarth as a case in point.

"Now you take Bearnarth," he said, apropos of nothing in particular. "When I was running this here ball club, I was too enthusiastic about Bearnarth. When I saw him at the Polo Grounds the first year, he could do eight or nine things and I said he can pitch in the big leagues. Then he commenced pitching too fast, and some men are amazing that way, but how can you be a starting pitcher that way? We're not talking about Koufax now, and besides he's got Perranoski."

"I was very disappointed," he went on, switching abruptly to his own medical stance. "I was doin' all right with the leg, and I got letters from all over the world, people telling me about their aches and pains. It was very sad."

"Then I tried to do too much," he said, not fully convincing anybody, "and set myself back."

Casey's next, and ultimate, challenge as one of the supposedly content Medicare set among the nation's "aging," came after the Mets had descended on St. Petersburg for their fifth spring training season—their first under another ringmaster. He showed a delicate sense of the occasion—in reverse, for a lifelong spotlight-stealer of his talent. He even gave Westrum a head start.

The "interim" "acting" manager, now the resident manager, arrived late in February and marshaled his men, including some established players like Ken Boyer and Dick Stuart, whom the Mets had bought since the change of command.

Then, one week after Westrum had hung out his shingle, Boyer bounded onto the little porch of the Mets' clubhouse at noon on March 4, glanced at the swarm of persons crowding around the old man with the cane and said: "You'd almost think Casey was in town."

Casey was in town. He had arrived by jet from California a dozen hours earlier, had almost got out of the house in a sports shirt, but then had been forced to change his "uniform" because Edna didn't think he should attend the races later in casual attire.

So then, dressed splendidly in maroon sports coat, dark slacks, white shirt and red tie, and carrying the black, crooked cane, he stood on the porch at Huggins-Stengel Field, held court and saw his amazing Mets for the first time in 1966 in the post-Stengel era.

"This club's got a chance to move," he said approvingly, with no trace of envy or resentment at his spot on the sidelines. "These fellows aren't as green as when I had them. You won 50 games last year, didn't you? Then why didn't you win 60? That's what I'd like to know."

Could the Mets go all the way from last place to the first division, as suggested by Westrum when he got the show on the road without help from the Great White Father?

"I saw it happen once," the Great White Father replied, reaching back a cool half-century to George Stallings's Boston Braves of 1914, who were last in July and still won the pennant and World Series. "That Boston club did it, but they had three pitchers that couldn't do nothing but win ball games."

"He's got a good power man at first base and a young man at first base, and they got the same problem in Los Angeles," he said, switching abruptly to Westrum, Stuart, Ed Kranepool and the Dodgers, in that order.

"He's got Scheffing, who knows about catching, and he's got Berra and he's got himself, which was fairly skilled for several clubs," he continued, ringing in Westrum, Bob Scheffing, Yogi Berra, and Westrum again. "And he got the best prospect from Los Angeles, too."

Now the subject was catching, the Mets' No. 1 problem at the moment, and the "best prospect" was 20-year-old Greg Goossen.

"The last coaches were terrific men," the Professor went on, starting a new paragraph on the coaching situation and saluting Don Heffner and Eddie Stanky, who left to manage the Cincinnati Reds and Chicago White Sox. "Two of them got employed running other clubs; three, counting our man. And now, can you fulfill the job?

"Now you got Virdon, a splendid high-class fella, and there's got to be something wrong with the outfield which he can help those young men. And his roommate at Pittsburgh was Groat, and they beat us out of the World Series and I got discharged."

Having thus covered Bill Virdon, the Mets' new manager at Williamsport, and Dick Groat, who helped beat the Yankees in 1960, the Professor switched back to the Mets, who were running onto the porch one by one, shaking hands and greeting their 75-year-old skipper emeritus with "Hello, Mr. Stengel," and "How you feeling, Casey?"

"McGraw," he said, meaning Tug McGraw, the young left-hander, "has got the earmarks of a splendid big league pitcher. When he's got 2-and-2 on the batter, you might get a foul off him. And having Stuart around would make Kranepool a better ball player, because Stuart bats in 90 runs and Kranepool is only 21 but you don't see him racing around the bases, do you?"

Westrum trotted over, posed affectionately with his predecessor and heard the Professor's final verdict on the 1966 Mets.

"And so," Casey concluded, "the youth got older guys playing in front of them, and that ain't bad."

Later, driving out to the Florida Downs racetrack, he summarized the overall situation.

"They say Koufax ain't signed and Drysdale ain't signed," he said, "and they done fairly splendid last year. And I'm supposed to know all about the English language and baseball and politics, but now all they want is a picture of this here cane."

"Yes, sir, these people down here want to put me in Sarasota," he said, referring to the Circus Hall of Fame. "But you can't get into the Baseball Hall of Fame unless you limp."

And four days later, that's exactly how he did get in. Leaning on the crooked black cane and wearing a shiny blue New York Mets' cap, he unexpectedly limped into the Hall of Fame—the 104th person elected and only the second elected on a special ballot after an extraordinary poll conducted quietly by mail during the previous month.

The secret had been kept even from Casey, in spite of a furor raised because the rules at Cooperstown required a waiting period of five years after a candidate had retired. The idea was to avoid hasty installations based on fervor, passion or enthusiasm, and to allow a respectable time for the eyes of "history" to grow accustomed to the light. But the Baseball Writers Association of America had petitioned the Hall of Fame to waive or ease the rule for Stengel, and the hall had acceded.

The next problem was to get the Professor into position for the announcement without letting the cat out of the bag. The ruse was elaborately staged.

Casey was roused at 5:30 on the morning of March 8 to attend a civic breakfast for the members of the Mets and St. Louis Cardinals, who also trained in St. Petersburg, and Edna recalled that as she combed his slightly tinted reddish gray hair over to the side he had groused mildly about wearing the same suit and shirt he had worn the night before. But she had—innocently, she insisted—pointed out that he had worn them only to dinner in the Colonial Inn and that they would be perfectly neat. So he stepped into the morning sunshine and declared in the first of four speeches he was to make that day that "this club is going to get out of 10th place and go very far upward."

When he was driven out to the ball park several hours later, the car radio was kept silent to avoid any unforeseen leak of the big news to come. He and Edna had been told that they were to make a presentation to Weiss and Westrum, and Casey even rehearsed a little speech en route about what a smart man Weiss was, with that Yale education and all.

When they pulled into the gravel parking lot at Huggins-Stengel

Field and walked over onto the grass in foul territory in right field, alongside the clubhouse porch, a spray of red carnations was handed to Edna, ostensibly for her to present to Joan Payson, who in fact was at her home on the east coast of Florida. Ford Frick, who had recently retired as Commissioner of Baseball in favor of William Dole Eckert, a former lieutenant general of the Air Force and a man widely teased as baseball's "Unknown Soldier," stepped before the gathering of newsmen and club officials and said into a cluster of microphones, as Casey stood by to deliver his "Weiss speech";

"We have had a special election and Charles Dillon Stengel was unanimously elected to the Hall of Fame."

The announcement touched off one of the most clamorous scenes since major league baseball teams had begun training on the west coast of Florida 53 years earlier. Edna, still carrying the immense spray of flowers, began to cry and leaned over and kissed Casey on the cheek.

He had just responded to Frick's announcement by saying "Thank you, very much," and now he turned toward Edna and said, in the same tone of acknowledgment as she planted the kiss: "Thank *you*, very much."

Eckert, who had been advised of the election only 24 hours before, shook Casey's hand and expressed cheer for "a great day."

Weiss wrung his old friend's hand and agreed that this was what he had had in mind in December when he had urged the Hall of Fame to "let him smell the flowers now."

"I guess," Casey finally said into the microphones, "I should say a thousand things. Being elected into the Hall of Fame is an amazing thing, and there are so many men which are skilled in various ways. So many noted men have got into the Hall of Fame and I think it's a terrific thing to get in while you're still alive."

Then, after throwing in a few sentences from his "Weiss speech" for good measure, and still leaning on his cane, he marched from the clubhouse terrace to the small bleachers along the first-base line and, without microphone or megaphone, stood before the overflow crowd. They were mostly old people of his own generation, who made St. Petersburg a mecca for the retired, and they had come to sit in the sun and see the Mets' first intrasquad game of the spring.

"They just put me in—if you don't know—the Hall of Fame,"

he said in a loud, hoarse voice that was promptly overridden by tremendous cheers.

Then, while Met players three generations younger gathered behind him like an honor guard, he limped to the third-base grandstand and repeated the announcement, to more thunderous cheers.

The holiday, town-meeting atmosphere was fanned by two things: his 55-year career as a player, coach and manager, and the unusual procedure followed to get him into the Hall of Fame. Only Lou Gehrig had been elected through a special vote since the shrine was established in 1939. He was inducted after announcing his retirement on May 2 that year when it was learned that he had been stricken by lateral sclerosis, which ended his life two years later.

Several other giants of the game had been honored under unusual circumstances, too. Connie Mack, who was born during the Civil War and who was a major league manager for 50 years until 1950, was elected with a special "pioneer" group while he was still managing. And Judge Landis was elected in 1944, two weeks before his death. Joe DiMaggio was enshrined in 1955, although he had retired only three years earlier, but as a result of this "haste" the five-year rule was adopted—until Stengel broke his hip and the regulations almost simultaneously.

Edna, signing autographs for fans who leaned over the fence behind first base, wiped another tear or two and said: "I can't get over it. This is greater even than winning the 1949 World Series."

A couple of hours later Casey, curiously serene and uncommonly pleased, slipped onto a stool in the lounge of the Colonial Inn and helped himself to a cocktail. Nat Holman, the pioneer basketball player and coach, who was vacationing at the inn, approached deferentially, introduced himself and was surprised when Stengel said brightly: "I know more about you than you know about me."

Then he launched a discussion of the Old Celtics and how he and some other baseball players used to sneak off at night to watch Holman play. Holman, incredulous, finally beat a respectful retreat and wandered down the mall behind the inn toward the Gulf of Mexico. He stopped outside the Stengels' double suite, where Edna was gabbing with the neighbors, and told her:

"I had a dream in the still of the night. It was of you and Casey arriving in Cooperstown, and there was a Rolls-Royce waiting at the airport, and you entered the Hall of Fame in style."

Edna, in a typical Stengelese recovery from grandeur to the economics of life, shot back: "That's nice. Who pays for the Rolls-Royce?"

The problem did not materialize, though several others did, such as an airline strike, but the Professor and his bride arrived in Cooperstown in a style that would have fulfilled Holman's fantasy, anyway.

Eight days before Casey's 76th birthday, they flew from Los Angeles to New York (on a non-striking airline), switched to a regional line and hopped right back out to Utica, then arrived in Cooperstown by car and swept into the Otesaga Hotel in plenty of time for the induction ceremony. Like three days early.

So by the time Ted Williams arrived for his induction at the same ceremony, Casey was already the toast of Main Street, and the surrounding country could not have been more astonished by his verve if he had paddled a canoe across Otsego Lake, jumped ashore like the Deerslayer and begun to stalk Indians with a baseball bat.

This was the Leatherstocking country of James Fenimore Cooper, country that was in the business of "selling history" through a series of museums that chronicled the adventures of the American Indian, the American farmer and the American baseball player. Williams, who had been accused during his magnificent 22-year career with the Boston Red Sox of being uncommunicative, even hostile, immediately communicated the fact that "I know what I want to say" at the installation ceremony, closeted himself in a motel room and composed a speech. Stengel, at the other extreme as a communicator, wrote and even rehearsed a speech, and then, as at St. Petersburg, disregarded it when the great moment came.

In any event, they added a few memorable paragraphs to Cooperstown's history industry on Monday morning, July 25, when they were enshrined in the Hall of Fame in a resplendent ceremony that crowded, thrilled and touched the country village where baseball had been born a century and a quarter earlier.

They staged their performances before 10,000 persons, four times the resident population of Cooperstown, speaking from a platform on the tree-lined lawn behind the Hall of Fame while peo-

ple sat on folding chairs, stood along the slopes and even perched
in trees. The widows of Babe Ruth, Christy Mathewson and Eddie
Collins were introduced to loud cheers. Officials of the Yankees,
Mets and other teams basked in the sunshine alongside league
presidents and baseball brass of all levels. Edna sat in a front-row
chair in a bright yellow dress. Dr. LaMotte, as intrigued as anybody over his patient's galloping convalescence, sat nearby, as did
George Weiss, watching his lifelong friend "smell the flowers now."

Then the new Commissioner of Baseball, William D. Eckert, a
proper, erect, almost guarded man in a dark suit, introduced Williams. He noted that the great left-handed hitter had spent nearly
five years "in the service of his country" as a Marine Corps pilot,
and Eckert, an Air Force pilot and officer for 35 years, said he was
pleased to share that bond with him. He recited some of Ted's remarkable statistics as a slugger: a career batting average of .344, a
slugging percentage of .634 (second to Ruth), a 1941 batting average
of .406 (making him the last man to reach .400), a career total of
521 home runs, 6 batting championships and 18 All-Star Games.

"It is difficult for me to say what's in my heart," replied Williams,
a towering, suntanned, curly-haired man, looking like Rock Hudson and sounding like John Wayne. "Today, I am thinking of my
playground director, my high school coach, my managers and
Tom Yawkey, the greatest owner in baseball."

He went on, in a moving, almost reverent speech, to express
"pride and humility" at "the greatest thing that ever happened to
me."

Williams, who had been elected to the Hall of Fame in January
after the minimum "waiting time" of five years, stirred the crowd
by his sincerity and solemnity. He was the 103rd person installed
into baseball's colonnade. Then Charles Dillon Stengel became No.
104.

He was introduced by General Eckert as "one of the greatest
managers of all time and a great judge of men," and no one, Eckert
said, "could get more out of players." Then the Professor was off
and running in a great, rambling, splendid reminiscence of his life
and times.

"Mr. Eckert," he began, in acknowledgment when the cheering
had died down, "and those distinguished notables that are sitting on the rostrum. I want to thank everybody. I want to thank

some of the owners who were amazing to me, and those big presidents of the leagues who were kind to me when I was so obnoxious. I want to thank everybody for my first managerial experience at Worcester, which was last in the Eastern League, and where I met that fine fellow George Weiss, who ran the New Haven club and who would find out whenever I was discharged and would re-employ me.

"I want to thank my parents for letting me play baseball, and I'm thankful I had baseball knuckles and couldn't become a dentist.

"I got $2,100 a year when I started in the big league and lived at Broadway and Forty-seventh Street. And they get more money now.

"I chased the balls that Babe Ruth hit. We couldn't play on Sundays, that was the preacher's day to collect. But in Baltimore we played at a racetrack even, and Ruth hit one over my head and Robby said, 'You'd think you'd play back on a guy who swings like that.' So I replied, 'who's Babe Ruth? He's a kid who just came out of that school.' But I backed up 50 feet more and called over to Hy Myers, 'Far enough?' And he said okay. And Ruth hit it way over my head just the same.

"And Grover Cleveland Alexander pitched in a bandbox in those days and still won 30 games. And there was Walter Johnson, who could pitch for a second-division club. And there was Joe McCarthy, whose teams were called lucky in the minor league, and so I told my players at Toledo: 'Yeah, and they'll be lucky until 1999 if *we* keep playing them.' "

Williams, he said, was "the most aggressive batter who ever went up to home plate." And he recalled his own troubles as a manager against Boston, "which is in New England," saying: "Of course, with my English and the Boston English, we had a little trouble understanding each other."

But nobody had any trouble understanding Casey as he roared nonstop through a 21-minute valedictory that ended with the incongruous, incredible statement: "And I want to thank the tree-mendous fans. We appreciate every boys' group, girls' group, poem and song. And keep going to see the Mets play."

Then the man who had traveled 55 amazin' years from Kankakee to Cooperstown stood with the sunshine reflecting off his hair, carefully combed to the side by his Edna, and heard the cheers roll across the hamlet where Abner Doubleday had started playing the "new game."

Now he was surrounded by the memories of other cheering throngs, and by amazin' baseball players like Cobb, Wagner, Mathewson and Lajoie, who were great when he stepped off the train in Brooklyn in 1912. And players like Ruth, Collins and Johnson, who became great in games in which he played. And managers like McGraw and Robinson, who taught him to teach other players and lead them toward Cooperstown.

He was still surrounded by the criticisms of 55 years, too. He had "over-managed" players. He had been resented for being too curt with some players in the dugout. He had been arbitrary, self-righteous, rude at times. He had been "the last angry old man" to some. He had even confused people and issues by a colossally ego-centric outlook. He had even confused the nation into thinking he was going to retire, but then he had "clarified" his remarks, made at City Hall in New York in July 1965. Then he had broken his hip three days later and retired anyway.

Yet, he was surrounded by the huzzahs of half a century for things uncommonly well done.

"He was short and wiry," wrote Leonard Koppett in *The New York Times*, "and certainly not as strong as most top athletes. He could run fairly fast, threw accurately enough and hit the ball pretty well, but in no respect could he be called gifted. In no physical respect, that is; in mind and spirit, he was as gifted as they come.

"Because he had no children to tutor and lead, his craving to improve through knowledge was directed at the young players working for him. In short, he became a dedicated teacher.

"He didn't always succeed, but he didn't always fail, either. That is why his deepest feelings in all his years as manager of the Yankees and Mets have been involved in 'leaving something behind.' With the Yankees, already successful, it was a desire to 're-build'; with the Mets, it was a desire to build from nothing."

"He gave the Mets the momentum they needed when they needed it most," said Arthur Daley, summing up the Professor's final assignment. "He was the booster rocket that got them off the ground and on their journey. The smoke screen he generated to accompany the blast-off obscured the flaws and gave the Mets an acceptance and a following they could not have obtained without him. He and he alone could have done the job."

"Casey," said Ty Cobb a few years before Cooperstown, "deserves to be in the Hall of Fame. He has shown the greatest ability to successfully manage a ball club, and surely deserves credit as the top manager of all time."

"He's probably done more for baseball than anyone," said Eckert.

"I think," said a friend of Lillian Gish, the actress, trying to find words to describe Miss Gish, "she has vanity. She's wonderful and loyal. She's an American institution, and no one would take a crack at her any more than they would at Casey Stengel."

So, surrounded by the deeds that would live after him, the American institution stood in the sunshine of the Cooperstown morning, looking a bit like Cooper's last of the Mohicans, the great wrinkled face thrust toward the cheering crowd.

At least, he was probably the only "American institution" that at the age of 75 had gone out and bought a new tuxedo, a piece of wardrobe equipment not normally considered necessary at 75 —in any event, not a new one. But in Charles Dillon Stengel's case, it would add a touch of the splendor necessary for him to commence bein' amazin' all over again.

It was a little like the time Noel Coward and Gertrude Lawrence left the cast of "Private Lives," and their replacements, wrote Brooks Atkinson, were fine—"but something of insanity has gone out of the performance."

APPENDIX

On July 9, 1958, hearings were held in Washington by the Sub-committee on Anti-trust and Monopoly of the Committee of the Judiciary of the United States Senate. The subcommittee was considering H.R. 10378 and S. 4070: to limit anti-trust laws so as to exempt professional baseball, football, basketball and hockey. The chief witness: Charles Dillon Stengel. Following are excerpts of his testimony:

* * *

SENATOR ESTES KEFAUVER. Mr. Stengel, you are the manager of the New York Yankees. Will you give us very briefly your background and your views about this legislation?

MR. STENGEL. Well, I started in professional ball in 1910. I have been in professional ball, I would say, for 48 years. I have been employed by numerous ball clubs in the majors and in the minor leagues.

I started in the minor leagues with Kansas City. I played as low as Class D ball, which was at Shelbyville, Kentucky, and also Class C ball and Class A ball, and I have advanced in baseball as a ballplayer.

I had many years that I was not so successful as a ballplayer, as it is a game of skill. And then I was no doubt discharged by baseball in which I had to go back to the minor leagues as a manager, and after being in the minor leagues as a manager, I became a major league manager in several cities and was discharged, we call it discharged because there is no question I had to leave. [Laughter.]

And I returned to the minor leagues at Milwaukee, Kansas City and

197

Oakland, California, and then returned to the major leagues.

In the last 10 years, naturally, in major league baseball with the New York Yankees, the New York Yankees have had tremendous success and while I am not a ballplayer who does the work, I have no doubt worked for a ball club that is very capable in the office.

I have been up and down the ladder. I know there are some things in baseball 35 to 50 years ago that are better now than they were in those days. In those days, my goodness, you could not transfer a ball club in the minor leagues, class D, class C ball, class A ball.

How could you transfer a ball club when you did not have a highway? How could you transfer a ball club when the railroads then would take you to a town you got off and then you had to wait and sit up five hours to go to another ball club?

How could you run baseball then without night ball?

You had to have night ball to improve the proceeds, to pay larger salaries, and I went to work, the first year I received $135 a month.

I thought that was amazing. I had to put away enough money to go to dental college. I found out it was not better in dentistry. I stayed in baseball.

Any other questions you would like to ask me?

SENATOR KEFAUVER. Mr. Stengel, are you prepared to answer particularly why baseball wants this bill passed?

MR. STENGEL. Well, I would have to say at the present time, I think that baseball has advanced in this respect for the player help. That is an amazing statement for me to make, because you can retire with an annuity at 50 and what organization in America allows you to retire at 50 and receive money?

Now the second thing about baseball that I think is very interesting to the public or to all of us that it is the owner's own fault if he does not improve his club, along with the officials in the ball club and the players.

Now what causes that?

If I am going to go on the road and we are a traveling ball club and you know the cost of transportation now—we travel sometimes with three Pullman coaches, the New York Yankees, and I am just a salaried man and do not own stock in the New York Yankees, I found out that in traveling with the New York Yankees on the road and all, that it is the best, and we have broken records in Washington this year, we have broken them in every city but New York and we have lost two clubs that have gone out of the city of New York.

Of course, we have had some bad weather, I would say that they are mad at us in Chicago, we fill the parks.

They have come out to see good material. I will say they are mad at us in Kansas City, but we broke their attendance record.

Now on the road we only get possibly 27 cents. I am not positive of these figures, as I am not an official.

If you go back 15 years or if I owned stock in the club, I would give them to you.

SENATOR KEFAUVER. Mr. Stengel, I am not sure that I made my question clear. [Laughter.]

MR. STENGEL. Yes, sir. Well, that is all right. I am not sure I am going to answer yours perfectly, either. [Laughter.]

SENATOR JOSEPH C. O'MAHONEY. How many minor leagues were there in baseball when you began?

MR. STENGEL. Well, there were not so many at that time because of this fact: Anybody to go into baseball at that time with the educational schools that we had were small, while you were probably thoroughly educated at school, you had to be—we had only small cities that you could put a team in and they would go defunct.

Why, I remember the first year I was at Kankakee, Illinois, and a bank offered me $550 if I would let them have a little notice. I left there and took a uniform because they owed me two weeks' pay. But I either had to quit but I did not have enough money to go to dental college so I had to go with the manager down to Kentucky.

What happened there was if you got by July, that was the big date. You did not play night ball and you did not play Sundays in half of the cities on account of a Sunday observance, so in those days when things were tough, and all of it was, I mean to say, why they just closed up July 4 and there you were sitting there in the depot.

You could go to work some place else, but that was it.

So I got out of Kankakee, Illinois, and I just go there for the visit now. [Laughter.]

SENATOR JOHN A. CARROLL. The question Senator Kefauver asked you was what, in your honest opinion, with your 48 years of experience, is the need for this legislation in view of the fact that baseball has not been subject to anti-trust laws?

MR. STENGEL. No.

SENATOR CARROLL. I had a conference with one of the attorneys representing not only baseball but all of the sports, and I listened to your explanation to Senator Kefauver. It seemed to me it had some clarity. I asked the attorney this question: What was the need for this legislation? I wonder if you would accept his definition. He said they didn't want to be subjected to the *ipse dixit* of the Federal Government because they would throw a lot of damage suits on the *ad dammum* clause. He said, in the first place, the Toolson case was *sui generis*, it was *de minimus non curat lex*.

Do you call that a clear expression?

MR. STENGEL. Well, you are going to get me there for about two hours.

SENATOR KEFAUVER. Thank you, very much, Mr. Stengel. We appreciate your presence here.

Mr. Mickey Mantle, will you come around?

Mr. Mantle, do you have any observations with reference to the applicability of the anti-trust laws to baseball?

MR. MANTLE. My views are just about the same as Casey's.

CHARLES DILLON STENGEL

Born at Kansas City, Mo., July 30, 1890

Height, 5:10. Weight, 175.
Batted and threw left.

Record as a Player

YEAR	TEAM & LEAGUE	G.	AB.	R.	H.	2b	3b	HR	RBI	AVG.
1910	Kankakee, N.A.	59	203	27	51	7	1	1		.251
1910	Maysville, Bl.Gr.	69	233	27	52	10	5	2		.352
1911	Aurora, Wis.–Ill.	121	420	76	148	23	6	4		.352
1912	Montgomery, S.A.	136	479	85	139					.290
1912	Brooklyn, N.L.	17	57	9	18	1	0	1	12	.316
1913	Brooklyn, N.L.	124	438	60	119	16	8	7	44	.272
1914	Brooklyn, N.L.	126	412	55	130	13	10	4	56	.316
1915	Brooklyn, N.L.	132	459	52	109	20	12	3	43	.237
1916	Brooklyn, N.L.	127	462	66	129	27	8	8	53	.279
1917	Brooklyn, N.L.	150	549	69	141	23	12	6	69	.257
1918	Pittsburgh, N.L.	39	122	18	30	4	1	1	13	.246
1919	Pittsburgh, N.L.	89	321	38	94	10	10	4	40	.293
1920	Philadelphia, N.L.	129	445	53	130	25	6	9	50	.292
1921	Phila.–N.Y., N.L.	42	81	11	23	4	1	0	6	.284
1922	New York, N.L.	84	250	48	92	8	10	7	48	.368
1923	New York, N.L.	75	218	39	74	11	5	5	43	.339
1924	Boston, N.L.	131	461	57	129	20	6	5	39	.280
1925	Boston, N.L.	12	13	0	1	0	0	0	2	.077
1925	Worcester, E.L.	100	334	73	107	27	2	10		.320
1926	Toledo, A.A.	88	201	40	66	14	2	0	27	.328
1927	Toledo, A.A.	18	17	3	3	0	0	1	3	.176
1928	Toledo, A.A.	26	32	5	14	5	0	0	12	.438
1929	Toledo, A.A.	20	31	2	7	1	1	0	9	.226
1931	Toledo, A.A.	2	8	1	3	2	0	0	0	.375
Major league totals		1277	4288	575	1219	182	89	60	518	.284

N.A.—Northern Association
Bl.Gr.—Blue Grass League
Wis.–Ill.—Wisconsin–Illinois League
S.A.—Southern Association
N.L.—National League
E.L.—Eastern League
A.A.—American Association

World Series Record

YEAR	TEAM	G	AB	R	H	2b	3b	HR	RBI	AVG.
1916	Brooklyn	4	11	2	4	0	0	0	0	.364
1922	New York	2	5	0	2	0	0	0	0	.400
1923	New York	6	12	3	5	0	0	2	4	.417
World Series Totals		12	20	5	11	0	0	2	4	.393

Record as a Manager

YEAR	CLUB & LEAGUE	FINISHED	WON	LOST	PCT.
1925	Worcester, E.L.	3	70	55	.560
1926	Toledo, A.A.	4	87	77	.530
1927	Toledo, A.A.	1	101	67	.601
1928	Toledo, A.A.	6	79	88	.473
1929	Toledo, A.A.	8	67	100	.401
1930	Toledo, A.A.	3	88	66	.571
1931	Toledo, A.A.	8	68	100	.405
1934	Brooklyn, N.L.	6	71	81	.467
1935	Brooklyn, N.L.	5	70	83	.458
1936	Brooklyn, N.L.	7	67	87	.435
1938	Boston, N.L.	5	77	75	.507
1939	Boston, N.L.	7	63	88	.417
1940	Boston, N.L.	7	65	87	.428
1941	Boston, N.L.	7	62	92	.403
1942	Boston, N.L.	7	59	89	.399
1943	Boston, N.L.	6	68	85	.444
1944	Milwaukee, A.A.	1	91	49	.650
1945	Kansas City, A.A.	7	65	86	.430
1946	Oakland, P.C.L.	2	111	72	.607
1947	Oakland, P.C.L.	4	96	90	.516
1948	Oakland, P.C.L.	1	114	74	.606
1949	New York, A.L.*	1	97	57	.630
1950	New York, A.L.*	1	98	56	.636
1951	New York, A.L.*	1	98	56	.636
1952	New York, A.L.*	1	95	59	.617

YEAR	CLUB & LEAGUE	FINISHED	WON	LOST	PCT.
1953	New York, A.L.*	1	99	52	.656
1954	New York, A.L.	2	103	51	.669
1955	New York, A.L.	1	96	58	.623
1956	New York, A.L.*	1	97	57	.630
1957	New York, A.L.	1	98	56	.636
1958	New York, A.L.*	1	92	62	.597
1959	New York, A.L.	3	79	75	.513
1960	New York, A.L.	1	97	57	.630
1962	New York Mets	10	40	120	.250
1963	New York, N.L.	10	51	111	.315
1964	New York, N.L.	10	53	109	.327
1965	New York, N.L.	—	31	64	.326
Major league totals		—	1926	1867	.508

E.L.— Eastern League
A.A.— American Association
N.L.— National League
P.C.L.— Pacific Coast League
A.L.— American League
N.L.— National League

* Won World Series.
Elected to the Baseball Hall of Fame—March 8, 1966.
Inducted—July 25, 1966.

INDEX